Shakespeare

Programs

Praise for the first edition of *Shakespeare* by David Bevington

'David Bevington's knowledge of Shakespeare is formidable. In this wonderful new book, Bevington uses the "Seven Ages of Man" speech from *As You Like It* to weave together Shakespeare's plays and poems with what is known of Shakespeare's life.'

Barbara Mowat, Folger Shakespeare Institute

'Recommended for all public and academic libraries in need of fresh introductory materials on Shakespeare.'

Library Journal

'Essential. A must for lower- and upper-division undergraduates; a pleasure for graduate students through faculty and for general readers.'

Choice

DAVID BEVINGTON

SHAKESPEARE

The Seven Ages of Human Experience

Second Edition

Blackwell
Publishing

BLACKWELL PUBLISHING
350 Main Street, Malden, MA 02148-5020, USA
9600 Garsington Road, Oxford OX4 2DQ, UK
550 Swanston Street, Carlton, Victoria 3053, Australia

First edition published 2002
Second edition published 2005 Blackwell Publishing Ltd
1 2005

Library of Congress Cataloging-in-Publication Data

Bevington, David M.
Shakespeare : the seven ages of human experience /
David Bevington.—2nd ed.
p. cm.
Includes bibliographical references (p.) and index.
ISBN-13: 978-1-4051-2753-0 (pbk. : alk. paper)
ISBN-10: 1-4051-2753-8 (pbk. : alk. paper)
1. Shakespeare, William, 1564–1616—Criticism and interpretation.
2. Maturation (Psychology) in literature.   3. Human beings
in literature.   4. Aging in literature.   I. Title.
PR2976.B443 2005
822.3′3—dc22
2004065960

A catalogue record for this title is available from the British Library.

Set in 10/13pt Galliard
by SNP Best-set Typesetter Ltd, Hong Kong
Printed and bound in the United Kingdom
by TJ International Ltd, Padstow, Cornwall

The publisher's policy is to use permanent paper from mills that operate a
sustainable forestry policy, and which has been manufactured from pulp
processed using acid-free and elementary chlorine-free practices.
Furthermore, the publisher ensures that the text paper and cover board
used have met acceptable environmental accreditation standards.

For further information on
Blackwell Publishing, visit our website:
www.blackwellpublishing.com

For
Laura, Peter, Sylvia, and Zeke

Contents

Illustrations

To the Reader

By design, this book moves around quite a bit from play to play, from prose to poetry, from early to late, in order to pursue themes and topics that seem to have fascinated Shakespeare and that certainly fascinate me. I hope they will interest you as well. One result is that discussions touch on only certain aspects of a given play or poem in a particular chapter. I keep coming back to some plays especially, such as *Hamlet, King Lear, A Midsummer Night's Dream, Othello,* and *The Tempest,* from different directions. If you find yourself wondering, for example, why a particular discussion of *King Lear* seems to centre on Edmund and his family without saying much about King Lear or Cordelia, just wait. I'll be back later in the book.

I did not realize how much I wanted to write this book until Andrew McNeillie pointed the way. I owe him my special thanks. I am eternally grateful also to the many friends and writers about Shakespeare whose ideas I have not directly acknowledged in this generally unfootnoted book and whose innovative ideas about Shakespeare I have so mingled with my own that I am not always sure which are whose. Among those to whom I am most consciously indebted are Janet Adelman, Richard Wheeler, Arthur Kirsch, Robert G. Hunter, Fredson Bowers, Alfred Harbage, Northrop Frye, A. C. Bradley, Lynda Boose, Frank Kermode, Claude Lévi-Strauss, Victor Turner, David Kastan, Patricia Parker, Barbara Mowat, Paul Werstine, C. L. Barber, Coppélia Kahn, Meredith Skura, Robert Watson, Stephen Orgel, James Calderwood, John Velz, Inga-Stina Ewbank, Sigurd Burckhardt, Linda Charnes, Norman Rabkin, Alvin Kernan, and Juliet Dusinberre. These people have changed my life in some way, often through a single, focused, seminal idea. My list here is of course very incomplete. In addition, I owe more than I can say to the many superb students at Harvard, the University of Virginia, and the University of Chicago who have challenged and sharpened what I have tried to teach with their questions and often surprising observations. It has been a privilege to be invited to think out loud about Shakespeare with them on a continuing journey of discovery. This little book represents, in distilled form, something of where I have gotten to at present.

I am grateful to Blackwell Publishing for a chance to bring out a second edition. In it I have corrected a number of errors and infelicities of style that escaped me on first passage. I have tried to say more about fathers and sons than in the first edition, about the perils of courtship, about the circumstances of Shakespeare's own life that may bear on his written work, about performance history of his plays on stage and screen, about his delicate representation of gender relations in all their ambiguous uncertainties, about his sources, and still more. Two inserted passages, on *Romeo and Juliet* and on fathers and sons, are of substantial length. In a new final chapter on 'Shakespeare Today', I look at the remarkable diversity of interpretations in modern criticism and performance of Shakespeare as a key to his malleability, his 'infinite variety', his ability to adapt to a changing world. Other changes deal with particular paragraphs. The book is a little longer than the earlier version, but develops the same idea of a life cycle that never ceases to fascinate me in Shakespeare.

David Bevington

CHAPTER ONE

◆

All the World's a Stage
Poetry and Theatre

This whole creation is essentially subjective, and the dream is the theater where the dreamer is at once scene, actor, prompter, stage manager, author, audience, and critic.
    Carl Jung, General Aspects of Dream Psychology *(1928)*

What makes Shakespeare so great? Everyone wonders about that. Is he simply a cultural icon, a great name, the study of whose works has become entrenched in high school and college curricula out of inertia? Are students being obliged to make their way through the difficulties of Elizabethan English and the thickets of early modern politics simply because their elders have done so? Is the study of Shakespeare an elaborate hazing ritual? How can he speak to the twenty-first century, given his experience in a culture that was monarchist, patriarchal, pre-industrial, and unacquainted for the most part with any peoples that were not Anglo-Saxon native-born English? In our day, when dead European white males are being expunged from the curriculum, why still read Shakespeare? He is unquestionably dead, European, white, and male. In what way, if at all, does he deserve to be celebrated as the greatest English writer, perhaps the greatest writer of all time?

One can begin to answer these questions by simply observing the factual evidence of a genuine popularity that is continuing and even growing today. In an era when college enrolments in most older authors – Chaucer, Milton, Spenser, Jonson, Marlowe, Pope, etc., not to mention Homer, Sophocles, Virgil, and Dante – are on the decline, Shakespeare courses are thriving. The film industry has discovered anew that

Shakespeare can be good box-office. Postmodern criticism, after declaring its own liberation from canonical authors, turns again and again to Shakespeare to test its most acute theoretical problems about genre, sexuality, language, and politics. Ask Shakespeare a question about anything and he is likely to come back with an amazing answer, or, more importantly, a still more puzzling question. As a character in George Bernard Shaw's *Misalliance* declares in wonderment (when a thief has just quoted Shakespeare to him), 'Good. Read Shakespeare: he has a word for every occasion'. One proof of Shakespeare's sturdy endurability is that, in these days when the curriculum has been liberated, teachers and critics and students turn to him by choice. He is a central text for feminists, deconstructionists, Marxists, traditional close readers, Christian interpreters, students of cultural studies, you name it. Despite his chronological antiquity, he speaks today to the condition of each of these methodologies.

Shakespeare is cited by more modern writers than any other writer in the canon, other than the Bible. This, presumably, is because he has become a by-word for situations we encounter daily. 'It's Greek to me', we say, when something is obscure, not realizing perhaps that we are paraphrasing Casca in *Julius Caesar*, having reported to Cassius that Cicero spoke 'in Greek' on the occasion of Caesar's refusing the crown, and asked 'to what effect' Cicero spoke, Casca answers that he couldn't follow the speech: 'it was Greek to me'.

Hamlet is full of lines that we appropriate to our daily lives. We see something 'in [the] mind's eye'. We agree with Polonius that one has a duty 'to thine own self' to 'be true'. We acknowledge his worldly wisdom that 'the apparel oft proclaims the man' and that it is best 'Neither a borrower nor a lender' to be. We concur with Hamlet that drinking or any other injurious overindulgence 'is a custom / More honoured in the breach than the observance'. We exclaim, with Hamlet, 'What a piece of work is a man!' When a speech or sample of writing is too long, 'It shall to the barber's with your beard'. If a speech is overacted 'It out-Herods Herod'. We know too well that 'conscience does make cowards of us all'. We nod in assent to the proposition that art must 'hold . . . the mirror up to nature'. When we wish to speak cuttingly, we 'speak daggers'. We resonate to the proposition that 'There are more things in heaven and earth . . . Than are dreamt of in your philosophy' and that 'There's a divinity that shapes our ends, / Rough-hew them how we will'. Most of all, perhaps, we ponder what it means 'To be or not to be', and celebrate Shakespeare's theatre with the splendid truism that 'The play's the thing'.

These are all remarkably memorable lines that have made their way into the language. They have done so because they eloquently address issues that we deeply care about: the nature of humanity, the purposes of art, the role of divinity in our lives, the puzzling temptations of suicide, and much more.

The argument of this book, indeed, is that Shakespeare lives among us today with such vitality because he speaks, with unrivalled eloquence and grace of language, to just about any human condition one can think of: infancy and childhood, early schooling, friendships, rivalry among siblings, courtship, the competitive way in which sons must learn to become their fathers' heirs, career choices and ambitions, sceptical disillusionment and loss of traditional faith, marriage, jealousy, midlife crisis, fathers' worries about the marriages of their daughters, old age, retirement, and the approach of death.

Shakespeare has immortalized for us the parabolic shape of this life cycle in the so-called 'Seven Ages of Man' speech delivered by Jaques in *As You Like It*, act 2, scene 7.[1] Jaques is prompted to his reflection on human existence by spectacles of suffering and injustice: the banishment of Duke Senior and his followers from the envious court of the usurping Duke Frederick, and the near-death by starvation of Orlando and his faithful servant Adam, now rescued from extremity by the charity of the forest dwellers. In his response to this situation, Duke Senior introduces the idea of our lives as a kind of theatre:

> Thou see'st we are not all alone unhappy.
> This wide and universal theatre
> Presents more woeful pageants than the scene
> Wherein we play in.
> $$(2.7.135–8)^2$$

Jaques elaborates on this wonderful commonplace in an extended theatrical metaphor:

> All the world's a stage,
> And all the men and women merely players.
> They have their exits and their entrances,
> And one man in his time plays many parts,
> His acts being seven ages. At first the infant,
> Mewling and puking in the nurse's arms.
> Then the whining schoolboy, with his satchel

And shining morning face, creeping like snail
Unwillingly to school. And then the lover,
Sighing like furnace, with a woeful ballad
Made to his mistress' eyebrow. Then a soldier,
Full of strange oaths and bearded like the pard,
Jealous in honour, sudden, and quick in quarrel,
Seeking the bubble reputation
Even in the cannon's mouth. And then the justice,
In fair round belly with good capon lined,
With eyes severe and beard of formal cut,
Full of wise saws and modern instances;
And so he plays his part. The sixth age shifts
Into the lean and slippered pantaloon,
With spectacles on nose and pouch on side,
His youthful hose, well saved, a world too wide
For his shrunk shank; and his big manly voice,
Turning again toward childish treble, pipes
And whistles in his sound. Last scene of all,
That ends this strange, eventful history,
Is second childishness and mere oblivion,
Sans teeth, sans eyes, sans taste, sans everything.

(2.7.138–65)

We might observe several things about this remarkable speech. First, it is masculine in its point of view. This is the story of a male child growing up to be a man and then circling back to second childhood (another common phrase for which we are indebted to Shakespeare). The occupations here are male: courtship of women, soldiership, profession, respectability of a judicial appointment, ownership of property. Is there such a thing as the Seven Ages of Woman? Well, in fact the Folger Library in Washington DC has a poem called *Seven Ages of Woman*, by Agnes Strickland (London, 1827), that traces the lifespan of women from childhood to maturity to old age, and guess what? Their only discernible occupation is childbearing and tending the family. The pattern is precisely that of a sixteenth-century German woodcut illustrating the same subject, in which, as the seven partly undraped female figures mature, their breasts become enlarged and attractive; as they age, the breasts droop until they are unsightly dugs hanging to the waist. The posture too goes from erect gracefulness to arthritic stooping. The contrast with Shakespeare's Seven Ages of Man could not be more instructive. Moreover, discussion of the Seven Ages of Woman is rare; Shakespeare's generation did not think consciously about women's careers as it did about men's, and not until the nineteenth century did a woman writer venture to suggest that Shakespeare's often-cited paradigm was in need of a feminist corrective. Shakespeare's portrayal of the life cycle is male, and he himself was a male. We will want to explore ways in which, thoughtfully and even anxiously, he seems to have confronted the problem of understanding the profound differences in gender that separate men and women, but we should begin by acknowledging that his point of view was inescapably that of the man.

Another point about Jaques' speech is that it is ironic. The individual portraits are uniformly wry in tone: the infant 'mewling and puking in the nurse's arms', the boy manifesting his unwillingness to go to school, the lover making a fool of himself over some young woman whom he insists on idolizing, the soldier pursuing illusory reputation and honour 'Even in the cannon's mouth', the justice complacent with worldly success, the old man covetous of possessions that will soon say goodbye to him, the dying man a child again. Life is indeed a cycle. What does it amount to? In Jaques' mordant view, it all comes to 'mere oblivion', without teeth to chew one's food, or eyesight, or taste, or anything at all.

This sounds remarkably like the plaintive chant in T. S. Eliot's 'A Fragment of an Agon': 'Birth, and copulation, and death. / That's all, that's all, that's all, that's all, / Birth, and copulation, and death.' One thinks too of Hamlet's meditations on death and oblivion in the graveyard where Yorick and so many others lie buried. Why might not the dusty remains of Emperor Alexander the Great be subject to the same kinds of indignity that Yorick's skull suffers at the hands of the gravedigger? 'As thus: Alexander died, Alexander was buried, Alexander returneth to dust, the dust is earth, of earth we make loam, and why of that loam whereto he was converted might they not stop a beer barrel?' Or, earlier in the play, 'What is a man, / If his chief good and market of his time / Be but to sleep and feed? A beast, no more.'

The ironies in Jaques' speech remind us of other passages in Shakespeare as well. The description of the infant 'mewling and puking' brings to mind King Lear, when he laments that 'We came crying hither' into this world. 'Thou know'st the first time that we smell the air / We wawl and cry' when we are come 'To this great stage of fools'. Falstaff's wry disquisition on honour in *1 Henry IV* ('Who hath it? He that died o' Wednesday') reads like a comment on Jaques' soldier 'Seeking the bubble reputation / Even in the cannon's mouth'. Touchstone's amusement at the clichéd verse that Orlando hangs on the trees of the forest in

As You Like It in praise of his Rosalind ('I'll rhyme you so eight years together, dinners and suppers and sleeping hours excepted', says Touchstone) is an amusing instance of Jaques' lover 'Sighing like furnace, with a woeful ballad / Made to his mistress' eyebrow'. The aged justices, Shallow and Silence, in *2 Henry IV* ('We have heard the chimes at midnight, Master Shallow', says Falstaff to one of them) seem to march right out of Jaques' vignette on 'the lean and slippered pantaloon'. Jaques' Seven Ages of Man reads like a blueprint for Shakespeare's dramatic portraiture of the crazy, funny, sad life of mortals on this earth.

This is not to say that Shakespeare is only, or even chiefly, an ironist, a satirical observer in the vein of Voltaire or Swift or Aristophanes. Instead, the Seven Ages of Man speech helps us to see that Shakespeare is an unsurpassed observer of *la comédie humaine*, along with Leo Tolstoi, Jane Austen, William Faulkner, E. M. Forster, and Honoré de Balzac. Shakespeare's observations of human folly are both acute and compassionate. Jaques' speech, to be fully understood, must be read in the context of a scene in which human charity and forgiveness do much to atone for Jaques' witty indictment of the existential meaninglessness of human existence. The present book, using Jaques' speech as a kind of outline, hopes to explore the ways in which Shakespeare sought to balance ironic and satiric observation with charity and compassion. It is in this balance that we find what is so deeply humane in him.

The young Shakespeare, turning up in London some time before 1592 in search of a career, found himself drawn to the theatre and to the writing of poetry. We know rather little about his life prior to that time. He was born in 1564, in Stratford-upon-Avon, the son of a man who prospered as a manufacturer and salesman of leather goods and who became the equivalent of mayor of the town, though he also seems to have experienced financial difficulties and to have been fined for absence from town meetings – probably as the result of his having overextended himself in his business dealings, though the possibility that he incurred official disfavour for clinging to the Catholic faith of his youth continues to intrigue those who wonder if Shakespeare himself was Catholic in his sympathies. Shakespeare's mother, Mary Arden, came from a good family of well-to-do yeoman farmer's stock. Though the school records have perished owing to the ravages of time, we cannot doubt that the son of the town's leading citizen would have gone to the King's New School there, where, tuition free, he would have received instruction chiefly in Latin, along with some Greek.

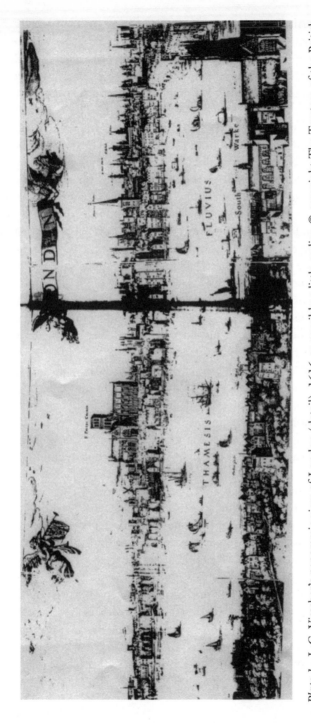

Plate 1 J. C. Visscher's panoramic view of London (detail), 1616 or possibly a little earlier. © copyright The Trustees of the British Museum.

He married, at eighteen, Anne Hathaway, who was eight years his senior and already some three months pregnant; a special licence had to be obtained to marry quickly, without the customary reading of the 'banns' or announcement of intent to marry that normally proceeded over three successive Sundays. The implications of a 'shotgun' wedding are clear, and is a matter to which we will return. The couple's first child, Susanna, was born on May 26, 1583. Two other children, the twins Hamnet and Judith, were born on February 5, 1585. ('Hamnet' was the name of a Stratford neighbor.) These were the last children born to William and Anne. Although the absence of any other children could have been the result of some medical condition, the circumstance may suggest instead that William and Anne did not continue to share a bed. Birth control, rudimentary at best, was essentially non-existent; families tended to be large, though this was by no means uniformly the case. At all events, Shakespeare appears to have left home some time after the birth of the twins. He never brought his family to live with him in London. Once he became prosperous he did acquire property in Stratford in which his wife and children were able to live handsomely, and he must have visited home when not occupied with his work in the big city, but he and his family did live apart much or most of the time.

I should say something, briefly, about the authorship controversy that has swirled about Shakespeare's head since the mid-nineteenth century. To many non-academics the issue remains unsettled. How could a provincial lad who never attended one of the universities of his day (Oxford and Cambridge) turn out to be the greatest writer in the English language? Why is it that we have no papers of his? How could a country boy depict with such acumen the lives of rulers and courtiers? Surely the work that survives shows the hand of a university-educated wit, like Christopher Marlowe, or an aristocrat, like the Earl of Oxford – who wrote sonnets and whose father-in-law, Lord Burghley, bears a passable resemblance to Polonius. Are there not clues in *Hamlet* and other plays that reveal biographical details more pertinent to the Earl of Oxford than to the boy from Stratford?

The Earl of Oxford is the leading contender currently as the rival author of Shakespeare's works. He is, however, only one of several who have been put forth. The first was Sir Francis Bacon, proposed briefly in the middle of the eighteenth century and then championed in America in 1852 and afterwards by Delia Bacon. Attracted perhaps to the idea by her sharing a last name with Sir Francis, she promoted the thesis that the plays were not by Shakespeare but by Bacon, Sir Walter Ralegh, and Edmund Spenser as a means of spreading secretly a liberal philosophy. In her estimate, William Shakespeare of Stratford was nothing more than an 'ignorant, low-bred, vulgar country fellow, who had never inhaled in all his life one breath of that social atmosphere that fills his plays'. Although her book in 1857 on the subject was not well received, and although she went on to suffer delusions that she was herself 'the Holy Ghost and surrounded by devils', the movement lived on; an English Bacon Society came into being in 1885, followed by an American counterpart in 1892. Christopher Marlowe has been another candidate; so have others. The very existence of this plethora of candidates is suspicious. So is the fact that the so-called 'anti-Stratfordian' theory did not emerge for two centuries or more after Shakespeare's death, and not with any noticeable following until well into the nineteenth century. Prior to that time, no one doubted that the plays and poems were by William Shakespeare. Mark Twain, himself an anti-Stratfordian, saw the humour of this. The works, he said, are not by Shakespeare but by another person of the same name.[3]

Well, a rose by any other name would smell as sweet, as someone once said, but is it true that it doesn't really matter if someone other than Shakespeare wrote these plays? Oxfordian apologists allow that a man called Shakespeare did live and act in the London theatre, but not as a playwright. (Shakespeare is listed at the top of 'the principal comedians' in Ben Jonson's *Every Man in His Humour*, performed by 'the then Lord Chamberlain His Servants' in 1598, and as one of 'the principal tragedians' in Jonson's *Sejanus*, acted in 1603.) The Earl of Oxford, according to this theory, being inspired to write but ashamed to sully his aristocratic name by lending it to a disreputable enterprise like playwriting, needed a front man. Shakespeare, an actor and 'actor-sharer' (that is, company member and part owner) of England's premier acting company, the Lord Chamberlain's Men (renamed the King's Men in 1603), was deemed a suitable candidate. This argument, unprovable by any documentary evidence, rests instead on the assumption that we need to find an author for the plays and poems who was suitably well-born and university educated. It presupposes that the many persons in London who knew Oxford and Shakespeare must have agreed not to talk about the arrangement and thus to keep the 'true' identity of the plays' author a secret. Authors did sometimes use pseudonyms in the Renaissance, but I know of no instance in which an author concealed his identity by adopting as a fictional cover the name of a theatre professional who was known to have written plays. (Robert Greene, in 1592, had warned his fellow playwrights to watch out for a young 'upstart crow' who was, 'in his own conceit, the only Shake-scene in a country'.) The theory of a widespread conspiracy of silence is also suspect in that it involves a lot of people, and it implicates a man like Ben Jonson, who was notoriously outspoken and undaunted by authority in high places. It implicates John Heminges and Henry Condell, Shakespeare's fellow actors who put together the great Folio edition of his plays in 1623. And why construct such a hypothesis in the first place? Only because of a conviction that a young man not educated at a university would have been unable to observe and describe the rich pageantry of London and court life that we find in the works.

The most telling argument against Oxford's authorship is that he died in 1604.[4] Centuries of scholarly study, unconcerned with the problem of Oxford's putative authorship, have dated many of Shakespeare's greatest plays – including *King Lear*, *Macbeth*, *Antony and Cleopatra*, *The Winter's Tale*, and *The Tempest* – well after 1604. Recent scholarship keeps refining the process. Dating is not always easy, and allowance must be made for some uncertainty of a year or two. Those who argue in favour of Oxford's authorship contend that posthumous publication was not unusual, and that the dating of the later plays, all of which remained unpublished after *King Lear* (in quarto, 1608) for the rest of Shakespeare's lifetime, rests on uncertain internal evidence and considerations of style. Among those who teach and write about Shakespeare in today's colleges and universities, nonetheless, the opinion is virtually unanimous that the canon of supposedly late plays does indeed depict an artistic journey that extends well beyond 1604 down to *The Tempest*, first presented at court in late 1611 (for which Shakespeare appears to have made use of accounts of shipwreck written in 1610), and then on to *Henry VIII* (first performed in mid-1613, resulting most unfortunately in the burning down of the Globe Theatre). Stylistically, the late plays display many features of run-on lines, pauses in the midst of a line of verse, feminine endings, and other characteristics that are significantly less identifiable in earlier plays. No less unlikely, in the view of most Shakespeare scholars, is the argument that if some plays were indeed written after 1604, topical references in them could have been covertly added by Oxford's heirs as a way of making them appear timely.

Actually, Shakespeare was just the sort of person who might have written the works we have. The Renaissance was a period of astonishing literary output, almost all of it by writers who came from social and educational backgrounds similar to Shakespeare's. John Webster's *The Duchess of Malfi* (1612–14) is arguably as great a play as most in the Shakespeare canon; Webster was a man of ordinary social background about whom we know considerably less than we do about Shakespeare. Christopher Marlowe's *Doctor Faustus* (*c*. 1589) is a great and moving tragedy; Marlowe came from a shoemaker's family in Canterbury, whence he was sent to Cambridge on a scholarship. Ben Jonson's stepfather was a bricklayer, and for a time Ben seemed destined to become one as well. Edmund Spenser's family were in sail-making. These men had a motive for writing; they had to earn a living by it, as Oxford certainly did not.

Moreover, university training in England at that time focused predominantly on the study of Latin, Greek, and Hebrew texts, many of them theological treatises chosen to train young men for the Anglican clergy or for administrative positions in government. Our modern notion of higher education as the mark of a liberally-educated person is a misperception when it is applied to Oxford and Cambridge in the late sixteenth century. A would-be writer like Shakespeare was far better off going to London where, like a reporter for a journal or newspaper today, he would pick up gossip about the court in the street and in the tavern. No self-respecting reporter today belongs to the Establishment he writes about; he learns his trade by writing, by talking with people, by reading, and by seeing plays.

Shakespeare's early writings display just the kind of learning that Shakespeare would have obtained at the King's New School in Stratford. The texts he surely read there (as we know from studies of school curricula of the era) are precisely the ones he cites in his plays: Ovid, Virgil, Seneca, and some others. Shakespeare's evident preference for consulting English translations of these classical authors by William Golding and others also seems consistent with the portrait we can construct of Shakespeare as an ambitious young writer. (Golding was Oxford's uncle and may have been one of his tutors, but we needn't see this fact as bolstering the claim for Oxford's authorship of Shakespeare's plays; Golding's verse translation of Ovid was widely available, and Ovid was a staple of the new educational system from which Shakespeare evidently benefitted.) The early works also show us a playwright steeped in the lore and practice of the theatre to which he belonged. London and its theatre were his university.

The lack of any surviving manuscripts by Shakespeare is perfectly natural. Who of us today saves, or even reads, film scripts? Shakespeare's papers were ephemera. His few signatures are in a shaky and uncertain hand, in part no doubt because he was in terminally poor health when he signed his will. Whether they are indeed his remains a matter of dispute. Variations in spelling were legion in his day.

Enough. I am an academic; you know where I stand. I don't expect to convert anyone already persuaded of the opposite view. But believe me, there is nothing, absolutely nothing, to the Oxfordian hypothesis. It is the answer to a nonexistent problem. The amazing thing is that anyone could have written the works of Shakespeare. He was obviously a genius; genius is not limited to the upper classes, and is indeed sometimes in short supply there. Let us return to a Shakespeare who lived among the people of whom he wrote.

Soon after he came to London, Shakespeare evidently considered a career as a poet – not a writer of poetic drama, that is, but a writer of lyric verse for publication. Or perhaps he wanted to be a dramatist after all, with lyric poetry as an attractive diversion and sideline. To be a professional poet, at any rate, he needed a sponsor and a publisher. He found both in 1593–4, when the Earl of Southampton befriended him, and a Stratford friend of his father, Richard Field, agreed to publish separately two lengthy poems by Shakespeare. Serious outbreaks of the plague may also have given him the opportunity to write these poems; in such times, the London authorities closed down the theatres as a public health precaution, and Shakespeare may have been underemployed as an actor and playwright.

The poems, *Venus and Adonis* and *The Rape of Lucrece*, reveal in their dedicatory notes a warmth of gratitude for the dedicatee, Southampton. The letter attached to the second poem is especially affectionate: 'The love I dedicate to Your Lordship is without end', and so on. Granted that obsequious flattery was *de rigueur* in such missives, it does seem likely that Southampton provided some financial support, as well as the use of his influential name. One traditional speculation is that Southampton gave Shakespeare the 'stake' he needed to buy into his position as shareholder of the newly-formed Lord Chamberlain's acting company in 1594. Another is that Southampton is the young man addressed in the Sonnets. More about that in a moment. The most interesting speculation is to wonder if Shakespeare aimed at being dependent on such aristocratic patronage for a possible career as a professional poet. John Lyly had been secretary to the Earl of Oxford in the 1580s; Edmund Spenser served as secretary to Lord Grey in the 1590s. Then as now, one could not easily

Plate 2 Henry Wriothesley, third Earl of Southampton, portrait by Jon de Critz the Elder, 1603. By kind permission of His Grace the Duke of Buccleuch and Queensbury. Print supplied by the National Portrait Gallery.

make an independent living as a poet; sponsorship provided the ready answer, if one could find a generous sponsor. We will never know how seriously Shakespeare considered this alternative, since the theatre made it possible for him to be a successful and even wealthy writer. The theatre and its public audience became his sponsor.

Shakespeare's poems give us invaluable insight into his craft as a writer. His two long poems are certainly not among his greatest works, but they do reveal much about his approach to imagery and the rhetorical devices of the trade. *Venus and Adonis* is an amorous poem based primarily on a well-known legend found in Ovid's *Metamorphoses*. The plot is a slender one: the goddess Venus becomes enamoured of a mortal young man, who proves to be bashful and reluctant. She attempts to steer him away from his avid desire to hunt the boar, but does not prevail. He is mortally wounded by a gash from the boar's tusk in his flank, and is metamorphosed into a purple-and-white anemone. To this slender story Shakespeare adds touches from the legends of Hermaphroditus and Narcissus, both of them self-infatuated young men who are put off by erotic heterosexual love. These are themes well calculated to the tastes of Southampton, and they re-emerge in the Sonnets.

What interests us most in this early poem is its approach to poetic craftsmanship. The poem is written in six-line stanzas and is organized as a narrative. Much time is spent in erotic contemplation of Venus's physical charms and her unsuccessful blandishments. In the following sample, Venus has cornered her unwilling partner, enfolding him in her arms and refusing to let him go:

> 'Fondling', she saith, 'since I have hemmed thee here
> Within the circuit of this ivory pale,
> I'll be a park, and thou shalt be my deer.
> Feed where thou wilt, on mountain or in dale;
>   Graze on my lips; and if those hills be dry,
>   Stray lower, where the pleasant fountains lie.
>
> 'Within this limit is relief enough,
> Sweet bottom grass and high delightful plain,
> Round rising hillocks, brakes obscure and rough,
> To shelter thee from tempest and from rain.
>   Then be my deer, since I am such a park;
>   No dog shall rouse thee, though a thousand bark.'
>   (229–40)

The imagery here is designed to titillate the reader with the prospect of Venus's body as a landscape, complete with hills (breasts), bottom grass (pubic hair), a high plain (the Mons Veneris), hillocks (the buttocks), obscure brakes (the hair-covered sexual entrance to her body), and so on. She offers her body as a cave for Adonis to enter and shelter himself from the ravages of this world. The conventional wordplay on deer/dear reinforces the amorous double meaning of the passage. The language titillates, even while it also offers itself as an exercise in wit: poet and reader alike are invited to work out the details of the analogy, allowing the mind to picture a sexual topography in as vivid detail as is desired. The wit is comic, ironic, distancing; we are permitted to see what is risible in the situation of a very nubile and well-built goddess vamping a narcissistic young man. The male reader, especially, is given the opportunity to wonder what it would be like for him to feed on Venus's plenteous and willingly proffered body. It is a sexual fantasy, controlled as such by the counter-impulse for the young male to discipline himself instead to the art of hunting. The verbal devices in this passage fit the occasion: the pleasing alternative rhyme (abab) leading to the final couplet (cc) of each stanza, the delight in antithesis (mountain/dale, upper body/lower body, hills/fountains, bottom grass/high plain), the use of recurrent sound effects to reinforce these antitheses (round rising/rough), and still more.

Such were the arts of rhetoric that would-be poets studied to perfect their craft in Shakespeare's day. Manuals of rhetoric by George Puttenham (*The Art of English Poesie*, 1589) and others were plentifully available, like how-to books. Poetry was seen as a branch of rhetoric; one learned to make one's ideas more persuasive and affective by adorning those ideas with images, extended metaphors, and 'conceits' (as they were called). The art of *Venus and Adonis* is the art of rhetoric, here being practised by an eager apprentice.

The Rape of Lucrece (1594) is more lugubrious and tragic. It chooses as its narrative a well-known account (as told in Ovid's *Fasti*) of the wife of a Roman nobleman who takes her own life after she has been raped by the son and heir of Tarquin the Proud, tyrant of the early Roman state. Lucretia, or Lucrece, chooses to die rather than live to bring shame on her husband's name; though blameless, she is now polluted and unchaste. Lucrece is thus presented as the model of innocent, dutiful, and victimized wifehood. The poem does not question her motives or her moral view of right and wrong in choosing to die. The poem thus envisages a subservient role for women, placing an extraordinary premium on chastity and the husband's right to possess his wife to the exclusion of other men. At the same time it presents a dark view of male sexual importunity. The rape is described in painful detail: Tarquin's guilty turning of the latch as he steals into her chamber at night, her radiant beauty as she lies asleep (revealing, demurely, 'Her breasts like ivory globes circled with blue'), Tarquin's unavailing struggles with his conscience, his rude hand advancing on her breasts ('round turrets') made pale and destitute by this outrage, her imploring him to remember his knightly oaths, his obduracy, his suppressing her piteous clamours by wrapping her night-linen around her head, and, in the aftermath, remorse, self-loathing, and disgrace. Like *Venus and Adonis*, this poem invites the male reader to participate vicariously in a sexual encounter, but it does so in such a way as to make male sexuality seem dirty and violent.

The poetic method relies again on extended metaphor applied as ornament. Here is a description of Tarquin as he first stands over the sleeping Lucrece in her bed:

> As the grim lion fawneth o'er his prey,
> Sharp hunger by the conquest satisfied,
> So o'er this sleeping soul doth Tarquin stay,
> His rage of lust by gazing qualified –
> Slaked, not suppressed, for, standing by her side,
>   His eye, which late this mutiny restrains,
>   Unto a greater uproar tempts his veins.
>
> (421–7)

The conventional image of a lion menacing its prey is linked in the poem to other such metaphors of assault drawn from the world of nature: a falcon towering in the skies over its victim, a black-faced cloud obscuring the sun, a 'foul night-waking cat' playing sadistically with a poor little mouse, weeds that overgrow the corn, frosts threatening the spring, a cockatrice or basilisk stalking a white female deer, a vulture, and so on. These images crowd into the poem at the moment of the atrocity to heighten the effects of pity and terror. The seven-line stanza (ababbcc) is the so-called rhyme royal, used to splendid effect by Chaucer in his *Troilus and Criseyde*, and is appropriate here to a serious subject.

As in *Venus and Adonis*, part of the aesthetic pleasure for the reader lies in the analogy; one is asked to picture the scene by imagining at once a brutal man standing over a sleeping woman and a lion slaking its hunger in torn flesh. The analogy suggests a deep and troubling connection between male sexual importunity and brute animal instinct. The man here, Tarquin, is torn by desire and compunction. The stanza, and the poem as a whole, is interested in the psychology of desire: pleasure enters at the eye, and might be satisfied with gazing on beauty were it not for the 'greater uproar' tempting Tarquin's 'veins' in the form of raging lust.

We do not know when Shakespeare began writing sonnets, since they were not published until 1609, and even on that occasion they appeared in print without his direct involvement. Yet clearly he was writing sonnets earlier. Frances Meres, in his *Palladis Tamia* of 1598, praises Shakespeare for his 'sugared sonnets among his private friends' along with his achievements as a dramatist. This testimony suggests that the sonnets were privately circulated in manuscript among the literati, as was indeed the custom with much poetry of the period; the calculated amateurism of non-published poetry had considerable cachet, whereas the writing of plays for public performance might be regarded as crassly commercial. Shakespeare had to earn a living, of course, but he also must have cared about his reputation as a poet; and privately circulated sonnets were just the thing. Sonnets had been in vogue since the late 1580s (when Shakespeare presumably arrived in London) and had been given a considerable boost by the appearance in print of Philip Sidney's *Astrophel and Stella* (1591) and Edmund Spenser's *Amoretti* (1595), among others.

These writings were presented as sonnet sequences, and so were Shakespeare's when they finally appeared in print. Whether they are entirely consistent internally as the narrative of a relationship is to be questioned, especially since they appear to have been written over a period of time, but nowadays the consensus is that the ordering is plausibly intentional and sequential. So too with the vexed question as to whether they are autobiographical: the general view today is that they probably are so, at least to the extent of registering powerful emotions in a relationship not unlike one that Shakespeare may have experienced personally.

In narrative terms, Shakespeare's sonnet sequence begins with a deep and loving affection between the speaker of the poems and a young man who appears to be well-born. The poet advises the young man to marry and beget heirs, since his beauty and achievements will be lost to posterity otherwise. The desires of his family for an heir are cited as a further motive for the young man not to waste his youth and beauty without begetting progeny. A corresponding theme is the achieving of immortality through poetry, and it is with this in mind that the poet urges his own vital function in the young man's life. The relationship soon takes on a pleading character, with the poet more importunate in his affections than the young man. Rival poets appear on the scene, prompting a jealous response from the poet-speaker. At times the relationship seems steadfast and immeasurably rewarding for the poet; at others, he seems insecure and anxious. Poems of longing express a desire for the young man's presence, or seek consolation in a time of separation with the thought that distance and time cannot conquer true affection. At other times, separation is an agony because the poet mistrusts its consequences. Toward the end of the sequence, an alarming new development manifests itself: the young man takes up with the poet's own mistress, the 'Dark Lady' of the Sonnets. The late sonnets are filled with bitterness, remorse, misogynistic resentment of women generally, and a hatred by the poet of his own sexual drive.

The most devastating manifestation of this last emotional experience is to be found in sonnet 129:

> Th'expense of spirit in a waste of shame
> Is lust in action; and, till action, lust
> Is perjured, murd'rous, bloody, full of blame,
> Savage, extreme, rude, cruel, not to trust,
> Enjoyed no sooner but despisèd straight,   5
> Past reason hunted, and no sooner had
> Past reason hated, as a swallowed bait
> On purpose laid to make the taker mad;
> Mad in pursuit, and in possession so;
> Had, having, and in quest to have, extreme;   10
> A bliss in proof, and proved, a very woe;
> Before, a joy proposed; behind, a dream.
>   All this the world well knows; yet none knows well
>   To shun the heaven that leads men to this hell.

The poet might almost be glossing the experience of Tarquin in Lucrece's bedchamber, lusting uncontrollably despite his understanding of the painful consequences of desire, and then loathing the very experience of orgasm as the prelude to remorse. This sad, repressed view of the male sexual experience, in which the entrance to the woman's sexual body is equated with the gates of hell, is one to which we will have occasion to return in exploring Shakespeare's later works.

A happier and earlier sonnet reveals not only the more upbeat themes of marriage and procreation as a means of immortalizing oneself, but also the poetic techniques that Shakespeare practised at the start of his writing career. Here is sonnet 7:

> Lo, in the orient when the gracious light
> Lifts up his burning head, each under eye
> Doth homage to his new-appearing sight,
> Serving with looks his sacred majesty;
> And having climbed the steep-up heavenly hill,   5
> Resembling strong youth in his middle age,
> Yet mortal looks adore his beauty still,
> Attending on his golden pilgrimage;
> But when from highmost pitch, with weary car,
> Like feeble age, he reeleth from the day,   10
> The eyes, 'fore duteous, now converted are
> From his low tract and look another way.
>   So thou, thyself outgoing in thy noon,
>   Unlooked on diest, unless thou get a son.

Here the young poet again pursues an extended analogy, a metaphor linking the daily passage of the sun across the sky to the life of a human being. The sun metaphor occupies the first twelve lines, down to the word 'So' in line 13 that introduces, in a final couplet, the application of the metaphor to the poet's young friend. The first twelve lines, arranged meaningfully in three four-line units or quatrains rhymed alternately in a pattern of abab, cdcd, efef, follow the course of the sun as it rises, shines brightly in mid-day, and then sets. The quatrains are set apart from one another by the rhyme scheme and by heavily end-stopped punctuation at the conclusion of each. At the same time, the thought moves forward by logical links, as the image proceeds from the burning light of morning sun toward the feeble glow of sunset.

The sun is strongly personified throughout, and is indeed vested with royal majesty. We humans do homage to the sun when it appears in its oriental splendour. Toward the end, we condescend to the sun now that it has lost its potency; we turn the other way, as ungrateful subjects might do in a declining monarchy. The pun on 'sun' and the 'son' of line 14, a favourite of Renaissance poets, reinforces a correlation between the extended metaphor and the final couplet's application of the image to the young man being addressed. The point of course is to urge procreation of children, since time will not stand still and beauty will inevitably fade.

The only recourse offered here to the ravages of time and ageing is the act of begetting progeny in a lawful marriage.

The verse reinforces, through strategies of sight and sound, the patterned movement of this sonnet. The first quatrain, introduced by the vocative 'Lo!' so expressive of wonder and worship, moves with assurance and calm. The second quatrain labours in its diction as it emulates the sun's climbing of the heavens; the scansion of line 5, 'And having climbed the steep-up heavenly hill' requires additional accents inserted into the iambic pattern ('stéep-úp héavenly) to achieve its effect. The third stanza, describing the decline of the sun, introduces an unusual number of pauses or caesuras calculated to slow down the lines: 'from highmost pitch, with weary car, / Like feeble age, he reeleth . . .' The final couplet, set apart from the rest of the sonnet by its couplet form, is similarly set apart by its didactic spelling out of the object-lesson to be learned by the young man, and by its abandonment of the sun metaphor that has governed the logic and rhetoric of this wonderfully contrived piece of writing for its first twelve lines.

Rather than boring you by discussing what you undoubtedly already know and feel about Shakespeare's best-known sonnets, such as 'Shall I compare thee to a summer's day' (sonnet 18) and 'Let me not to the marriage of true minds / Admit impediments' (sonnet 116), let me show you instead one more example that demonstrates the highly self-conscious and rhetorical manner of Shakespeare's incomparable sonneteering. Sonnet 29 explores the consolation that a poet can find in loving friendship when he needs that consolation most:

> When, in disgrace with fortune and men's eyes,
> I all alone beweep my outcast state,
> And trouble deaf heaven with my bootless cries,
> And look upon myself and curse my fate,
> Wishing me like to one more rich in hope,   5
> Featured like him, like him with friends possessed,
> Desiring this man's art and that man's scope,
> With what I most enjoy contented least;
> Yet in these thoughts myself almost despising,
> Haply I think on thee, and then my state,   10
> Like to the lark at break of day arising
> From sullen earth, sings hymns at heaven's gate;
>   For thy sweet love remembered such wealth brings
>   That then I scorn to change my state with kings.

This poem, like sonnet 7, employs a metaphor drawn from the natural world, but in this present instance the image of the lark does not govern the entire first twelve lines; its arrival is postponed until line 11. Instead, the poem moves toward this image in a prolonged and suspended dependent clause. That is to say, the subject and verb of the poem's one long sentence do not appear until line 10: 'Haply I think on thee'. The 'When' clause preceding that point continually looks forward to the payoff: what is the poet's anxiety a prelude to?

As in sonnet 7, Shakespeare carefully marshals the resources of the four-line quatrain. The first quatrain expresses the poet's dismay at lack of worldly success. It does so repeatedly, in the rhetorical device of amplification that Shakespeare often uses, and introduces those iterated instances with a repeated 'And': 'And trouble deaf heaven', 'And look . . .' This device of beginning successive lines with the same word is called anaphora, in case you wanted to know. ('Nay, I care not for their names', says Jaques in *As You Like It.* 'They owe me nothing.') The second stanza moves on to instances of the poet's unhappy jealousy toward those who prosper more than he. Again, the idea is amplified through repetition, affording Shakespeare an opportunity for some artfully contrived verbal gymnastics. Notice the repetition of sound and sense in line 6: 'Featured like him, like him with friends possessed'. This figure is known to the rhetoricians as anadiplosis, or the beginning of a phrase with the final words of the previous phrase; it is also ploce, the insistent repetition of a word within the same line or phrase. Line 7, 'Desiring this man's art and that man's scope', deftly displays the figure of rhetoric known as parison, or the symmetrical repetition of words in grammatically parallel phrases. 'This man's art' and 'that man's scope' are recurrent in their pattern since they both begin with a demonstrative, then a possessive, and then the noun. The parallelism here also employs isocolon, or the repetition of units of equal length of sound: in 'this man's art' and 'that man's scope' the words of the second phrase repeat the monosyllabic length of the first. Sounds are repeated as well: 'this' and 'that' begin with the same letters (alliteration again), and 'man's' is repeated. Repetition is of course a fundamental element of poetry, and lends itself to antithesis, as in line 8, where 'what I most enjoy' is explicitly contrasted with 'contented least' through the antithesis of most/least. It is here practised as a contrived art that a young poet can learn through experience and imitation.

Following this brilliant though unobtrusive demonstration of what were known as the 'flowers' of rhetoric, the sonnet develops a new strategy of upward movement. The mood through the first two quatrains is one of deep discouragement. At that point, turning his thought around with the functional word 'Yet', the sonneteer finds consolation in friendship. With this uplifting thought, the poem too ascends. The image of the lark rising at break of day, which any English person who has been out in the fields at dawn can witness to, is indeed heavenly. The lark's voice seems to pour down from way up there. It soars far above this 'sullen earth', and does indeed seem to sing 'hymns at heaven's gate'. The poem provides language for this ascent as it moves forward past the end of the verse line in 11–12: 'at break of day arising / From sullen earth'. And, once the poem has reached its triumphant affirmation in loving friendship, it finds its own high plateau of sound. The concluding couplet, after the onrush of ascent in lines 11–12, is steady, confident, sublimely monosyllabic (except for 'remembered') and Anglo-Saxon in its choice of plain, simple words: 'For thy sweet love remembered such wealth brings / That then I scorn to change my state with kings'.

Shakespeare did not need to confine his artistry as poet to his narrative poems and sonnets. The drama of his time was very often written in verse, especially blank verse, which had been invented only a few decades earlier (1557) by the poet Henry Howard, the Earl of Surrey, in his translation of Virgil's *Aeneid*; blank verse was meant to provide an English equivalent for Virgil's Latin hexameters. Shakespeare's early plays in all genres – comedy, history, tragedy – are largely in verse. The language is tightly controlled and rhetorically stylized, as in the examples we have seen in the poems. Take for instance the justly famous opening of *Richard III*:

> Now is the winter of our discontent
> Made glorious summer by this son of York,
> And all the clouds that loured upon our house
> In the deep bosom of the ocean buried.
> Now are our brows bound with victorious wreaths,   5
> Our bruisèd arms hung up for monuments,
> Our stern alarums changed to merry meetings,
> Our dreadful marches to delightful measures.
> Grim-visaged War hath smoothed his wrinkled front;
> And now, instead of mounting barbèd steeds   10
> To fright the souls of fearful adversaries,
> He capers nimbly in a lady's chamber
> To the lascivious pleasing of a lute.

This passage is in blank verse, that is, iambic pentameter, which is to say in a five-stress line composed of five 'feet' ('penta' means 'five') that move iambically from an unstressed to a stressed syllable: 'And áll the clóuds that lóured upón our hóuse'. This pattern may be varied at times, since perfect rhythmic repetition becomes monotonous: 'Nów is the wínter of our díscontént' begins with an inversion in the first foot and asks for little if any stress on the unimportant 'of'. Still, the basic rhythmic beat is unmistakable. The metrical form is well suited to English speech; the accents in these lines fall where we would expect them, and the stresses call our attention to the important words. The lines in this passage are generally end-stopped, that is, with a marked pause at the end of each, and the individual lines are not interrupted in the middle by pauses. Run-on lines that move uninterruptedly past the end of the line, together with caesuras or marked pauses in the middle of lines, are increasingly frequent as we move into Shakespeare's middle and late career. The present passage is manifestly early.

This passage is not part of a lyric or narrative poem; it is a dramatic monologue, spoken by an actor in soliloquy. Yet the verse is almost as organized as a sonnet. The speech begins with two quatrains, marked at the transitions by end punctuation. In the first four lines, Richard mockingly congratulates his native country for having achieved peace after the so-called Wars of the Roses between Lancaster and York; his party, of York, has won, and his powerful family members are now celebrating. The verbal adroitness of Richard's speech depends rhetorically on antithesis: the contrasts of winter and summer, cloudy skies and clear skies, war and peace. These antitheses proceed in this first quatrain in two-line segments, first winter to summer in two lines (with a familiar pun on 'sun' and 'son'), then clouds to clear skies in lines 3–4. Then, in the second four-line unit, we encounter the same antithesis, only this time repeated four times, one to each line: unadorned brows to wreath-bound brows, battered arms ('bruisèd arms') to trophies of victory ('monuments'), military sorties ('alarums') to merry meetings, the awesome march of soldiers to delightful dancing ('measures').

Along with the repeated and rhythmic use of antithesis, which mockingly emphasizes Richard's thesis that war has given way to peace, Shakespeare uses amplification by saying essentially the same thing a number of times in different words and employing different metaphors. Moreover, the passage is replete with the rhetorical figures we have seen in the narrative poems and sonnets. Antithesis positively invites the repetition in grammatically identical patterns: 'stern alarums' changed to 'merry meetings' (adjective-noun), 'dreadful marches' to 'delightful measures' (adjective-noun). These two lines, 7 and 8, are virtually identical to one another in their pattern of antithetical repetition. The second of these lines makes notable use of alliteration in the repetition of first letters of words: *d*readful *m*arches, *d*elightful *m*easures. The lines are organized and connected to one another by anaphora, or repetition of the initial first word: in lines 6–8, 'Our', 'Our', 'Our'.

Line 9 stands by itself as a personification of War, though the antithesis is the same as before: the god of war, no longer frowning, is now smiling. What then follows is a third quatrain in lines 10–13. This time, Shakespeare extends his antithetical war-peace pattern over the entire four lines, describing rather comically how the god of war has given up his customary pursuit of mounting steeds and is instead capering nimbly in a lady's chamber 'To the lascivious pleasing of a lute'. A musical metaphor extends the vocabulary of antithesis as we move from the sounds of war to those of chamber music and dancing. The pleasingly irregular cadences of line 13, with its numerous unaccented syllables – 'To the lascívious pléasing of a lúte' – captures the lightness and frivolity of the occasion that Richard wishes to characterize. Richard's distaste for England's turning from war to peace is by now evident, so much so that we perceive another antithesis: from masculine assertiveness to soft effeminacy. Peace, to Richard, is enervating and corrupting.

The first thirteen lines of this play are thus almost sonnet-like in their organization: three quatrains and a one-line unit (line 9), rather than three quatrains and a concluding couplet. Let us go on a bit further:

> But I, that am not shaped for sportive tricks,
> Nor made to court an amorous looking-glass;   15
> I, that am rudely stamped, and want love's majesty
> To strut before a wanton, ambling nymph;
> I, that am curtailed of this fair proportion,
> Cheated of feature by dissembling Nature,
> Deformed, unfinished, sent before my time   20
> Into this breathing world scarce half made up,
> And that so lamely and unfashionable
> That dogs bark at me as I halt by them –
> Why, I, in this weak piping time of peace,
> Have no delight to pass away the time,   25
> Unless to see my shadow in the sun
> And descant on mine own deformity.

Here, with his abrupt 'But I', Richard turns to himself and his place in a time of corrupting peace. He has no function in it. His distaste is conveyed through a series of proofs that he is not fit for a lady's bedchamber. The proofs repeat the point, in the pattern of amplification, making strong use of anaphora to introduce each new instance: 'But I, that', 'I, that', 'I, that', 'Why, I' (lines 14, 16, 18, 24). The long sentence from lines 14 through 27 is a suspended sentence; that is, the main verb is postponed until line 25 ('I . . . Have no delight to pass away the time'), in order that Richard may dazzle us with an array of illustrations of his deformity and his rage. The verse mimics what he is saying, as in the halting meter of this purposefully ragged line: 'That dógs bárk at me as I hált bý them'. Renaissance rhetoricians would call attention to the spondees, or feet with two heavy stresses: 'dógs bárk', 'hált bý', as expressive of limping.

Shakespeare's early plays are often filled with lyrical poetic forms embedded in the dramatic dialogue. Not everyone notices, perhaps, that when Romeo and Juliet first speak to each other at the Capulets' masked ball, they do so in the form of a perfect Shakespearean sonnet, in which the quatrain form governs the pace of the dialogue:

ROMEO: If I profane with my unworthiest hand
This holy shrine, the gentle sin is this: 95
My lips, two blushing pilgrims, ready stand
To smooth that rough touch with a tender kiss.
JULIET: Good pilgrim, you do wrong your hand too much,
Which mannerly devotion shows in this:
For saints have hands that pilgrims' hands do touch,   100
And palm to palm is holy palmers' kiss.
ROMEO: Have not saints lips, and holy palmers too?
JULIET: Ay, pilgrim, lips that they must use in prayer.
ROMEO: Oh, then, dear saint, let lips do what hands do.
They pray; grant thou, lest faith turn to despair.   105
JULIET: Saints do not move, though grant for prayers' sake.
ROMEO: Then move not, while my prayer's effect I take.
[*He kisses her.*]
(1.5.94–107)

Astonishingly, this moment of romantic ecstasy is rendered in a verse form that requires absolute control of language. Three quatrains (rhymed abab cdcd efef) lead on to the final couplet (gg). The lovers' first kiss comes after the couplet. How does Shakespeare manage to combine tight rhetorical contrivance with passionate and deeply personal utterance?

The controlling metaphor in the sonnet is that of a pilgrimage to a shrine: Romeo is the pilgrim, Juliet's hand is the shrine he hopes to worship with a kiss. The worship of a woman is a commonplace of Renaissance poetry, borrowing (blasphemously, if you like) from the language of religious devotion. Romeo uses the arch and frayed metaphor of the courtly love tradition, in which the man prostrates himself before the object of his desire; the male is importunate, self-abnegating, pleading. Romeo seizes the initiative; the first four-line unit of the sonnet is his, and he exploits it to fashion an elaborate, extended metaphor of imploring his 'saint' to save his life by returning his ardour.

Juliet, attracted to Romeo but caught off guard, parries his metaphor with language that displays both her wit and her prudent sense of caution. Romeo is coming on pretty strong, and his metaphor betrays the very sort of fashionable sonneteering that Juliet will try to wean him from in their first extended conversation in the garden below her window. (It is not a balcony, by the way, it is a window.) In the sonnet's second quatrain, given entirely to her, Juliet matches image for image in the game of metaphorical interchange that Romeo's gambit has laid down for her. She continues to speak of him as a pilgrim, since he has chosen that role, but she mildly rebukes him for his self-abnegation, and offers as much encouragement as she decorously can by insisting that she is no saint, or, if he insists on calling her one, then she is a saint with real hands and real feelings. Her parrying his move takes the form of suggesting that a touch of hands may be sufficient at the moment, as they dance together; a kiss would be presumptuous and too sudden.

When Romeo takes advantage of her extending his metaphor to argue that saints must have lips as well as hands, she again has a witty and decorous reply: lips are to be used in prayer. We notice that in this third quatrain the lovers are now sharing the lines; we have moved from a quatrain apiece to one in which Romeo and Juliet are singing in rapid alternation. The astute logic of their argument leads into Romeo's final use of the pilgrim metaphor: he pleads with his 'saint' to save him as only she can do. The move allows Juliet to accede out of compassion and without taking the initiative (which would be improper for her to do), since saints are the passive objects of veneration. In this fashion, the lovers and the sonnet form arrive at the same point of conclusion, and they kiss.

Shakespeare's early comedies are filled with songs and other lyrical expressions. *A Midsummer Night's Dream* (*c.* 1595) is largely in verse, except for the broad comedy scenes of Bottom the Weaver and company;

at this stage in his career, Shakespeare tends to use verse for his romantic characters and prose for the clowns. The play is a *tour de force* of verse forms. Theseus and his courtiers speak generally in blank verse, and it is the serviceable vehicle for dialogue in other parts of the plays as well. When the lovers are engaging in one-line exchanges (or stichomythia, as it is called), they sometimes use rhymed couplets, as when Helena and Hermia are comparing notes on how they should respond to Demetrius's unwelcome paying of attention to Hermia and his spurning of Helena:

> HERMIA: I frown upon him, yet he loves me still.
> HELENA: Oh, that your frowns would teach my smiles such skill!
> HERMIA: I give him curses, yet he gives me love.
> HELENA: Oh, that my prayers could such affection move!
> (1.1.194–7)

Note the rhetorical use of alternating repetitions here – 'I . . . yet he . . .' in lines 1 and 3, 'Oh, that . . .' in 2 and 4 – running across the rhyming pattern which links lines 1 with 2 and 3 with 4.

The fairies sometimes use a shorter verse line, like this chant at the start of the second act:

> FAIRY: Over hill, over dale,
>   Thorough bush, thorough brier,
> Over park, over pale,
>   Thorough flood, thorough fire,
> I do wander everywhere,
> Swifter than the moon's sphere.
> (2.1.2–7)

Two-stress lines in alternating rhyme culminate in a rhymed couplet. The shorter line accentuates the rhymes, since they occur so frequently; the effect is like the lyric of a song, and who is to say whether the fairy says or sings these lines? The anaphora and repetitions within lines are no less marked: 'Thorough . . . thorough', 'Over' . . . 'over'. The rhythm is reinforced by alliteration: 'bush . . . briar', 'park . . . pale', 'flood . . . fire'. The rhythmic repetition in these same instances of equal-sounding words of equal length in identical grammatical positions is essential to the songlike quality of the passage.

Puck is fond of trochaic tetrameter in couplets, that is, four-beat verse starting off on a stressed syllable:

> Through the forest have I gone,
> But Athenian found I none
> On whose eyes I might approve
> This flower's force in stirring love.
>   (2.2.72–5)

Oberon uses this verse pattern as well, when he applies love-juice to the lovers' eyes; and when he and Titania are reconciled, she answers his rhymed trochaic tetrameters in kind. When the fairies sing a song, they add pleasing variety to the play's ample store of lyric forms: for their 'roundel' or dancing in a ring, they sing a lullaby. 'Pyramus and Thisbe', the godawful entertainment put on by Bottom and company before the Duke and his Duchess in act five, is a delicious travesty of verse forms that shows how easy it is to do this sort of thing badly:

> But stay, oh, spite!
> But mark, poor knight,
> What dreadful dole is here?
> Eyes, do you see?
> How can it be?
> Oh, dainty duck! Oh, dear!
>   (5.1.272–7)

The astonishing thing is that these verses display so many of the rhetorical devices through which Shakespeare learned to write so well: anaphora ('But', 'But'), the mix of rhymed couplets and alternating rhyme, alliteration ('dreadful dole', 'dainty duck . . . Oh, dear'), grammatical repetitions ('But stay', 'But mark'), personification and apostrophe ('Eyes, do you see?'), and so on. What it is that distinguishes great lyrical verse from utter banality is almost indefinably subtle. Learning the difference is a matter of taste and genius; it is also a matter of practice. Shakespeare apprenticed himself to his trade.

CHAPTER TWO

◆

Creeping Like Snail

Childhood, Education, Early Friendship, Sibling Rivalries

Mon semblable, mon frère.[1]
Baudelaire, 'Au lecteur'

Shakespeare's children are an odd lot generally. They are precocious; they speak like little adults, except that they cling to an innocence which presumably they are to lose as they grow older. Infancy and childhood are remembered later in life as golden moments. They are remembered too, of course, as painful and awkward: Jaques, in his Seven Ages of Man speech, pities the infant 'Mewling and puking in the nurse's arms', and King Lear escalates this wry view into an indictment of the very process of being born: 'the first time that we smell the air / We wawl and cry'. Still, most children in Shakespeare are happy enough to be alive. If only they knew!

The oddness and precocity can be seen, for example, in the two young princes of *Richard III* who are destined to be murdered at their uncle's command. Both are brought to London (3.1) after the untimely death of their father, King Edward IV. Young Richard exhibits his precocity in the form of a 'sharp-provided wit' that comes dangerously close to mocking his namesake uncle Richard for his humped back. The older brother, Edward, now the young king of England though not yet crowned, can only dimly perceive the power struggle that is circling around him in the shape of uncles and other family members professing to be his well-wishers and guardians; he knows only that some of his uncles on his mother's side have been executed, and he wishes they were still alive to counsel him. His talk is full of the idealism of youth. 'Methinks the truth should live from age to age', he insists, as he reflects on the legend that Julius Caesar built the Tower of London. Richard of Gloucester, commenting *sotto voce*, warns us that such idealism cannot fare well in a cruel world: 'So wise so young, they say, do never live long'. When Edward vows that he will, if he lives to be a man, 'win our ancient right in France again / Or die a soldier, as I lived a king', Richard again chills us with a private choric response: 'Short summers lightly have a forward spring'. Precocity is at once attractive and doomed.

Both princes fear that their other uncle, the Duke of Clarence, has been murdered in the Tower and that his ghost haunts that place. This anxiety produces an exchange between Edward and his uncle Richard that shows the youngster's verbal dexterity in the rhetorical figure of antimetabole, or the symmetrical repetition of words in inverted order:

PRINCE EDWARD: I fear no uncles dead.
RICHARD OF GLOUCESTER: Nor none that live, I hope.
EDWARD: An if they live, I hope I need not fear.
                                                      (3.1.146–8)

Beginning and ending in 'fear' (an effect also known as epanalepsis), the passage plays with 'dead' and 'live', 'hope' and 'fear' in a way that is at once witty and heartbreaking, since we know that the boys' lives will soon end. Shakespeare uses younger persons in a tragic drama like *Richard III* to highlight the painful contrast between youthful idealism and an older, worldly-wise cynicism that preys upon innocence and destroys it.[2]

Prince Arthur in *King John* (*c.* 1594–6) is a remarkable part for a boy actor on the Shakespearean stage. Surrounded by older men grasping for power in an era of dynastic uncertainty and kept in custody by his uncle (King John) who occupies a throne belonging by right of inheritance to Arthur himself, the boy is thus the inevitable focus of a struggle that involves the French as well as various interested parties in England. He himself seems motivated by nothing more complex than a deep fondness for his keeper, Hubert. The scene in which he learns that Hubert has been ordered to put out his eyes (since the last thing John needs around is a relative with a better claim to the throne than his own) is deeply moving and personal. Hubert sees at last that he cannot do this thing to such a lovely young person, at whatever risk to himself. Yet the danger if he disobeys is delayed, not ended, since the mere fact of Arthur's existence is enough to keep alive John's political difficulties. Arthur jumps from the walls of the castle where he has been kept prisoner and dies on the unyielding stones below,

> Oh, me! My uncle's spirit is in these stones.
> Heaven take my soul, and England keep my bones!
> (4.3.9–10)

thereby setting in motion a baronial rebellion against John and a French alliance against him that is only barely defeated.[3] Arthur's childhood innocence is the only glimmer of hope in a fallen world, and is not enough to prevent political disaster. Yet the image of his tender goodness is ineradicable, both as an indictment of adult human folly and as a promise of something better.

Macduff's young son has a similar role to play in *Macbeth*. Like Arthur, he is the victim of a power struggle over which he has no control. His very innocence tells against him. His father's great enemy, Macbeth, in seeking to terrify his nobility into compliance with his usurped and now tyrannical rule, vows to 'give to th'edge o'the sword' Macduff's wife, his babes, 'and all unfortunate souls / That trace him in his line'. Macbeth cannot bear that his aristocrats and rivals for power should have children while he has none; he has already done his best to eradicate the lineage of his chief rival, Banquo. In that he fails, because prophecy dictates that Banquo's progeny shall be kings, but Macduff's children are afforded no such supernatural protection.

The scene (4.2) in which Lady Macduff and her son learn of impending butchery and then confront the butchers sent against them is representative of Shakespeare's use of children in tragic drama. The boy is young, naive, bright, and trusting. He knows that birds manage to live by eating worms and flies, so why may he not somehow survive too? His naive questioning of his mother looks at death and danger in such a way as to call into question the supposed wisdom of his elders. If his father is dead, as his mother reports (untruly, lest the boy wonder why the father is not at home protecting them), why may not his mother buy another husband at the market? If traitors are executed for swearing and telling lies, why should not the swearers and liars hang up the honest men instead, since there are more swearers and liars? The boy is, as his mother says, a 'poor prattler' speaking 'with all thy wit', and yet in his innocence he sees more truth about human folly than his supposed betters can imagine. These inversions remind us of the Fool in *King Lear*, Lear's 'boy', a child in mind if not in years, whose seemingly foolish speech repeatedly perceives truths that can be discerned only by those who are children, or fools, or the victimized.

Childhood is not always such an endangered state, of course. In the comedies, pertness and precocious wit can be part of the fun. The page called Mote in *Love's Labour's Lost* (the word 'moth' in the original can mean a 'mote' or speck dancing in a sunbeam or else a moth) takes pleasure in spoofing the affected mannerisms of his master, Don Armado, the fantastical Spaniard. Armado calls his page 'boy', 'imp', and 'my tender juvenal', plainly indicating the need for a boy actor in the role. Uppity servants are often called 'boy', as for example in *The Comedy of Errors* and *The Two Gentlemen of Verona*, and indeed their wit runs to the adolescent or even infantile in its wordplay on scatological functions or the parts of the woman's body. Their comic routines of sassing their elders are dramaturgical effects that Shakespeare learned at least in part from the plays of John Lyly, whose theatrical successes in the 1580s (*Campaspe, Sappho and Phao, Galatea, Endymion*) were written for acting companies made up almost entirely of boy actors. Shakespeare's plays always employ boy actors for the women's parts, but also in the portrayal of pages, young servants, and children.

One of the most endearing portraits of childhood, and especially of schooling, is to be found in *The Merry Wives of Windsor* (1597–1601). The scene (4.1) is too often cut from production because it is quite detachable. William, the son of Mistress Page (one of the 'merry wives' of the title), is being taken to school by his mother when they happen to encounter the Welsh-born schoolmaster, Sir Hugh Evans. Evans puts his pupil through his Latin paces in order to impress Mrs Page with how well her son is being taught. The pedagogy, truly offputting, involves nothing but a catechism of memorized definitions and declensions in Latin. Asked by Evans to explain 'What is he, William, that does lend articles?' (meaning, evidently, How does one decline demonstrative pronouns like 'this' and 'that'?), William parrots the standard answer out of a Latin grammar book written by John Lyly's grandfather, William Lilly: 'Articles are borrowed of the pronoun, and be thus declined, *singulariter, nominativo, hic, haec, hoc*'. Prodded by his interrogator, William goes on from the nominative to the accusative case, though he makes a mistake here and has to be chastised for it. The accusative, in Evans's droll Welsh manner of speaking, comes out as '*hung, hang, hog*' – i.e., '*hunc, hanc, hoc*'. Evans's attempt to be serious about this method of instruction is not enhanced by the fact that Mistress Quickly, ignorant of Latin, keeps hearing risible English analogues: ' "Hang-hog" is Latin for bacon, I warrant you', she helpfully suggests.

The boy is partly pleased to show off his learning and partly cowed by his tendency to forget and thus stand in jeopardy of a spanking. 'You must be preeches', the schoolmaster warns, meaning that the boy must be spanked with his breeches pulled down. Shakespeare amiably displays the inanity of it all, in recollection no doubt of his own school days in Stratford. Whether spanking was pedagogically conducive to learning was a lively topic in his day, with schoolmasters generally in favour. The pedant Holofernes in *Love's Labour's Lost*, with his teeth-gnashing puns and his zealotry about scansion, is an even more daunting caricature of the schoolmaster. One wonders if Shakespeare, who certainly could not have learned all that he eventually learned from memorizing Latin declensions, felt about his formal instruction pretty much the way that the 'whining schoolboy' does in Jaques' Seven Ages of Man speech, 'creeping like snail / Unwillingly to school'.

The innocent idealism of childhood and youth is often remembered in Shakespeare as a time of unsullied friendship between young persons of the same sex; it is also a time when rivalries begin among siblings. The memory of their friendship is very dear to the hearts of Polixenes and Leontes in *The Winter's Tale*, for example. King Polixenes of Bohemia, at the end of a nine-month visit to King Leontes of Sicilia, recalls how much they meant to each other as youths:

> We were as twinned lambs that did frisk i'the sun
> And bleat the one at th'other. What we changed
> Was innocence for innocence; we knew not
> The doctrine of ill-doing, nor dreamed
> That any did. Had we pursued that life,
> And our weak spirits ne'er been higher reared
> With stronger blood, we should have answered heaven
> Boldly 'Not guilty', the imposition cleared
> Hereditary ours.
>
> (1.2.67–75)

The exact ages of these two persons is not specified, but implicitly they had not yet reached the age of sexual maturation, because when Leontes' queen, Hermione, playfully suggests 'By this we gather / You have tripped since', Polixenes takes up her suggested line of reasoning by blaming the young men's fall from innocence on sexual desire:

> Oh, my most sacred lady,
> Temptations have since then been born to 's, for
> In those unfledged days was my wife a girl;
> Your precious self had then not crossed the eyes
> Of my young playfellow.
>
> (1.2.76–80)

Puberty brings with it a consciousness of and a potentiality for sin that had previously been absent, because of the absence of desire. Sex is directly associated with the very beginning of sin in human history, the fall of man and the expulsion from the Garden of Eden. In the equivalent of that garden, Polixenes and Leontes 'knew not / The doctrine of ill-doing', and did not even know of its existence among other humans. They were, so to speak, unaware of their nakedness, or at least that nakedness might be shameful. They were 'not guilty', cleared of the hereditary 'imposition' – that is, of original sin. The conversation is a playful one, but it does bespeak a mind-set like that we encounter in some of Shakespeare's sonnets: sex is revulsive and brings on self-loathing. We were all of us in a better place before we became sexually conscious. And indeed, in this play the adult friendship of Leontes and Polixenes soon falls prey to the debilitating and nearly tragic consequences of jealousy.

The image of twinned lambs brings to mind a lovely passage in *A Midsummer Night's Dream* when Helena, one of the four young persons who have fled to the forest of Athens in pursuit of love only to find that their amorous longings are being frustrated at every turn, appeals to Hermia to remember the mutual fondness they have previously shared as loving friends. Again, what Helena recalls is innocence and twinning. That blissful state stands out in memory as wholly unlike the anxious jealousies that they are now encountering in the forest. Helena is speaking, in an attempt to persuade Hermia to side with her and not with the men, who, she thinks, are mocking her by their courtship of her:

> Is all the counsel that we two have shared –
> The sisters' vows, the hours that we have spent
> When we have chid the hasty-footed time
> For parting us – oh, is all forgot?
> All schooldays' friendship, childhood innocence?

> We, Hermia, like two artificial gods
> Have with our needles created both one flower,
> Both on one sampler, sitting on one cushion,
> Both warbling of one song, both in one key,
> As if our hands, our sides, voices, and minds
> Had been incorporate. So we grew together,
> Like to a double cherry, seeming parted,
> But yet an union in partition,
> Two lovely berries moulded on one stem;
> So, with two seeming bodies but one heart,
> Two of the first, like coats in heraldry,
> Due but to one and crownèd with one crest.
>   (3.2.198–214)

Helena speaks of her childhood friendship with Hermia as though they were not only twins but Siamese twins, sharing one body with one heart, their hands and sides incorporate, joined like a double cherry. So too their voices and minds were as one: they sang the same songs, as they sat working on the same 'sampler' or decorative piece of needlework.

The image brilliantly captures what is so attractive and psychologically vital about same-sex friendship in childhood. As the infant matures into the young child, he or she inevitably seeks new relationships outside the family and discovers thereby an alter ego, an image of the self embodied in some other child of the same age and sex. Friendship is of course possible between boys and girls at this age, but Shakespeare tends to dramatize same-sex friendship in the pre-adolescent years. This kind of friendship affords a relationship that the family cannot provide. The other person to whom one now becomes firmly attached is not a sibling, competing with oneself for parental attention and approval; nor is that person an adult. That other person is a version of oneself. 'Horatio – or I do forget myself!' says Hamlet when, in a moment of intense personal crisis and disgust with the members of his own family, he encounters once again the best friend that he has ever known. A friend of one's age and sex becomes, in childhood, the person with whom one can be truly confidential. One need not trust others; friendship in Shakespeare is often a matter of choosing that one soul-mate with the hope of some permanence, as in the sonnets. Even if there are more than one, they must be few in number. As Polonius advises his son Laertes in *Hamlet*, 'Those friends thou hast, and their adoption tried, / Grapple them unto thy soul with hoops of steel', while avoiding shallow friendships with 'each new-hatched, unfledged courage'. These examples are drawn from the time when Hamlet, Horatio, and Laertes are no longer children, and yet the intense appeal of same-sex friendship remains as strong as in childhood, or even stronger.

Like Polixenes and Leontes in *The Winter's Tale*, Helena and Hermia of *A Midsummer Night's Dream* go through a sort of nightmare as they encounter the opposite sex. The encounter is bracing, at times intensely rewarding, and eventually successful, but the transition is a time of peril. Helena begs Hermia to share with her the memory of their perfect complementarity as young girls, discovering in each other a chance to see themselves, as it were, from the outside. Shakespeare chooses names for them that are similar almost to the point of interchangeability: Hermia, Helena, both trisyllabic, beginning in 'He' with the stress on the first syllable and ending in 'a'. The relationship is in one sense narcissistic: it replicates beautifully the legend of Narcissus, falling in love with his own reflection in a pool, with the crucial difference that the young person falls in love with someone who is Other and can thus provide a seeming escape from the solipsism of being locked inside one's own psyche. This new experience of loving friendship is intensely liberating and euphoric. As in *The Winter's Tale*, it is seen as prelapsarian: it recuperates the imagined experience of the Garden of Eden before the fall. 'Childhood innocence' is celebrated not simply in being a child; it takes the self-enlarging form of same-sex friendship. Through the recurrent image of Siamese-like physical and emotional bonding, it enables the individual child to move beyond single selfhood into community.

Innocent friendship among young people is especially tender when it exists between two girls or young women.[4] Celia and Rosalind in *As You Like It* are inseparable friends. They are no longer children, but we do meet them before romantic opportunities arise to pull them in different directions. They are cousins, not sisters, and thus are separated enough to be friends without the direct competition of being in the same nuclear family. In fact the bitter rivalry of their two fathers, who as brothers cannot stand each other, intensifies the young women's need for each other. Celia talks of their companionship in images of union that recall those of Helena as she appeals to Hermia's remembrance of their childhood friendship in *A Midsummer Night's Dream*. Speaking to her father of Rosalind, Celia declares,

> We still have slept together,
> Rose at an instant, learned, played, eat together,

And wheresoe'er we went, like Juno's swans
Still we went coupled and inseparable.

(1.3.71–4)

Celia is probably confusing Juno's swans with Venus' swans, that were
yoked together to draw Venus' chariot, but both goddesses rode in char-
iots, and in any case the image is of physical yoking. The young women's
occupations are described as being the same as in *A Midsummer Night's
Dream*: studying (presumably in a private tutorial at home), playing,
eating together. We learn that they were 'ever from their cradles bred
together' and would suffer any misfortune before allowing themselves to
be separated.

Celia's father vigorously opposes this friendship, and tries to wean his
daughter away from Rosalind by a piece of worldly advice. His reply to
Celia's description of that friendship is to argue that Rosalind's very goodness is a reason for Celia to part company from her:

She is too subtle for thee; and her smoothness,
Her very silence, and her patience
Speak to the people, and they pity her.
Thou art a fool. She robs thee of thy name,
And thou wilt show more bright and seem more virtuous
When she is gone.

(1.3.75–80)

Duke Frederick knows whereof he speaks. Having stolen the dukedom
from his older brother, Duke Senior, Frederick rules through tyranny and
intimidation. His advice to Celia is to emulate his practice by distancing
herself from a relative of her own age and sex whom the people will
inevitably compare with her, and to Celia's disadvantage. Young and innocent friendship, in this equation, is presented by Shakespeare as entirely
opposite to the rivalry of older siblings. Duke Frederick rules over 'the
envious court', where envy produces hatred and murderous intent. Celia
and Rosalind's only option is to flee to the Forest of Arden as a refuge,
a place of innocence even if it also contains the dangers that are inherent
in the natural world. Celia leaves her father and exposes herself to these
dangers in the name of friendship with Rosalind, who must, as the daughter of the banished Duke Senior, also seek exile. In the forest they find a
true father and, ultimately, a husband for both young women.

Beatrice and Hero in *Much Ado about Nothing* are also cousins who are close to each other in age. Theirs too is chiefly a story of courtship to which we will return, but in the present context of same-sex friendship we might note here the same kind of closely knit sisterhood that is discernible in Helena and Hermia, or Rosalind and Celia. Beatrice and Hero sleep together: 'I have this twelvemonth been her bedfellow', avows Beatrice, in an attempt to confute the horrible accusation that Hero has been sleeping around with various men, even on the very eve of her intended wedding to Claudio. Beatrice concedes that she absented herself from Hero's bed on the night in question, presumably so that Hero could ready herself emotionally for the new experience of sleeping with a man in lawful marriage, but Beatrice hotly denies the possibility of any wanton behaviour on Hero's part. She has shared a room with her, knows her heart, her habits, her thoughts about men. Beatrice possesses a special knowledge, based on intimacy, love, and faith, that sees the truth of Hero's plight when most of the men, including Hero's own father, are misled by their own fearful prejudices against women and their credulous willingness to believe what any man will say against women. Female friendship is here more certain and true than the morally compromising fashion in which men generally share attitudes and convictions.

Friendship among women is, on the whole, a wonderful thing in Shakespeare. (Let us set aside for the moment the ominous collaboration of the three Weird Sisters in *Macbeth*, or that of Goneril and Regan in *King Lear*!) We see it, briefly but poignantly, in Titania's explanation, in *A Midsummer Night's Dream*, of her reasons for wanting to keep the changeling boy that she and Oberon are quarrelling over:

> The fairy land buys not the child of me.
> His mother was a vot'ress of my order,
> And in the spicèd Indian air by night
> Full often hath she gossiped by my side
> And sat with me on Neptune's yellow sands,
> Marking th'embarkèd traders on the flood,
> When we have laughed to see the sails conceive
> And grow big-bellied with the wanton wind;
> Which she, with pretty and with swimming gait,
> Following – her womb then rich with my young squire –
> Would imitate, and sail upon the land
> To fetch me trifles, and return again
> As from a voyage, rich with merchandise.

But she, being mortal, of that boy did die;
And for her sake do I rear up her boy,
And for her sake I will not part with him.

(2.1.122–37)

This shared intimacy between two women stands out in vivid contrast to the quarrel between the King and Queen of Fairies. Because Titania's faithful attendant died in pregnancy, Titania feels that she owes it to that woman, whom she dearly loved, to rear the child in her memory rather than turn the boy over to the very male Oberon (whose motive, so far as we can tell, is chiefly one of wanting to teach Titania a lesson as to who is boss, but who may also be amorously inclined toward 'the lovèd boy' whom he desires to have as his 'henchman' or attendant page). Titania's love for the dear mother of the child is prompted by recollection of a magical time together when they shared experiences as only women can, celebrating pregnancy. The woman's graceful gestures, with her big-bellied stance and gait, imitated those of the sailing ships visible offshore; like the sails, she conceived and was full. The passage is so beautiful that one is prompted to wonder if Oberon's insistence on having the child is prompted also by the jealousy of longing for something that Oberon simply cannot have. Women share a special world in which men have no place.

For a manifestation of this same feminine close relationship in the tragic context of male hostility and resentment, we might look at Emilia and Desdemona in *Othello*. Emilia knows that she herself is unhappily married to Iago. She tries at least intermittently to please him, if only to keep peace (divorce being, in early modern Europe, usually out of the question), but to no avail. Infinitely more precious to Emilia is her relationship to the virtuous and generous woman she serves as a companion and lady-in-waiting, Desdemona. The scene (4.3) in which Emilia prepares Desdemona to go to bed and await the arrival of the bridegroom who will, as we already know, murder her is an extraordinary one of intimate conversation between women. Their difference in rank is of no consequence; it matters to neither of them. They wish to talk about marriage. Desdemona has good reason to ask questions; men are a puzzling, even a frightening, lot, and her husband has begun to treat her very badly. The conversation turns to Lodovico, a Venetian nobleman who has just come from Venice to Cyprus with letters from the Venetian governors removing Othello from his command and deputing Cassio in his place. 'This Lodovico is a proper man', comments Desdemona to her companion in the privacy of her apartments, and Emilia readily agrees: 'A very handsome man'. 'He speaks well', adds Desdemona, to which Emilia replies with an observation that plainly reveals her own warmth of feeling toward Lodovico's handsomeness: 'I know a lady in Venice would have walked barefoot to Palestine for a touch of his nether lip'. The frankness is disarming and revealing. Both women, we feel sure, have not the slightest intention of doing anything about their fascination with Lodovico, but they can look if not touch, and they can establish a confidence with each other in admitting that Lodovico is, for them, something of a male god.

Desdemona's willow song, famously set to music by Verdi in his *Otello*, puts before the two women a sad tale of a maiden made desolate by her false lover's accusation that she will 'couch with more men'. 'Oh, these men, these men!' exclaims Desdemona as she finishes her song. 'Dost thou in conscience think – tell me, Emilia – / That there be women do abuse their husbands / In such gross kind?' Emilia matter-of-factly allows that there are 'some such, no question'. 'Wouldst thou do such a deed for all the world?' pursues Desdemona. Emilia's droll answer is that she would do so indeed 'for all the whole world' – in the literal sense of doing it for infinite wealth. Who wouldn't make her husband a cuckold in order to make him a monarch? The women are bantering on a serious topic, about an absurdly hypothetical situation that nonetheless keeps coming back to the reality of marriage in which women are too often abused. Emilia is experienced enough in the bitterness of marital strife to have imagined what her revenge might be, especially if her husband were to strike her, or chase after other women. (Iago has certainly struck Emilia; about the other allegation we cannot be sure, though he does confess to lusting after Desdemona.) Speaking now in the frank intimacy of her close relation with Desdemona, Emilia ponders the nature of a woman's moral duty to her husband in a thoroughly unhappy marriage:

> And have not we affections,
> Desires for sport, and frailty, as men have?
> Then let them use us well; else let them know.
> The ills we do, their ills instruct us so.
>
> (4.3.103–6)

So far as we can tell, Emilia never acts on her own advice, or even really contemplates doing so. She is simply responding to the remarkable intimacy of a conversation between two women who are loving and belea-guered friends. Though of course no longer children, Emilia and Desdemona discover anew the kind of innocent friendship that offers a refuge against the fallen condition of humanity. As in *A Midsummer Night's Dream*, one could argue here that the animus of the men against these goodhearted women is accentuated by a jealous fear of a special world that women occupy and can share only among themselves. Iago especially wishes to destroy Desdemona because she is the embodiment of womanly virtue.

Shakespeare is fascinated with the paradox of two in one in his por-trayal of innocent friendship, or, for that matter, of a romantic relation-ship at its ideal best. So indeed was John Donne in a poem like 'The Ecstasy'; the idea was a Renaissance commonplace. For all its familiar fea-tures, nonetheless, the paradox is deeply expressive of a longing for com-munion with another human being that is ethereal, prelapsarian, and so incomprehensibly mysterious that words can hint at it only through logical impossibilities. One example is in Shakespeare's 'The Phoenix and Turtle', a poem written for a collection of such verses published in 1601. The occasion is to celebrate the union of the phoenix and the turtledove, one a legendary Arabian bird supposed to be reborn in its own ashes as a symbol of immortality, the other a symbol of constancy in love. The turtledove is spoken of as the male, although sex really does not matter. Their eternal, innocent love can be conveyed only through a series of para-doxes about the numbers one and two:

> So they loved, as love in twain
> Had the essence but in one,
> Two distincts, division none;
> Number there in love was slain.
>
> Hearts remote yet not asunder,
> Distance and no space was seen
> 'Twixt the turtle and his queen;
> But in them it were a wonder.
> (25–32)

The poem goes on to state that 'Reason, in itself confounded, / Saw division grow together'. The experience is explicitly nonrational, even supra-rational. One can understand the paradox of two becoming one only through a contemplative meditation akin to the experience of faith;

one's reason cannot show how this is possible, since it is manifestly impossible, and so one must take this larger and mysterious truth on faith. Poetry is pre-eminently a genre in which such explorations are possible, precisely because those explorations go beyond the capabilities of denotative language.

Friendship among young males in Shakespeare tends to be more of a sparring match. To be sure, Polixenes and Leontes of *The Winter's Tale* idealize their childhood friendship as an innocent and tender relationship not unlike that of Helena and Hermia; but as boys grow up in Shakespeare they often become noisy, argumentative, anxious to show off their wit among their friends, and very susceptible to peer pressures governing what is acceptable and unacceptable behaviour according to the code of the male pack. A case in point is *Romeo and Juliet*, where Romeo's conduct as a male is heavily influenced by the actions and attitudes of his friends.

In the early scenes of this famous love story, we see Romeo not with Juliet but with Benvolio and Mercutio. When Romeo mopes and frets about his unproductive non-relationship with a certain Rosaline, who never appears in the play but is instead the disembodied goddess whom he fruitlessly worships, Mercutio mocks his misplaced adoration. 'You are a lover', he jeers. 'Borrow Cupid's wings / And soar with them above a common bound.' The thing to do with love if it gets rough with you is to get rough with it; 'Prick love for pricking, and you beat love down'. Mercutio's endless delight in bawdy puns about pricks and the like adds to the abrasive humour. His Queen Mab speech (1.4.53–94) is a bravura put-down of all kinds of human folly, most of all love. Queen Mab gallops through lovers' brains, 'and then they dream of love'. She rides 'O'er ladies' lips', and is especially present with maids that 'lie on their backs'. Mercutio seems intent on warning Romeo away from the enervating effects of love, urging his return to the companionship of young men. When, later on (2.4), Romeo does indeed act more companionably, Mercutio welcomes him back to the fold; 'Why, is not this better now than groaning for love? Now art thou sociable, now art thou Romeo, now art thou what thou art.' Mercutio does not know that Romeo's more 'manly' behaviour is prompted by his having fallen truly in love with Juliet, rather than pining after the unresponsive Rosaline.

As attractive as this jolly friendship appears to be, Romeo's need for the approbation of his friends will prove his undoing at the play's moment of tragic decision (3.1). When Tybalt issues his insulting challenge to

Romeo for having courted Juliet at the Capulets' evening masqued entertainment, prompting Mercutio's no less angry response, Romeo finds
himself caught between his new-found devotion to Juliet and his commitment to the male code of honour. He cannot reply mildly to Tybalt's
challenge without seeming to be guilty of appeasement. 'Oh, calm, dishonourable, vile submission!' exclaims Mercutio, who thereupon challenges Tybalt himself, and is killed in the encounter when Romeo attempts
to intervene. This is too much for Romeo, that his friend should die on
his behalf and that he, Romeo, should thus suffer to see his reputation
'stained / With Tybalt's slander'. Romeo faces what is for him a perilous
choice: either he must respond as Juliet would wish, in patient forgiveness, or else he must obey the code of honour among men. He chooses
to do the latter, explicitly rejecting the counsel of love: 'O sweet Juliet,
/ Thy beauty hath made me effeminate, / And in my temper softened
valour's steel'. The macho ties between young males have prevailed over
reason and charity; for the moment, Romeo cares more about proving to
his friends that he is a 'man' than he does about what the consequences
will be to his new love for Juliet. Youthful male behaviour in Shakespeare
commonly polarizes the differences between the sexes; the men need to
show that they are tough lest they appear 'effeminate'.

We see this combative, supermasculine aggressiveness everywhere in
the plays. Demetrius and Lysander in *A Midsummer Night's Dream*,
friends as the play begins, are ready to slay each other in the forest of
Athens, egged on by the mischief-loving Puck, who mocks their homici-
dal virility: 'Here, villain, drawn and ready. Where art thou?' Whereas the
young women weep and flee from each other when they fall out, the
young men insult one another and issue challenges (3.2). To be sure, Puck
guarantees that no harm will be done, and that the weary lovers will lie
down together as they should, man with woman: 'Two of both kinds
makes up four'. Puck helps resolve their differences, but only after he has
shown how very differently young men and women respond to the hazardous game of courtship.[5]

We see the same competitiveness of young men in *Love's Labour's Lost*,
when four young aristocrats, having vowed to eschew romantic love in
the cause of academic pursuit and studiously male companionship, grow
secretive and ashamed in their dealings with one another once young
women are on the scene. The males of *The Taming of the Shrew* are drawn
to one another's company by their horror of the prospect of dealing with
a shrew; their first impulse, once three of them are married, is to bet

against one another on the obedience of their wives. Claudio and Benedick in *Much Ado about Nothing*, best of friends as the play begins, are eventually at swords' points over the slander of Hero; Beatrice's most solemn requirement of Benedick is that he 'kill Claudio'. The male competitive instinct is exacerbated by rivalries in wooing. In Shakespeare's earliest tragedy, *Titus Andronicus*, the vicious brothers Demetrius and Chiron vie with each other to see who gets to enjoy Lavinia.

The ties of friendship in early childhood, whether male to male or female to female (or, more rarely in Shakespeare, across the barrier of gender), are all the more necessary because they escape and transcend the rivalries of siblings. Within the family, relationships are often portrayed in Shakespeare as being intensely competitive. Ultimately that competition may give way to reconciliation: long-separated siblings are usually destined to be reunited in Shakespeare's plays, and young siblings, faced with outward dangers, may well band together, like the two doomed young princes in *Richard III*. Nevertheless, the competition is omnipresent and usually keen. We should hardly be surprised at this. Sibling rivalry is the very stuff of folklore, as in the tale of Cinderella and her churlish sisters, and indeed that story of rivalry among sisters is at the heart of Shakespeare's *King Lear*.

Rivalry is often most keen between siblings of the same sex. This hardly comes as a surprise. We must therefore be cautious in looking for autobiographical hints in Shakespeare's portrayal of emulous siblings. Even so, we cannot help being intrigued by the fact that Shakespeare had a younger brother named Edmund. This Edmund died in 1607, close to the time (perhaps soon after the time) when Shakespeare wrote *King Lear* and included in it the terrifying villainy of Edmund against his brother Edgar. Whether Shakespeare and his own brother Edmund seriously quarreled we have no way of knowing, and we should credit them both by assuming that Shakespeare certainly need not have experienced betrayal by his brother in order to write *King Lear*, but the choice of name does suggest at least that Shakespeare sought out stories and names for his characters that would allow him to create fiction out of imaginary parallels between life and art. The nuclear family is by its very nature both loving and rivalrous, providing to the dramatist the very stuff out of which dramatic conflict can arise.

Rivalrous relationships between brothers extend from one end of Shakespeare's career to the other, from the *Henry VI* plays to *The Tempest*. Although Shakespeare does not show us childhood rivalries directly, he is plainly interested in the consequences of vexed relationships that appear to have begun early in life. Orlando in *As You Like It* has never received a decent upbringing as a gentleman because his older brother, Oliver, has disobeyed their father's injunction that Orlando be bred well. Orlando justly complains that his 'keeping' differs little 'from the stalling of an ox'. He eats with the farm hands and is denied any education. The situation is parallel to another competitive rivalry in the same play between brothers at the court of Duke Frederick, albeit with the inversion of younger and older: here the younger brother has usurped the authority of his elder brother and sent him into banishment. The play is structured around this pairing of fraternal rivalries. It ends rather suddenly with a restoration of order and harmony – Oliver is taught to love his brother by the transforming influence of charitable love in the Forest of Arden, while Duke Frederick unexpectedly determines to 'put on a religious life' and throw 'into neglect the pompous court' – but not before the rivalries have caused a good deal of dislocation.

At the heart of both animosities of brother against brother is envy of lovable goodness. Oliver confesses in soliloquy, once he has dispatched the wrestler Charles with a commission to break Orlando's neck in an upcoming wrestling contest, that he is perplexed by the violence of his dislike for Orlando: 'my soul, yet I know not why, hates nothing more than he'. Why indeed? Oliver confesses the utter perversity of his hating someone who is not only his brother but a fine, lovable young man:

> He's gentle, never schooled and yet learned, full of noble device, of all sorts enchantingly beloved, and indeed so much in the heart of the world and especially of my own people, who best know him, than I am altogether misprized.

> (1.1.157–61)

Oliver's last phrase here, about being 'altogether misprized,' explains to us what has seemed mysterious to him. His rivalrous hatred of Orlando grows out of resentment for the affection that others bestow on Orlando instead of on Oliver himself. Part of Oliver realizes that he is only making things worse by acting in the churlish and even murderous way that he does, but he has not yet found a way out of this box. He knows only that he needs to kill his brother, thus getting him out of the way so that others will forget Orlando and pay attention to Oliver instead. This competition for attention is most keen in their own family. Oliver is uncomfortably aware that Orlando has always been the favourite of their father, Sir Rowland de Boys. Oliver, as inheritor of the family fortune and possessed with powerful authority as head of household, now has a way of getting back at the favoured child, the hated sibling.

Frederick's resentment of Duke Senior is of the same sort. Frederick too has found that his brother is more beloved than he. Asked to give his reasons for banishing Rosalind now after having earlier banished her father, Duke Senior, Frederick explains curtly: 'Thou art thy father's daughter. There's enough.' His advice to his daughter, as we have seen, is that she distance herself from Rosalind simply because 'thou wilt show more bright and seem more virtuous / When she is gone'. Frederick has a reputation for being 'humorous', that is, given to dangerous and unpredictable whims of vengeance. Conversely, his older brother is dearly loved by those who have followed him into exile as 'co-mates and brothers'. These polarities explain the animosities of jealousy; they also make sense of the play's sudden and apparently surprising happy ending. Both Oliver and Frederick are unhappy being tyrants; their envy of goodness bespeaks a wish that they too could be lovable, just as any rebellious child in a family is really asking to be loved. They do not know how to find that lovability, but it exists still as an ideal, and the phenomenon of sudden conversion for both brothers at the end of the play is a way of providing the answer.

In the leitmotif of rivalrous brothers that seems to have fascinated Shakespeare from start to finish, the older, banished brother is usually seen as bookish and impractical while the younger is more of a machiavel. Duke Senior loves to talk philosophy with his banished friends; Frederick calculates his every move. Orlando (the younger brother in this instance) is occupied with falling in love, or with caring for a dear old servant, Adam, who has devoted his life to his young master; Oliver uses the word 'love' (in his conversation with Charles the wrestler, for example) as a term of cynical obligation; Charles's 'love' for Oliver is such that Charles will obligingly break Orlando's neck. Similarly, in *The Tempest* (*c.* 1611) we find that Prospero's younger brother, Antonio, is the calculating rival who knows how to take advantage of his brother's bookish ways.

Prospero freely confesses to having neglected 'worldly ends' that he might dedicate all his energies in retirement and seclusion to 'the bettering of my mind'. His books have been his chief and only concern, to the ignoring of his state duties. Shakespeare is probably thinking of the age-old paradox of the philosopher-king (as expounded in Plato's *Republic*):

is it possible for one person to be both humanely wise and politically saga-cious? Well, apparently not. As the saying goes, those who can, do; those who can't, teach. Prospero is a teacher and scholar, and as such is unfit for rule.

Antonio, back in the days when he and Prospero were brothers in the court of Milan, became the one who tended shop while his brother pursued 'secret studies'. Antonio perfected the political art of 'how to grant suits, / How to deny them, who t'advance and who / To trash for overtopping'. That is, he learned how to acquire power through dis-pensing political favours, distributing and then collecting IOUs. He did so with a takeover in mind. Once he had lined up his support in this fashion, he formed a secret alliance with an old enemy of Milan, Alonso, King of Naples, according to which Alonso's army would oust Prospero in return for Antonio's promise of homage and tribute to Naples. Having gained power through this *coup d'état*, Antonio then proceeded to 'banish' his brother in such a way as to ensure the death of Prospero and his infant daughter, casting them adrift in an unseaworthy ship with only the supply of food and water provided for them by a kindly old courtier named Gonzalo. The intent was no less murderous than Oliver's designs on Orlando.

Doubtless the most terrifying younger brother in Shakespeare is Edmund in *King Lear*. He is illegitimate, having been begotten by his father, the Earl of Gloucester, in a moment of stolen sexual pleasure. Gloucester has every intention of providing for his illegitimate son, as gentlemen generally did in the early modern period; they expected to have bastards, and usually had enough money to care for them. As Gloucester condescendingly puts it, 'there was good sport at his making, and the whoreson must be acknowledged'. Edmund's half-brother Edgar is not only legitimate, but the elder, so that his claim to inheritance of the family fortune is doubly strong.

Like Hermia and Helena in *A Midsummer Night's Dream*, these two are alliteratively named, and are indeed a pair. On the evidence of their two brief conversations together (1.2 and 2.1), they have been close as brothers. Edgar appears to trust and like his younger half-brother, and treats him as an equal. Yet Edmund deeply resents his older brother's ascendancy over him, and despises the custom of primogeniture (whereby property descends wholly to the oldest son) as an ancient and arbitrary custom among men that has no sanction in Edmund's amoral world of 'nature'.

> Wherefore should I
> Stand in the plague of custom and permit
> The curiosity of nations to deprive me,
> For that I am some twelve or fourteen moonshines
> Lag of a brother? Why bastard? Wherefore base?
> When my dimensions are as well compact,
> My mind as generous, and my shape as true
> As honest madam's issue?
>
> (1.2.2–9)

The inescapable rivalry between older and younger sons that is built into the system of primogeniture is here intensified by the issue of bastardy and by Edmund's intellectual candour and ruthlessness.

Once again too, as with Duke Frederick in *As You Like It* and Antonio in *The Tempest*, the younger brother's resentment is exacerbated by his perception that his older brother is the more beloved. Edgar is plainly the favourite of his father, however much the Earl wishes to do the right thing by Edmund as well. Once Gloucester has been blinded and has become an outcast, his only hope is that he might 'see' once more the son whom he has wronged:

> O dear son Edgar,
> The food of thy abusèd father's wrath!
> Might I but live to see thee in my touch,
> I'd say I had eyes again.
>
> (4.1.21–4)

Such tender feeling, and the touching relationship that Gloucester subsequently develops with the 'naked fellow' who is indeed his son though he does not know this, does much to atone for the tribulations that Gloucester and Edgar have suffered. It also helps to gain perspective on the depth of Edmund's jealous resentment of his father's favourite. Indeed, one can look at Edmund as a young man who, made to feel unwanted by the society in which he finds himself, seeks his revenge by aiming at not only the life of his half-brother but those of his father and of a succession of fathers that includes the Duke of Cornwall and King Lear.

Iago in *Othello* is not literally the younger brother of Cassio, but we can discern in their relationship a metaphoric family constellation in which Iago is bound to Othello and Cassio. One is his commanding officer; the other is his fellow-officer and superior to him in the chain of command. Clearly, one of the events that precipitates Iago's vengeful plotting at the start of the play is Othello's choice of Cassio to be his lieutenant instead of Iago, who must ignobly remain 'his Moorship's "ancient"' or ensign.

Iago's scorn for Cassio's inexperience in the field ('Mere prattle without practice / Is all his soldiership'), and his cynical impatience with the system of favouritism in which, as he sees it, one must flatter those in power to get ahead, are his ostensible reasons for being angry at having been passed over for promotion. We quickly sense that the resentment is more personal: the problem is that Othello prefers Cassio. He has chosen Cassio because Cassio, an old friend, often served as intermediary between Othello and Desdemona in the general's wooing of her, as a kind of go-between facilitating the match. Cassio is, moreover, handsome, smartly dressed, and naturally attractive to other people, men and women alike. He is, as Iago says, a 'proper man' – that is, good-looking. He is 'handsome, young, and hath all those requisites in him that folly and green minds look after'. Iago is eaten by jealousy, an affliction that is greatly augmented at this critical moment in his life because Othello has just married – another betrayal, another choice to love someone other than Iago himself. Never mind that Iago hates Othello because he is black and more successful than he, in love and in war; despite that hatred, Iago cannot bear it that Othello should prefer the handsome Cassio and the lovely Desdemona before him. Iago's revenge is to use the very attractiveness of Cassio that Iago so loathes as a weapon with which to insinuate to Othello that Desdemona is in love with Cassio. Iago is so all-embracingly evil, so lacking in any semblance of conscience, and so pleased and amused by his own cleverness in wanton destruction that his malignancy seems finally inexplicable, as if he were some kind of devil driven by pure hatred of all good; yet what is so terrifying about him is that he is a human being after all, needing to punish and destroy those who have awakened his insatiable jealousy.

Don John in *Much Ado about Nothing* is, like Edmund in *King Lear*, a bastard younger brother of a charismatic and much-loved figure, in this case Don Pedro, commander of the army in which Benedick and Claudio have served. As such, Don John is, virtually by definition, the villain of this comedy. (Shakespeare's comedies not infrequently have villains, because of Shakespeare's love of threatening his romantic comedies with near-tragic circumstances.) Don John is the engineer of a great deal of malicious mischief in this play. He nearly succeeds in spoiling the impending marriage of Claudio and Hero by leading Claudio to believe, on the occasion of a masqued ball (2.1), that Don Pedro is wooing the lady for himself and not for Claudio; and then, undaunted by his final lack of success in this gambit, Don John proceeds to unfix the marriage once again by devising a tale about Hero's supposed sexual profligacy.

Don John shares with Iago a wantonness of evil purpose so universal in its animus that it seems ready to light on any opportunity for mischief. At the same time, he is driven by much the same envy and resentment that motivates Edmund, Iago, and Duke Frederick: he finds it intolerable that his older brother should be so much beloved and that the people around him should be so happy. Marriage he regards as the perfect emblem of the foolish search for happy companionship that he so detests. 'What is he for a fool that betroths himself to unquietness?' he asks his chief henchman, Borachio, who has brought him intelligence of an intended marriage. Who is being so unwise as to subject himself to the nagging of a wife? Simultaneously, Don John thinks to ask his other question of this marriage plan: 'Will it serve for any model to build mischief on?' (1.3). Don John is proud to be 'a plain-dealing villain'; 'I cannot hide what I am'. Without even knowing who it is that hopes to marry, his instinct is to be the spoiler, the undoer of merriment. He is the churl and misogynist whose machinations must be foiled in order for the play to end happily. More profoundly, he is the embodiment of a spirit of resentment and wary cynicism that resides in the hearts of other men as well, and that they must come to terms with before they can truly know themselves and enter fully into a mature loving relationship.

Richard of Gloucester is a younger brother in *3 Henry VI* and *Richard III* whose pathway to the throne, once the Yorkists have defeated their Lancastrian opponents, must make its way against his older siblings as his first steps to power. The newly installed King Edward IV, eldest of the three brothers, obligingly dies of illness brought on in part by dissipation, but the Duke of Clarence is another matter. He is in good health, and must be dispatched by being drowned in a butt of malmsey wine by two of Richard's henchmen. The gripping scene of Clarence's murder, in which he pleads with the consciences of his assailants and nearly succeeds in winning one of them over until he is cravenly struck down from behind, is designed to amplify Clarence's goodheartedness as opposed to the sinister and gloating evil of his younger brother. Clarence has sinned, he knows, in the Wars of the Roses, and has blood on his hands, but he is truly sorry and begs forgiveness of his Maker. His trusting of Richard makes that brother's villainy all the more reprehensible. Younger brothers in Shakespeare need careful watching.

Claudius is the younger brother of Hamlet Senior, whom he murders in order to gain not only the throne but also the love of his brother's wife. Shakespeare makes this crime appalling in every imaginable way: it is a murder, it is a regicide, and it is incestuous. Hamlet and his father's ghost are agreed on this last point. 'That incestuous, that adulterate beast!' the ghost exclaims. 'Let not the royal bed of Denmark be / A couch for luxury and damnèd incest,' the ghost admonishes his son. Hamlet is readily disposed to concur: he has already deplored his mother's unseemly willingness 'to post / With such dexterity to incestuous sheets'. At the very last, as Hamlet stabs Claudius and forces him to swallow the dregs of the poison prepared for Hamlet himself, the dying hero accounts incest as among the chief justifications of his act of killing. 'Here, thou incestuous, murderous, damnèd Dane, / Drink off this potion.' We might regard marriage with one's sister-in-law, unrelated by blood, as not incestuous, but canon law has often taken an opposite view, and the play clearly condemns the marriage as incestuous. The murder is, moreover, a re-enactment of the first crime committed on earth after the expulsion of Adam and Eve from the Garden of Eden: the slaying of Abel by his younger brother, Cain. In an attempt at prayer, Claudius sees all too clearly the awful truth about his crime in these biblical terms. 'Oh, my offence is rank!' he laments. 'It smells to heaven. / It hath the primal eldest curse upon't, / A brother's murder.' No crime could be more ancient or more heinous.

Cain slew Abel out of resentment and envy. As John Steinbeck psychologizes the story of Genesis in *East of Eden*, the younger son resents the fact that their father (rather transparently named Adam in Steinbeck's account) prefers his eldest born to the younger son. The Book of Genesis makes clear that the real disapproving and denying father is God Almighty. When Abel offers the firstlings of his flock as a grateful sacrifice, 'the Lord had respect unto Abel and to his offering. / But unto Cain and to his offering he had not respect' (Genesis 4.4–5). Abel is a shepherd, Cain a 'tiller of the ground'; the rivalry is ancient and rooted in a competition for survival. We understand why Cain was 'very wroth' against Abel, though we of course are not supposed to countenance the murder. Most of all, we can see that the Genesis story is an archetype for Shakespeare's fascination with the jealous emulation of younger brothers.

Claudius and Hamlet as brothers are not unlike Duke Frederick and Duke Senior, or Antonio and Prospero. The older Hamlet, brave soldier that he was, is remembered for his chivalry and above all for his almost uxorious fondness of his queen, Gertrude. He would not 'beteem the winds of heaven' to 'Visit her face too roughly', Hamlet recalls. The interlude of 'The Murder of Gonzago', which Hamlet commissions from the visiting players to 'catch the conscience of the King', portrays the Player King (a stand-in for Hamlet Senior) as gentle and indulgent in his conversation with his wife. We never hear of this king as especially businesslike. Claudius, on the other hand, takes a firm and capable grip on the helm of state at his first public audience (1.2). He explains the reason for his hasty marriage to Gertrude, arranges passport matters for Laertes, and, most important, dispatches ambassadors to head off with immediate success a threatened Norwegian invasion of Denmark. Claudius is, like Antonio in *The Tempest*, one for whom the exercise of power is pleasurable and rewarding. He does it well. We sense that he craved power in Denmark out of a conviction that he could rule more effectively than his brother. He has the support of counsellors like Polonius who, though they certainly would not have countenanced the murder, are not unhappy to see the Danish throne occupied by such an administrative expert. Claudius earns the admiration of Rosencrantz and Guildenstern for the no-nonsense manner in which he goes about protecting his own life by guarding against Hamlet's dangerously eccentric ways. Claudius is not a lovable king, but he really knows his job and the pragmatic necessity of self-preservation. Hamlet Senior, like Prospero, was more trusting, unsuspecting, open. Such men, if they are rulers, are apt to wake up in a boat headed for exile, or not wake up at all.

Bassianus, in *Titus Andronicus*, suffers fearfully and unjustly at the hands of his older (not younger) brother, Saturninus, whom the play's title figure has unwisely assisted to the throne of ancient Rome. For having married his beloved Lavinia, whom Saturninus had wanted for himself, Bassianus loses both the lady and his life. King John's political difficulties arise out of the fact that he has usurped the throne that would have been his older brother Geoffrey's right and has now descended to Geoffrey's son Arthur. The list of envious brothers is extensive.

Elsewhere in Shakespeare, the rivalry of brothers is displaced into patterns that seem less threatening but that still grow out of competition within the family. Philip the Bastard in *King John* is partly a benign earlier version of Edmund: although he is the older rather than the younger brother of Robert Faulconbridge, Philip is, like Edmund, illegitimate. The two brothers are certainly in contention, and over much the same issue as in *King Lear*: who is to inherit the family name and fortune. Old Sir Robert Faulconbridge has died, leaving two sons, both of whom claim to be his true-born son, but the younger has charged Philip with bastardy. If that is true, the estate is Robert's, but the allegation may be hard to prove. King John, to whom the matter is appealed, inclines to the claim of Philip, since that son was first-born to a married couple; in marriage, the husband is assumed to be the father of children born to his wife. Young Robert's counter-argument is that he was told by their father, on his deathbed, that the father was abroad on a diplomatic mission when Philip was conceived. The heated argument is resolved only when Philip decides of his own free will that he would rather be known as the reputed son of King Richard I, Richard the Lionhearted. He is confirmed in his desire when his widowed mother confesses that she did indeed yield to the importunities of that princely man. With the patronage of King John's mother Eleanor, who is persuaded by Philip's dashing style that he is indeed her grandson, and having been knighted by King John as Sir Richard Plantagenet, Philip the Bastard embraces a new future as his own man. This amusing episode, occurring in the play's opening scene, bears a significant thematic connection to John's own dynastic ambiguities: he has taken the throne from his nephew Arthur, and is himself a rival brother (younger, in this case) vying for the birthright of his recently dead older brother Geoffrey. Fraternal rivalry is at the heart of England's dynastic uncertainties.

Indeed, the seesaw battle of the Wars of the Roses depicted in the *Henry VI* plays and *Richard III* is often described as a contest of brother against brother, even when the antagonists are in fact cousins, like Henry VI and the cousin who rises to become Edward IV. At times, brothers do in fact end up on opposite sides of the conflict, as when the Duke of Clarence defects to the Lancastrian cause in protest over his brother Edward's folly in marrying Lady Elizabeth Grey, although eventually Clarence switches back to his Yorkist allegiance. Throughout, the metaphor of brother against brother is a kind of metonymy for civil butchery in which family members slaughter one another in a grim contest of reciprocity. The words 'brother' and 'brothers' turn up more frequently in *3 Henry VI* than anywhere else in the canon, and *Richard III* is not far behind (along with *Measure for Measure* and *As You Like It*). The recurrence of names on the two sides of the quarrel lends symmetry to the carnage: an Edward for an Edward, a Richard for a Richard (*Richard III*, 4.4). In a poignant emblematic scene in *3 Henry VI* (2.5), King Henry, sitting on a molehill and contemplating the deep perversities of human life, must witness the parallel spectacles of a son that has unknowingly killed his father in battle and then a father that has unknowingly killed his son. Every family disruption takes part in the conflict more broadly known as brother against brother.

Interestingly, the relationship of sister to sister is not often explored by Shakespeare; he is far more interested in brothers. The few sister relationships we are shown can be disruptively competitive, as, notoriously, in *King Lear* and its tragic re-imagining of the story of Cinderella and her haughty sisters. Kate mistreats her younger sister Bianca in *The Taming of the Shrew*, partly out of jealousy for all the devoted male attention that Bianca receives, partly out of an understandable impatience with the marriage game. Adriana and Luciana in *The Comedy of Errors* differ sharply, like Kate and Bianca, as to whether women should be wary of suitors or acquiescent. Shakespeare is less interested in portraying how sisters relate to one another than he is in the relationship of sister to brother or brother to brother.

The Comedy of Errors is about the separation and eventual reunion of two pairs of brothers, both of them identical twins. (Shakespeare was the father of twins, born in 1585.) The two Antipholuses were born in an hour, 'the one so like the other / As could not be distinguished but by names'. At the selfsame hour two other identical twins were delivered to a woman of lower social station, thus providing, in time, a pair of servants (the Dromios) for the Antipholuses. Both sets of twins are separated by a storm at sea, one pair ending up in Ephesus, and the other in Syracuse. The search of the Syracusan twin for his long-lost brother brings him and his Dromio to Ephesus, where all the hilarious mix-ups occur as a result of mistaken identity. Eventually a recognition scene restores the brothers not only to each other but to their long-separated mother and father.

At its heart, this comic farce, taken out of Plautus's *Menaechmi*, or *Twins*, is a story of the search for one's other self. Identical twins are a special case in the phenomenon of siblinghood. Stories abound in every culture about identical twins whose spouses cannot tell them apart, even in bed. *The Comedy of Errors* toys with this titillating fantasy: one of the play's funniest scenes (2.2) is when Adriana, the wife of Antipholus of Ephesus, invites the man she takes to be her husband into 'their' house. 'What, was I married to her in my dream?' ponders Antipholus of

Syracuse to himself. He decides to 'entertain the offered fantasy'. Why not? What man would turn down the chance to sleep with a beautiful woman who suddenly invites him into her bedchamber?

The potentially transgressive and even incestuous thrust of this plot (compare Claudius in *Hamlet*, who marries his sister-in-law with tragic consequences) is deflected by the fact that Adriana has a spinster sister whom Antipholus of Syracuse can safely marry instead of his own sister-in-law. *The Comedy of Errors* explores one of our most needful dreams, that of finding a long-lost sibling and thereby rediscovering ourselves. The person we find is, in the words of Baudelaire's 'Au lecteur', 'mon semblable, mon frère', my likeness, my doppelganger. Richard of Gloucester addresses the Duke of Buckingham as 'my other self' when he wants to make the point that they think alike. Our imaginings about twins are so piquant because they heighten the appeal and also the threat of sibling relationships. Brothers are our enemy because they are us. Edmund discovers this at the end of *King Lear*, when the unknown knight who successfully challenges him to a duel turns out to be his brother Edgar. 'My name is Edgar, and thy father's son', says the challenger, and Edmund knows that his destiny has somehow come back to bring him to account: 'The wheel is come full circle; I am here'. Cain and Abel confront each other once more, in a replay of the oldest crime on earth.

Twins are at the heart of *Twelfth Night*, except that here the identical twins are sister and brother, not siblings of the same sex. Shakespeare's own twins, Judith and Hamnet, were sister and brother. Elizabethan stage conventions give Shakespeare a wonderful opportunity to play with illusions here, since a boy actor takes the role of Viola, who then disguises herself as a youngster, Cesario. The Countess Olivia is also played by a boy. *Twelfth Night* revisits the enduring fantasy we encountered in *The Comedy of Errors*, in which a young man (Sebastian) finds himself accosted by a beautiful woman (Olivia) and invited into her house to be her husband. As in *The Comedy of Errors*, this is a male fantasy, a dream of unexpected good fortune. Emerging moments later from this encounter (4.3), Sebastian cannot believe that he is awake; he pinches himself, as it were, to be sure. What has happened to him is 'some error', and yet a happy error. Again, the comedy depends on twinning. Viola and Sebastian may be girl and boy, but until the very end of the play they are easily mistaken for the other; Viola, after all, is wearing the guise of a young man. Stage productions of the play invariably elicit a gasp from the audience when the two are finally seen together. Here the rivalries inherent in siblinghood are muted, partly because twins are emblematic of similarity rather than difference, and partly because brother–sister relationships are presented as less hostile and threatening by Shakespeare than brother-to-brother relationships.

Imogen and Cloten in *Cymbeline* are an apparent exception in that they are very antipathetic siblings, but here the difference is ascribable to the fact that they are not blood-related at all: the repulsive Cloten is the son of King Cymbeline's second wife by a former husband, whereas Imogen is the daughter of the King by his dead first wife. Arviragus and Guiderius, on the other hand, are indeed related to Imogen as her true brothers, though they cannot know so when they first meet; this relationship is precious to them all. Isabella and her brother Claudio quarrel in *Measure for Measure*, but are soon reconciled, and are remorseful for their momentary loss of faith in each other. Octavius Caesar, in *Antony and Cleopatra*, manoeuvres his sister into an unfortunate marriage with the most deplorable of motives (he hopes that the marriage with Antony will fail, so that he can break a treaty with him), but Octavia is still the one human being for whom Octavius feels a loving affection. Ophelia in *Hamlet* has her troubles with Hamlet, but her brother Laertes is utterly loyal to her. The sons of Priam and Hecuba in *Troilus and Cressida* think that their sister Cassandra is mad, but they are protective of her all the same. The exceptions prove the rule. Viola and Sebastian in *Twelfth Night* are true sister and brother. In finding each other, they rediscover themselves, arriving at identities that enable them to enter into a world of heterosexual completion in marriage. It is this world of courtship and marriage to which we will next turn.

CHAPTER THREE

◆

Sighing Like Furnace

Courtship and Sexual Desire

The girl who strikes your fancy will need to be sought out;
she won't come floating down to you through the filmy air.

Ovid, The Art of Love[1]

A man who would woo a fair maid
Must prentice himself to the trade
And practise all day
In methodical way
How to flatter, cajole, and persuade.

W. S. Gilbert, The Yeomen of the Guard

Negotiating sexual desire in Shakespeare is the very stuff of dramatic conflict. It sets in motion the plots of his romantic comedies and provides dramatic closure through the working out of differences in the battle of the sexes. In tragedies like *Romeo and Juliet* and *Othello* that concern themselves with love and marriage, sexual desire is no less central to the story. Courtship is thus an essential element of plot construction.

It is also a subject on which Shakespeare dwells for its own sake. Writing comedies at a time when he was roughly between the ages of twenty-six (in 1590) and thirty-six or seven (in 1600–1), Shakespeare was still relatively young and yet old enough to appreciate what is so funny and even absurd about young people falling in love. Absurd the process may be, but it is also deeply serious, fraught with emotional perils, filled with frustrations and self-hatred. The time of falling in love is a time of discovery of the Other Sex – a jarring awakening of consciousness that brings with it the need for a wholesale reassessment of one's own sense of identity. To leave behind the intense competition of inter-family rivalries and the relatively contained world of same-sex friendship, with which we were concerned in the previous chapter, is to enter a bewildering and even hostile environment where anything can happen.

What are young men and women like as they encounter the ecstasies and the hazards of courtship? How, in Shakespeare's view, do young men and women differ in their responses to it? For his own reasons, partly dramatic, partly no doubt because of who he was as a human being, Shakespeare depicts men and women as extraordinarily dissimilar, so much so that the wonder is they are ever able to reach any accommodation.

The contrasts between men and women in love are not uniformly flattering to males. Far from it. With notable exceptions, like Petruchio in *The Taming of the Shrew*, men do not know themselves as well as young women do. They have a lot to learn, and their best hope is to learn better from the women they love. Young men in Shakespeare tend to idealize and worship women, putting them on a pedestal and expecting from them the attributes of some shining goddess. (We have already seen how Romeo courts Juliet at first as though he were a pilgrim and she a saint who alone can relieve his suffering.) Because young men are so apt to fantasize about women and project onto them desired qualities of perfect womanhood that are unrealizable, the men are prone to disillusionment. They are fearful of rejection, fearful above all that the object of their desire will unman them by turning to some other male, thereby displaying a scorn for the wooer's very virility. Men turn women into objects they long to possess. Their longing for such possession makes them vulnerable to a disappointment that again is deeply personal; it is an affront to the male ego to be denied his self-proclaimed right to own and control the object of his desire. Such a longing is inherently unstable. Perhaps for these reasons, men in Shakespeare are also inclined to be inconstant in their vows to women. Proteus in *The Two Gentlemen of Verona* is a classic instance; his very name, derived from the Old Man of the Sea who is capable of assuming an infinite variety of shapes, is symbolic of inconstancy.

Young women in Shakespeare, meanwhile, are for the most part witty, self-possessed, knowledgeable as to who they are, and strongly motivated by an awareness of what it is that they want. They are faithful to the young men to whom they are attached, even when those men prove unfaithful to them, and even when the women are wrongly suspected of casting their looks on other men. They enjoy torturing the young men with the prospect of competition from some other man, but only in game; they remain true. Having chosen not to wander in their affections, and having to deal with young men who are emotionally all over the map, young women must teach their partners what love should truly be about and must also learn to forgive. That forgiveness is often the reconstituting force through which Shakespearean romantic comedy achieves its closure.

Take, for example, *Love's Labour's Lost*, a comedy that may have been revised as late as 1597, shortly before its publication in 1598, but that could have been written in its original form as early as the late 1580s. The marked influence of John Lyly's comic style on this play argues for an early date. (Interestingly, *Love's Labour's Lost* is the first published play to bear Shakespeare's name on the title page, in 1598.) This play is all about wooing. At its centre are four young men and four young women, evenly paired and matched: the King of Navarre and three aristocratic friends who are attempting to institute an all-male academy devoted to study without the distracting presence of women, and the Princess of France, who, accompanied by three ladies-in-waiting, arrives at their doorstep on a diplomatic mission concerning a dowry and a territorial dispute about Aquitaine. The diplomatic issue is of little importance; it is a vehicle to bring the four young women into the lives of four young men who have just sworn not even to talk with a woman for a term of three years.

One can see immediately in the symmetry of four and four the shape of the love plot. The King of Navarre is destined to be the love partner of the Princess of France, while his most outspokenly witty friend, Berowne, is unmistakably meant for the wittiest of the ladies, Rosaline. That leaves two and two, who are quickly sorted out in the marriage game in such a way that Longaville is paired with Maria and Dumaine with Katharine. These last two pairs are more or less interchangeable; the symmetry is what counts.

The young men are astonishingly maladroit. They plainly do not see what we as audience see at once, that the arrangement of four on four necessitates romantic intrigue. The comedy of the play's first scene derives from the huge discrepancy between what the young men think they are going to do and what we know is sure to happen. They cannot even agree among themselves as to the feasibility of the oath proposed and taken, that they are not to see or speak with a woman during their three years of intense study, that they are to fast entirely one day in the week and are to eat but one meal a day otherwise, and that they are to sleep only three hours a night. Berowne is the realist:

> Oh, these are barren tasks, too hard to keep:
> Not to see ladies, study, fast, not sleep!
> (1.1.47–8)

As the news of the ladies' imminent arrival makes plain, the King himself must break the decree in order to negotiate dowry matters with the Princess of France. Of necessity, the gentlemen are forsworn even before they begin. Their bewilderment and lack of self-understanding make them look foolishly immature.

The ladies, by contrast, are cool, elegant, and realistically determined to have their way. At their first entrance (2.1), Maria delivers a judicious appraisal of Longaville, the target of her interest, as brave, cultured, and well reputed, but too sharp-witted. The two have met at some time in the past. Katharine knows Dumaine to be well accomplished and worthy, if also given to an excessive delight in wit. For Rosaline, Berowne is the most attractive of the three for his merriment. 'God bless my ladies!' the Princess mocks. 'Are they all in love, / That every one her own hath garnishèd / With such bedecking ornaments of praise?' Yet she too has a favourite choice, one best fitting her royal rank. The ladies know exactly what they are doing.

The comedy of the gentlemen's discomfiture grows by the hour. Though trying to be restrained and diplomatic, they are smitten at once and guiltily aware that they are in danger of perjuring themselves. Boyet, attending the ladies as a kind of gentleman usher, regales the ladies with accounts of how the gentlemen betray their secret curiosities. Berowne, the most voluble of the gentlemen, castigates himself in soliloquy for falling in love with a black-eyed beauty, Rosaline, who will, as wife, be 'like a German clock, / Still a-repairing, ever out of frame / And never going aright' (3.1). He sees his own folly but cannot amend it.

Berowne's greatest fear is that he will be caught out in his perjury by his friends. Peer pressure is all-important to him. He cringes at the prospect of being jeered at for his hypocrisies and lack of steadfastness. As it turns out, his friends all harbour the same anxiety. In an artfully constructed scene (4.3), they overhear one another in an overlapping series of spyings. Berowne enters first and then stands aside as the King arrives with a sonnet he has written to the Princess. The King in turn stands aside as Longaville enters on a similar mission; then Longaville is given a chance to eavesdrop on Dumaine. 'Four woodcocks in a dish!' exclaims Berowne, who enjoys the commanding position of knowing all. Once Dumaine has recited his sonnet (and we should note that their poetic effusions are all pathetically conventional), Longaville steps forward to confront Dumaine with his perjury; then Longaville is confronted in turn by the King. In last place, Berowne now steps forth 'to whip hypocrisy'. Will he be allowed to enjoy his triumphing over them all? Of course not. A comic mix-up delivers into their hands Berowne's own sonnet, intended for Rosaline. Berowne confesses, on their joint behalf, that they are all pick-purses in love and deserve chastisement.

Their unwilling confessions bring immense relief, for they are now free to acknowledge their passions and to act in concert. Hesitant before, the gentlemen are now manic in their pursuit of love. They vie with one another as to which of their mistresses is the fairest. They betray an adolescent curiosity about the women's sexual bodies: Berowne fantasizes a street paved with their eyes, able to see 'what upward lies' as the women walk overhead. Such eagerness, of course, is setting them up for a fall. The women, plainly in control, see through the Russian disguises that the gentlemen hope to surprise them with and coolly administer a put-down. To the ladies, this is sportful entertainment. As the Princess put it, 'There's no such sport as sport by sport o'erthrown'. Responding to the gentlemen's gambit of disguising themselves, Rosaline proposes that the ladies 'mock them still' by complaining to the gentlemen, after the 'Russian' visit, 'what fools were here, / Disguised like Muscovites in shapeless gear'. (Mozart and da Ponte later make use of a similar plot of mirthful deception in *Cosi Fan Tutte*.) The ladies best the gentlemen at their own game, administering a kind of comic justice that, as Berowne ruefully acknowledges, pours down plagues from the stars for perjury.

Resolving to speak honestly from now on, and to woo in all good conscience, the gentlemen of this play have plainly learned a lot through their discomfiture. They have not learned enough, though, it seems. *Love's Labour's Lost* is strikingly unlike other Shakespearean romantic comedies in its refusal to provide an ending in marriage. (Kenneth Branagh's recasting of the play (2000) as a musical film version set in 1939, on the eve of World War II, makes the point by picturing the young gentlemen as university students about to serve and perhaps die for their country.) The gentlemen must wait and do penance; perhaps then, after a year or so, the ladies will relent. When the King complains that love is unhappy with delay, the Princess rebukes him: a year is hardly too long 'To make a world-without-end bargain in'. The King and his fellows are 'perjured much'; they deserve and need the chastisement that the ladies deliver to them. The ending is a triumph for the ladies. As the desired love objects, they know how to maintain control. As the wiser sex, they have a right to demand that their lovers learn from them what a commitment to marriage realistically requires.

The Taming of the Shrew, on the other hand, is at least in part a fantasy of male control. What could be more daunting to the male psyche than to encounter a woman with the fearsome reputation of being 'Katharine the curst'? Such a title for an unmarried woman is 'of all titles the worst'. Indeed, the men all gravitate instead to her seemingly more docile younger sister, Bianca. All, that is, except Petruchio, who takes on the assignment of wooing Kate as though he were Houdini attempting the impossible. He is braced rather than intimidated by any obstacles.

> Be she as foul as was Florentius' love,
> As old as Sibyl, and as curst and shrewd
> As Socrates' Xanthippe, or a worse,
> She moves me not, or not removes, at least,
> Affection's edge in me, were she as rough
> As are the swelling Adriatic seas.
>
> (1.2.68–73)

His professed motive is wealth, for Kate is the older daughter of the wealthy Baptista Minola.

Yet we soon perceive that Petruchio is interested in Kate and attracted to her as a woman of spirit. He wishes to tame her, to be her lord in a marital relationship that bestows ascendancy on the husband. He succeeds in ways that appall us today if we think about them seriously, though we need to understand that they are part of the comedy's exaggerated effect. He overpowers her objections in their courtship, drags her away from the marriage feast, exhausts her on a forced-march journey to his estate, deprives her of sleep and of proper food, and displays a fearsome temper in denying her the garments that she would like to wear. His analogy in all of this is far from reassuring: she is his falcon, that must be kept hungry until she 'stoop'. He boasts to the audience of his technique, asserting triumphantly that he holds the key to man's quest for domestic tranquillity:

He that knows better how to tame a shrew,
Now let him speak. 'Tis charity to show.
(4.1.198–9)

This is no mere talk. By carrying out his program of sleep deprivation and continual harassment, he succeeds. Kate is no longer shrewish or rebellious at the end of the play. Petruchio has won in his own terms. In some feminist stage productions of recent years, as for example in Charles Marowitz's production at the Open Space Theatre in London in 1975, Kate becomes an automaton, mechanically responding as if she has been programmed to be docile by her controlling husband.

This reading of the play as antifeminist and of Petruchio as a sexist ogre is not the only interpretation possible, to be sure. Arguably, Kate is an unhappy person at the play's start. She scorns men for entirely plausible reasons, having observed how they compete commercially for women as though they were mere objects. She has no use for Bianca's spineless suitors. At the same time, Kate betrays a lack of completion in her own life. Perhaps she does not object to marriage itself so much as to the way the marriage game is cynically played. Petruchio is unlike any other man she has met: he is witty, assertive, and self-aware. In their first scene together, they prove well matched as wit combatants. Sensing perhaps that Petruchio is really interested in her as a person, despite his bravado and his talk of money (which begins to sound, in his mouth, like a witty parody of the venal wife-buying that other men practise), Kate finds herself drawn to his manly importunity despite her understandable wariness. Clearly they are a pair; no one other than Petruchio could hope to woo Kate, and no woman of less wit than Kate's could hope to capture Petruchio's attention. In film and on stage they have often been portrayed by famous married couples of the theatrical world whose own widely publicized domestic difficulties add spice to the play's depiction of the battle of the sexes: Mary Pickford, 'America's sweetheart' of the silent film era, gives as good as she takes in her contest for supremacy with Douglas Fairbanks (1929), while Elizabeth Taylor's set-to with Richard Burton (directed by Franco Zeffirelli, 1967), shortly before their divorce, is a titillating replay of their explosive verbal encounters in Edward Albee's *Who's Afraid of Virginia Woolf?* Petruchio and Kate are, as we shall see, a kind of study for Benedick and Beatrice in *Much Ado about Nothing*.

The hazing that Kate must undergo is inhumane, at least by our standards today, and it insults the dignity of her sex. At the same time,

Petruchio has a plan which is at least calculated in his terms to better her happiness. His temper tantrums are staged, not involuntary or spontaneous. They are designed to show Kate a picture of herself as an angry shrew. She gets the point. Whether she simply gives in to the inevitable or comes to share his point of view, she can be presented in her final long speech as a more confident and self-knowing woman than she was before. She perceives, as do we, an ironic inversion in the final scene: the supposedly tractable Bianca refuses to obey her husband's order to come to him and thus loses the wager he has placed on her obedience, while Kate's quick response to Petruchio's command makes him the winner of the bet. The orders given to the wives to leave what they are doing and come at their husbands' call are arbitrary commands, issued without explanation; they demand unhesitating obedience. Bianca (and the Widow who has married Hortensio) are mistrustful, and see no reason to obey without being given any explanation. Kate obeys Petruchio's order partly because she knows the price of refusal, but also perhaps because she trusts him by now to have some coherent purpose in asking what he demands of her. Perhaps she understands that he intends all this for her own good. Perhaps. The play can be interpreted in many different ways. Certainly Petruchio has his way with her, whether for her benefit or for his or, plausibly, for both.

Victory goes to the man. Petruchio is the clearsighted one who understands from the start what Kate must be taught. He has little to learn, whereas learning is the very substance of her story. Before we assume a sexist bias on the part of the dramatist, however, we must remember that women take the upper hand in *Love's Labour's Lost*. Perhaps we can say that Shakespeare's romantic comedies are beginning to air a debate on the subject of mastery in the battle of the sexes. By choosing different plots from different sources, Shakespeare opens up a range of possibilities. Perhaps, too, we hear the dramatist wrestling with his own inner feelings, his own longing for mastery of women and at the same time his sense of shame and abashment at male giddiness and importunity. This is not to make a biographical claim about Shakespeare other than to propose that, from his perspective, he sees incisively into the condition of both sexes and concedes, with a characteristic generosity of spirit, that men can do wrong to women. We have seen in the Sonnets how he can portray the experience of sexual orgasm as shameful and dirty.

A Midsummer Night's Dream argues both sides of the case regarding male supremacy. The framing plot of Theseus and Hippolyta features man on top. Theseus has conquered the Amazonian Hippolyta in battle. 'I wooed thee with my sword', he says to her, 'And won thy love doing thee injuries.' We are reminded of Petruchio. What sort of love is it that is won by the man's doing injuries to the woman? Even if Hippolyta is sometimes presented in current stage productions as the unwilling captive, still defiant in her Amazonian disdain for men and unsympathetic toward old Egeus's claim of absolute parental authority over his daughter Hermia, Hippolyta does become the bride of her powerful husband. Theseus controls their agenda. He sets the date for their wedding, plans the entertainment for it, and presides over the festivities.

In the world of fairydom as well, the male is undisputed victor. Oberon is determined to teach Titania a lesson in obedience by taking back from her the changeling boy over whom they are quarrelling. It matters not to him that Titania is attached to the boy by her loyal and loving remembrance of the boy's mother; perhaps, indeed, as we have seen, Oberon is jealous of such relationships among women that exclude him. His only professed motive in wishing to have the boy back is to put Titania in her place. He never expresses fondness for the boy, though he wants him as his 'henchman' or page – perhaps there is a hint of sexual favourite.

At all events, Oberon's methods of subduing Titania to his will are as rough and humiliating as those of Petruchio. At Oberon's behest, Puck installs an ass's head on Bottom the Weaver and then arranges matters so that, under the influence of the love juice that he and Oberon use for their purposes, Titania falls in love with an ass. Even if this seems an odd kind of punishment, with Oberon cuckolding himself by foisting on his queen a grossly mortal lover, it achieves its purpose. Puck cannot contain his glee in reporting to Oberon the ludicrous effects of the love juice. 'My mistress with a monster is in love!' he crows. Bottom's hee-hawing, scratching his hairy ears, calling for hay to eat, and the like are calculated to emphasize the monstrosity of the immortal–mortal liaison to which Titania has been unwillingly subjected. It all leads to the complete success that Oberon has wanted. Here is how he describes to Puck his wife's capitulation:

> When I had at my pleasure taunted her,
> And she in mild terms begged my patience,
> I then did ask of her her changeling child,
> Which straight she gave me, and her fairy sent
> To bear him to my bower in Fairyland.
>   (4.1.56–60)

When Titania is then awakened from her trancelike sleep, and finds herself lying beside the hairy fool whom she has entwined in her arms, she has nothing more cutting to say to her husband than 'How came these things to pass? / Oh, how mine eyes do loathe his visage now!' Oberon has won. So has Theseus. The theatrical convention in common practice today of doubling Oberon and Theseus, along with Titania and Hippolyta, reinforces the way in which male ascendancy over the female dominates the framing action of the play.

The tribulations of the young human lovers, on the other hand, pursue a very different course. We see by contrast that Theseus's marriage with Hippolyta is a state affair, governed by the dictates of political necessity, where male supremacy is more in accord with the ideology of the state and is perhaps all the more suspect for that reason; patriarchal authority is not seen in this play as an unmixed blessing. In the more ordinary realm of human experience, at any rate, and in the magical forest near Athens where societal and legal controls are both absent and inappropriate, the young lovers are struggling to find out who they are in relation to awakening sexual desire.

As we have seen, the pre-romantic attachments of Helena and Hermia, Demetrius and Lysander are to persons of the same sex. The young women in particular have shared a happy time when they were virtually twinned and inseparable. The call of sexual desire puts them to a new and frightening test. In one important sense, *A Midsummer Night's Dream* is a fable of the uncertain progression that young persons must make from the comforting and partly narcissistic adoration of a person closely resembling oneself, to a very different kind of attraction toward the Other Sex. That the genders are so very different accentuates the difficulties for the participants. The encounter takes the form, in this play, of a dream. It is pretty much a nightmare, and has increasingly been interpreted as such in criticism and in production, notably Jan Kott's *Shakespeare Our Contemporary* (1964) with its vision of the Athenian fairy world as a place of disturbingly erotic brutality, and Peter Brook's Kott-inspired kinetic stage production of 1970.

The lovers' difficulties precede their running away into the forest, of course. In part these are the external difficulties routinely encountered in stories of young lovers: a parent (Egeus) who opposes romantic attachment and insists on his own choice for his daughter Hermia, and an unfeeling social world of authority and male dominance that sides with the father against the daughter. This is the stuff of comedy as a genre derived from neoclassical writers like Ariosto and Machiavelli and, before them, the Roman comic dramatists Plautus and Terence. The plot of elopement is set in motion by the hostility to young lovers of the courtly and sophisticated world.

In the forest, on the other hand, temporarily no longer under the restraint of law, the lovers find the difficulties to be in themselves and with each other. Demetrius, insisting on his right to marry Hermia against her will, follows Helena into the forest not out of love for her but because he hopes that Helena will lead him to Hermia. Helena, for her part, is positively masochistic in her desire to be with Demetrius on even the worst of terms. She will continue to love him, she declares, even when he insists that he cannot love her. Her self-abasement is extreme:

> I am your spaniel; and, Demetrius,
> The more you beat me I will fawn on you.
> Use me but as your spaniel, spurn me, strike me,
> Neglect me, lose me; only give me leave,
> Unworthy as I am, to follow you.
>   (2.1.203–7)

Demetrius's response could not be more ignobly brutal. He warns her that her being with him alone in the forest at night might tempt him to seize 'the rich worth of your virginity'. In other words, he threatens to rape her. To him, evidently, violent sexual possession can more aptly arise out of hate than of love. Even this will not deter Helena; she is determined to be his slave.

The comic mix-ups of Puck's administering of the love juice lead to further impasse: he is supposed to apply it in order to prompt Demetrius to fall in love with Helena, but manages instead (because he was told to do this to 'an Athenian', and the young Athenian men are dressed alike) to cause Lysander to fall in love with Helena instead of Hermia. Puck is delighted, even though he did not intend this:

> Then will two at once woo one;
> That must needs be sport alone.
> And those things do best please me
> That befall preposterously.
>   (3.2.118–21)

The confusion, delightful as a means of dramatizing the varied complexities of plotting, is also a supreme test of the lovers in their first real encounter with the competitive world of sexual desire.

How will they react? Helena's response is wonderfully perverse. Although one might think that she would enjoy being avidly pursued now by two men, whereas she had no admirer at all such a short time before, Helena instead figures out a way to make herself thoroughly unhappy. The men have joined conspiratorially, she decides, to mock her. Their professions of love are only cruel teasing. Even worse, her dearest friend Hermia has deserted the cause to join in mockery of poor Helena. The test has shown Helena something she may not have known about herself before: she is prone to self-pity and insistent on imagining things to make herself unhappy. She is her own worst enemy. Hermia, for her part, is bewildered, hurt, astonished at first that Lysander could reject her so callously and suddenly. The women lash out at each other, calling each other names like 'puppet' and 'maypole', urging invidious comparisons of their respective heights and physical attractions. Friendship is perilously threatened by the business of mating to which they are all now unhappily committed.

The men respond with what we are invited to see as typically male behaviour. They scoff at Hermia, calling her 'dwarf' and 'minimus' and 'hindering knotgrass'. Lysander throws her off roughly when she attempts to cling to him. He exhibits a behaviour that Shakespeare dramatizes as all too normal, though it might seem strange to us today: Lysander cannot fall in love with a new woman without instantly hating the woman he loved until just this moment. The men also grow abusive and even murderous toward each other. All this hatred is prompted by competitiveness in love. The women are foolish to try to scratch each other's eyes out; the men are foolish to wish to kill each other. Their quest for love has turned into a nightmare.

Or so it seems. When they awaken early the next morning, sleeping on the ground in pairs, Lysander with Hermia and Demetrius with Helena, they do not understand how they came to lie in this amiable fashion or how it has come about that Lysander is once again in love with Hermia. (Demetrius presumably remains under the spell of the love juice that has prompted him to adore Helena, whereas Lysander has been released from his spell.) They only know that something magical and transformative has occurred. By some power that he cannot account for, Demetrius finds that his love for Hermia has melted as the snow. The images of the night seem now 'small and undistinguishable, / Like far-off mountains turnèd into clouds'. 'Are you sure / That we are awake?' asks Demetrius. 'It seems to me / That yet we sleep, we dream.' No longer a nightmare but a happy dream, their testing experience in the forest has revealed to them a rather frightening image of their capacity for self-pity, hatred, and murderous intent with the ultimate purpose of showing them a better way. The dream thus represents for them what it has been to encounter sexual difference, to find it frightening both in itself and in terms of what it provokes in them, and then to awaken into a self-knowledge and a sharing of heterosexual desire that is deepened and made more precious by the awareness of how it can save them from their potential worst selves. Mastery in a battle of the sexes is not at issue here; unlike Theseus and Hippolyta, or Oberon and Titania, these four lovers find an accommodation and seeming equality in love that does not require the humiliation of the woman. Helena need not now be Demetrius's spaniel.

This image of a progression toward love and marriage is one that gives priority to heterosexual fulfillment. To be sure, the Sonnets and other writings give us plenty of reason to see how complex and ambiguous is the matter of constructing gender and identity in Shakespeare; loving relationships between persons of the same sex can be extraordinarily strong and tender. Still, a comedy like *A Midsummer Night's Dream* opts for marriage between men and women as the final act of the drama. It is the psychological goal toward which the young people uncertainly make their way. They find the process hurtful and demeaning, but the ultimate reward is all the more rich and precious for their encountering of those difficulties.

Portia, in *The Merchant of Venice*, is very much of two minds about independence from men. She is the beautiful heir of a man who has left her lots of money. On the other hand, her father has circumscribed her choice of husbands by his device of the three caskets and the choice that her wooers must make in order to win her hand in marriage. She intends to abide by her father's will. Sometimes in modern stage productions she tilts the contest in favour of Bassanio by hinting to him which casket he is to choose (as in Theodore Komisarjevsky's 1932 production at Stratford-upon-Avon, in which the singing of 'Tell me where is fancy bred' laid undue stress on 'bred' because of its rhyme with 'lead'), but in the text the issue is more open. The play seems to suggest, in fact, that she is not unwise to leave matters this way: Bassanio does, after all, choose the correct one, perhaps because the father wisely knew that the right young man would have the philosophical wisdom and the problem-solving savvy to know that, paradoxically, the lead casket, with its harsh lesson of paying no attention to outward shows and ornament, would direct Bassanio to the lady he desires.

By giving her hand in marriage to Bassanio, according to her father's will, Portia accepts the traditional patriarchal pattern of marriages: her father has chosen for her, and in effect gives his daughter to the younger man of whom he approves. Along with her acceptance of this arrangement, Portia also willingly turns over her wealth and management of her estate to her new lord. The word 'lord' is hers. It betokens, in the following passage, the transfer of control from herself to Bassanio:

> Myself and what is mine to you and yours
> Is now converted. But now I was the lord
> Of this fair mansion, master of my servants,
> Queen o'er myself; and even now, but now,
> This house, these servants, and this same myself
> Are yours, my lord's.
>
> (3.2.166–71)

Portia is fully aware of the loss, along with the presumed gain. She wants it plainly understood that she is making a sacrifice of her independence and control of wealth, to a considerably greater degree than is now required of Bassanio.

She does relinquish control freely, it seems, and yet the play cannot finish without allowing her a chance to tease and even torment her new husband on the matter. The episode of the rings occupies our attention in the theatre after the dramatic excitement of the trial of Antonio and the downfall of Shylock. Portia, disguised as a young doctor of law, has accomplished what all the older males of Venice have found impossible: she has outwitted Shylock with a legal quibble and has defeated his case. Playfully, she asks of Bassanio a thing that appears but a trifle in return for her having saved the life of Bassanio's dear friend and patron, Antonio: she would like to have the ring on Bassanio's finger. The disguised Portia knows, of course, that the ring in question is the wedding ring with which Bassanio has solemnly vowed never to part. Disguise gives her a great advantage in this matter: she knows everything (as do we as audience), whereas Bassanio is in the dark, a bewildered character in a little drama that she is scripting. Unable to persuade Bellario (i.e., Portia) of the reasons forbidding him to part from the ring, and urged by Antonio, Bassanio gives in. He hopes that he can get away with this. We know that when he gets home he will be asked by Portia to account for the disappearance of the ring.

Portia teases Bassanio to the very limit. She is testing him. Yes, he has given away the ring, as he should not have done, but the circumstances were compelling. Portia pretends to find the excuse unallowable, and threatens to sleep with whichever man now owns the ring that she gave her husband in marriage; meanwhile her waiting-gentlewoman, Nerissa, plays a similar trick on Bassanio's follower, Gratiano. Yet Portia knows that Bassanio gave up the ring uncomfortably, and in the name of friendship – a friendship that is often interpreted on the modern stage as suffused with homoerotic feeling, at least on the part of Antonio.[2] Bassanio has put this friendship ahead of romantic love, under the pressure of the moment. That, to Portia, is not an ignoble choice. Better to love a man who is steadily loyal in his obligations of loving friendship. The choice elevates spiritualized love over carnal love, as indeed in Bassanio's choice of the lead casket, but the two need not be incompatible. Nor does heterosexual fulfillment deny the importance of a deeply loving relationship between men, though the play may suggest that such love is best fulfilled when it ripens into the completion of a heterosexual marriage capable of producing children. Portia can hope that Bassanio, who has shown such loyalty in male-to-male friendship, will also turn out to be the loyal husband she has been seeking. The contretemps of the rings has been a test for Bassanio, presenting him with a seemingly impossible choice, but one that, in its paradoxes, points to the reconciliation in marriage of the physical and the spiritual sides of human nature.

The episode of the rings also makes a point about mastery in the battle of the sexes. Portia has surrendered control of her worldly affairs to Bassanio; she has also, in a fantasy of disguised appearance, shown how a woman can outsmart a whole courtroom full of men, and has then reminded Bassanio forcefully through the ring business that she still knows how to control him. Marriage involves quid pro quo. Bassanio is all the more attractive as the male lead of the play and as her partner because he seems entirely willing to acknowledge her status and power in their relationship.

The seemingly deliberate replay of elements of *The Taming of the Shrew* in *Much Ado about Nothing* gives us some indication of the extent to which Shakespeare is inviting us to wrestle with and reevaluate the issue of supremacy in the war of the sexes. Benedick and Beatrice are reincarnations of Petruchio and Kate in several ways: they are the wittiest young people in the play, and yet are both so strong-minded, and so disarmingly frank in the things they say, that they are in real danger of missing their chance to be happy together. Like Kate, Beatrice has a deserved reputation for being a shrew. 'By my troth, niece', says her uncle Leonato to her, 'thou wilt never get thee a husband if thou be so shrewd of thy tongue.' Leonato's brother Antonio emphatically agrees: 'In faith, she's too curst'. Benedick is wary of Beatrice's sharp tongue, and is also cautious because of another universal danger he perceives in the married state. Benedick repeatedly dwells on the humiliating prospect of cuckoldry. When mockingly advised by his commanding officer, Don Pedro, that 'In time the savage bull doth bear the yoke,' Benedick has a ready answer: 'The savage bull may, but if ever the sensible Benedick bear it, pluck off the bull's horns and set them in my forehead'. The worst humiliation he can invent for himself is to be labelled with the sign, 'Here you may see Benedick the married man'. On her side, Beatrice is put off to no less a degree by the prospect of losing her independence to a man: 'he that is more than a youth is not for me, and he that is less than a man, I am not for him'. And yet we know that, like Petruchio and Kate, or Berowne and Rosaline in *Love's Labour's Lost*, these two are destined for each other. In their wit and creativity of spirit, they are an inevitable match.

The conflict for both is one of autonomy versus dependence, the lure of freedom in singleness versus the comforts of needing and being needed by another. The particular difficulty at issue is sharpness of tongue. They both speak so wittily and so cuttingly, having created for themselves a game of verbal one-upmanship, that they both are unable to assess the seriousness of each other's criticisms. Is the other person just indulging in the established game of clever insult, or does the other person really dislike me? This is the question they cannot answer with certainty. The masked ball in 2.1 exacerbates the difficulty by allowing them to play their hazardous game under false pretences. Benedick, disguised (he hopes) as a stranger, informs Beatrice that he has heard people say she is disdainful and dimwitted; Beatrice, not fooled by the disguise, revenges herself by answering as though to a complete stranger that, in her own opinion, Benedick is 'the Prince's jester, a very dull fool'. Benedick, taken in, is genuinely hurt; here, it seems, is objective evidence of what he has feared, that Beatrice truly scorns him. Beatrice has clearly won in their little game of one-upmanship, but at the expense of nearly losing Benedick, to whom she is, despite herself, really attracted.

Such an impasse, in which both are convinced of the other's dislike, requires the intervention of their friends. Don Pedro, Claudio, and the other men devise a ruse whereby Benedick is to overhear a discussion of Beatrice's unhappiness because of Benedick's scornful treatment of her. The ladies do the same for Beatrice. It is a learning experience for both, to be told that their best friends deplore their coldness of heart. The ruse works because they are both generous of spirit and open to criticism, and because the fondness they feel for each other is genuine. The only thing that has held back a rapprochement is each lover's fear of being triumphed over scornfully by the other person. Once they are persuaded that the scorn of the other person is only a defensive mask (which it is, after all), they are ready to take the real risk of surrendering their autonomy. The means used to persuade them is a ruse, but it is not really a lie.

The resolution of their difficulty, compared with that of Petruchio and Kate, is far more based on equality and mutual understanding between the sexes. Like Portia, Beatrice knows when she can command. 'Kill Claudio!' she orders her lover, when Claudio has slandered and rejected Beatrice's cousin Hero. The order is issued as a requirement: if you want me to love you, you will do this. Benedick, reluctant of course to threaten the life of his best friend, undertakes to do what Beatrice insists upon because he senses that she is right in saying that Hero has been slandered. A spirit of comedy in this play relieves him of actually having to carry out the assignment; once Hero has been redeemed from slander, the badly mistaken Claudio can be forgiven. Benedick can marry Beatrice without committing manslaughter. The point has been made, in any case, that she as a woman has the right to expect certain things from her man, as he from her. The fact that Beatrice is independently wealthy after her father's death, like Portia, has given her a choice. The final coupling of Beatrice and Benedick is remarkably free of any constraints of social custom other than their serious and mutual investigation as to what it would be like to live together permanently as wife and husband.

The young protagonists of *Romeo and Juliet* (1594–6) behave in ways that reinforce the pattern we have been exploring. This play is of course a tragedy, but it is isolated in time of composition from the other tragedies (*Titus Andronicus* is earlier; *Julius Caesar*, *Hamlet*, *Othello*, and the rest are later) and is more or less contemporary with *A Midsummer Night's Dream* and *The Merchant of Venice*. Then, too, *Romeo and Juliet* is a remarkably funny play, at least during the first half, and its delight in lyric poetic forms continually reminds us of comedies like *A Midsummer Night's Dream*.

Appropriately, then, Romeo and Juliet are more like Lysander and Hermia or Berowne and Rosaline than they are like Hamlet and Ophelia or Othello and Desdemona. Romeo, when we first meet him, is lovesick for an unresponsive young woman named Rosaline. Shakespeare never brings Rosaline onstage; she is instead the disembodied personification of the Petrarchan lady whom the young man idealizes adoringly without any hope of reciprocal ardour. She thus anticipates the shepherdess Phoebe in *As You Like It* (to be discussed next), who seemingly enjoys being cruel to the shepherd Silvius because it gives her the power of rejection and glorifies her beauty as unattainable by the grovelling, self-abasing male.

Why Rosaline in *Romeo and Juliet* is so unresponsive to Romeo is never exactly explained, but presumably her pleasure in denial is like that of Phoebe. Romeo's lovesickness is, at any rate, severe. We learn in the play's first scene that Romeo keeps to himself, denying his company to his friends and preferring to stay in his chambers during the day. There, he 'shuts up his windows, locks fair daylight out, / And makes himself an artificial night'. Occasionally his furtive presence can be glimpsed among a grove of sycamore trees to the west of Verona, as he hides from human society, 'With tears augmenting the fresh morning's dew, / Adding to clouds more clouds with his deep sighs'. When Benvolio manages to catch up with him, Romeo laments that he is not himself: 'This is not Romeo; he's some other where'. Romeo repeatedly invokes the rhetorical figure of oxymoron, or inherent contradiction, to characterize the love–hate antitheses of his distress: 'O heavy lightness, serious vanity, / Misshapen chaos of well-seeming forms, / Feather of lead, bright smoke, cold fire, sick health, / Still-waking sleep, that is not what it is'. Love to him is 'A choking gall, and a preserving sweet'. Romeo can talk of nothing other than his own unhappiness; his infatuation for Rosaline is narcissistic, self-absorbed, conventional. He seems almost to enjoy his pain, and has no will to remedy the situation. He refuses at first to go with his friends to the Capulets' ball, where he might meet other young ladies. Romeo is in love with his own misery.

Rosaline's part in this play is to serve as a foil for Juliet, whom Romeo does in fact meet at the ball. Rosaline is denying and cruel; Juliet is respon-sive and affectionate. To be sure, her modesty forbids her to take the initiative in wooing or appear too easily won, but when her words of

longing for Romeo are overheard by him in the garden behind her family's
house and below her window (2.2), she bids a quick farewell to 'com-
pliment' (i.e., conventional etiquette) and confesses her love for him
with disarming candour. She must become his instructor in true love.
Swooning with passion as he is for her, Romeo knows only the language
of courtly Petrarchan discourse and must be brought down to earth. His
fanciful talk of overleaping the walls of her orchard with love's light wings,
and his adoration of her as 'a wingèd messenger of heaven' manifesting
herself to the 'white-upturnèd wond'ring eyes' of mortals like himself as
the worshipped deity 'bestrides the lazy puffing clouds / And sails upon
the bosom of the air', must give way to her insistence that danger is
present and that they must think quickly if they are to escape the perils
of family hostility. She is the one who asks the pragmatic questions. Will
Romeo consent to marry her? Where and at what hour can he be reached
in the fast-approaching morning? How will they manage to come together
before a priest, given the rancour that divides their families?

Romeo's emotional narcissism as a male quickly accedes to the reciprocal affection and greater self-knowledge that he learns, paradoxically,
from a young woman who is 'not yet fourteen'. Yet his male callowness
is not to be gotten over all at once. It contributes significantly to the play's
sudden veering toward tragedy in act three, when Romeo, coming upon
a scene of violent confrontation in the streets of Verona, refuses at first
to answer Tybalt's taunting challenge to a duel for having had the audac-
ity to dance with Juliet at the Capulets' ball, but then, driven to desper-
ation by Tybalt's slaying of Mercutio, makes his fateful choice. Caught
between his newfound love for Juliet and the code of masculine honour
insisting that Mercutio's death be avenged, Romeo, as we have seen, capit-
ulates to the masculine demands of honour and thereby brings on himself
the banishment that separates him from his new bride. The nature of his
tragedy lies partly in the hostility of an incomprehending world, but also
in Romeo's own insufficient maturity as a male. Because he betrays the
lesson in love that Juliet has taught him but which he has only partly
assimilated, he and Juliet cannot live to celebrate the kind of reciprocal
affection and understanding that is ultimately achieved by Beatrice and
Benedick in *Much Ado* or by Rosalind and Orlando in *As You Like It* and
Viola and Orsino in *Twelfth Night*.

The male-to-male attachments that compete for Romeo's affection are
strong indeed. Both Benvolio and Mercutio offer him, in their varying
ways, the camaraderie and the role-modelling that a young man desper-

ately needs. Mercutio is sometimes played in modern productions as homoerotically attracted to Romeo (as in the films of Franco Zeffirelli, 1968, and Baz Luhrmann, 1996), brilliantly scoffing at love as a way of urging Romeo to rejoin his companions. 'Why, is not this better now than groaning for love?' he asks Romeo, offering him witty male companionship in place of enervating lovesickness. Yet in its unthinking aspect the intense group loyalty among friends is capable of turning into the mindless conflict that prompts two respectable families of Verona to inflict mayhem on one another. Romeo is the tragic inverse of the young male protagonists of the romantic comedies; they manage to survive their waywardness, while Romeo, despite Juliet's precious instruction, fails under pressure.

As You Like It and *Twelfth Night* achieve a kind of culmination in the genre of romantic comedy by using the disguise of the heroine as a way of exploring how young women can best help young men achieve the emotional maturity they so badly need in order to be fully marriageable. The transition from the single state to heterosexual union is, as we have seen, fraught with personal peril, especially for the male. What sort of young woman does the young man need, in order to traverse this difficult rite of passage? Writing from the male point of view, Shakespeare imagines at least two answers: Rosalind and Viola.

Rosalind reminds us of the Princess in *Love's Labour's Lost* and Portia in *The Merchant of Venice*: she is sharp-witted, she is independent, and she knows what she wants. She falls in love with Orlando the moment she sees him. Both she and Orlando are aware, however, that he needs a lot of bringing along. Having been neglected in his education and breeding by his churlish older brother, Orlando finds that he does not even know how to speak in the presence of someone as refined and beautiful as Rosalind. In the Forest of Arden, once he has fled there to escape his brother's wrath, he can think of nothing better to do than pen verses to the absent object of his affection and hang those verses on trees. Having met her only once, he dreams about her unrealistically: she is his goddess, his unattainable ideal.

Because Rosalind has also made her way to the forest, disguised as Ganymede, she is in a position to take Orlando in hand. Posing as a young man, she counsels him on his distress. She even agrees to play Rosalind to his Orlando, in a complex interplay of fantasy and reality: she is really Rosalind (though also 'really' a boy actor) disguised as Ganymede and now play-acting at being herself. In this role she undertakes to straighten him out about women. 'Maids are May when they are maids, but the sky changes when they are wives,' she warns Orlando. In her supposed role as Orlando's Rosalind she will 'be more jealous of thee than a Barbary cock-pigeon over his hen, more clamorous than a parrot against rain, more newfangled than an ape, more giddy in my desires than a monkey'. She will weep for nothing when he is disposed to be merry, and she will laugh 'like a hyena' when he is inclined to sleep.

Rosalind's insistent wish is to disabuse Orlando of his fatuous male tendency toward idolizing her as some goddess. She must disabuse him of the clichés of courtship. When he tritely protests that he will die if he cannot have his Rosalind, she is splendidly sceptical: 'The poor world is almost six thousand years old, and in all this time there was not any man died in his own person, *videlicet*, in a love cause'. The stories of Troilus and Cressida and of Hero and Leander are threadbare legends: the facts are that Troilus died in battle, not of lovesickness, whereas Leander caught a cramp swimming the Hellespont and drowned. 'Men have died from time to time, and worms have eaten them, but not for love,' she concludes. The object lesson is plain: Orlando must be instructed how to think of his Rosalind as a flesh and blood woman, capable of bad temper and other inappropriate moods, though not of inconstancy in her affections. If she can teach him this, in much the way that Juliet wants to show Romeo how to set aside his poetic hyperboles and think of her as a real woman, then Orlando may be on his way to discovering what marriage is really about.

The theatrical trick at Shakespeare's disposal here is that Rosalind is in disguise as a young man. This safe distancing from gender difference makes possible a candour and intimacy that would presumably not be possible if Rosalind came to the still uninstructed Orlando as her feminine self. That would be too daunting. As Orlando's friend, on the other hand, Rosalind can offer wholesome counsel and can at the same time test his capacity for friendship. Their closeness is a loving one, and not without the suggestion of a complex emotional relationship; her disguise name, Ganymede, is that of Jove's cupbearer and male favourite, and on the Elizabethan stage the part of Rosalind was taken by a boy. Building on such a friendship, once it is fully established, Rosalind can then resort to the theatrical trick Shakespeare has held up his sleeve: she can reveal her sexual identity as a woman and as the object of Orlando's desire. Friendship has come first, as also in *The Merchant of Venice*; sexual fulfillment can then safely follow.

Viola in *Twelfth Night* is similarly unthreatening in her relation to the man she comes to love, Duke Orsino. Viola adopts the disguise of Cesario for reasons of prudence, but that disguise soon provides a more meaningful function: she can counsel Orsino as his young friend. Orsino is getting nowhere in his courtship of the Countess Olivia; it is another of those fruitless courtly-love fantasies of pursuit of the beautiful but unobtainable lady. For Olivia, the corresponding fantasy is one of being the desired object with the power to say no. Olivia and Orsino are so perfectly matched in their unproductive role-playing that they could go on thus forever.

Both of them find Viola different from what they both have come to expect in a relationship. She is fresh, breezy, and iconoclastic (as is Rosalind) about the posturings of Petrarchan love-sonneteering. No wonder Olivia falls at once in love with this seeming young man. Cesario is so unlike Orsino, so direct and spontaneous, so cheeky, so practical, so real. For his part, Orsino finds Cesario no less attractive, though ostensibly at least in a different way. Physical sexual desire is not a part of Orsino's interest in Cesario, at least, not consciously so. Like Olivia he finds the young 'man' disarmingly candid and surprisingly sympathetic. Cesario is a good listener. Orsino quickly discovers that no one in his court means as much to him as Cesario. He depends on Cesario not just for the sending of hopeless messages to Olivia, but for advice about this thing called love. Orsino sends away his courtiers in order that he and Cesario may discuss what men and women are like, how they differ from men in their emotional needs. Cesario soon becomes the best friend Orsino has ever had. Their differences in social station quickly fade into the background.

As in the case of Orlando and Rosalind, these repeated conversations of Orsino and Viola/Cesario give the young woman, in her unthreatening guise as a young man, the opportunity to educate Orsino, to show him the emptiness of his imaginings for a woman (Olivia) whom he in fact scarcely ever sees and never thinks about in realistic terms. Orsino at the end of the play is manifestly more ready for the give-and-take of the daily life of marriage than he was when Viola/Cesario first appeared on his doorstep.

When Orsino learns that his young friend has evidently married Olivia in secret, Orsino is furious. Is he angry because he has lost Olivia, or because he has lost Cesario? To say that he loves Cesario is hardly a misstatement; he has come to depend on that young man's company and counsel. Earlier, the sea captain Antonio's deeply loving attachment to

Viola's brother Sebastian, a feeling so intense that physical separation is virtually unbearable, is still another indication in the play of ways in which male-to-male love can anticipate and prepare for the heterosexual denouement. In modern stage productions, Antonio is often portrayed as homosexually attracted to Sebastian, just as his namesake in *The Merchant of Venice* is often portrayed as in love with Bassanio. Whether there is also a muted physical attraction in Orsino's fondness for the seemingly male Cesario is hard to tell, though the convention in the early modern theatre of a boy playing the role of Viola/Cesario certainly adds to the interesting ambiguities. The playful uncertainties of gender are no less captivating in the theatre when the Countess Olivia becomes enamoured of 'Cesario' (i.e., Viola in disguise) and then marries Sebastian thinking that person to be Cesario, when all of these dramatic characters were played on Shakespeare's stage by young males. When, at any rate, the time comes for Viola to reveal her sexual identity, this theatrical trick provides a completion of Orsino's odyssey like that of Orlando in *As You Like It*. A deep, loving friendship, made possible in the first instance by the seeming lack of disparity in gender between Orsino and Cesario, now ripens into a sexual partnership between Orsino and Viola. Friendship needs to come first because that is the more spiritual relationship; thereafter, sex is not only permissible but wonderful. A companionate marriage is in prospect because husband and wife began their relationship as friends. At the height of his achievement in romantic comedy, Shakespeare perfects a pattern of emotional development that enables the male to move through friendship to erotic desire with as little trauma as possible. The process requires a Rosalind or a Viola or a Juliet to ensure success; she is the theatrical artist and magician needed for this purpose.

CHAPTER FOUR

◆

Full of Strange Oaths and Bearded Like the Pard

The Coming-of-Age of the Male

Thou? Why, thou wilt quarrel with a man that hath a hair more or or a hair less in his beard than thou hast. Thou wilt quarrel with a man for cracking nuts, having no other reason but because thou hast hazel eyes.

Romeo and Juliet, 3.1

Even while he explored sexuality and companionship in his romantic comedies of the 1590s, Shakespeare also devoted himself to a kind of drama in which men act out their conflicts with one another in an essentially male arena. Women do sometimes play a significant part in his English history plays, especially those of the early 1590s dramatizing the Wars of the Roses and the reign of King John. In the second four-play sequence of historical plays that Shakespeare wrote in the late 1590s, on the other hand, women are to be found at the margins of human action. The young Prince Hal who is to become Henry V has no mother in these plays. He also lacks any relationship with a woman other than a passing acquaintance with Mistress Quickly, the keeper of the tavern where he revels with Falstaff. To be more precise, Prince Henry befriends and courts no woman until the very end of the entire saga. *Henry V* culminates, like a romantic comedy, in the marriage of Henry with fair Katharine of France. Marriage provides closure, albeit with a brief and dispiriting historical reminder that Henry V's son, Henry VI, will manage to undo all that his father has accomplished in France. At all events, this marriage comes very late in the game. Young Henry avoids all commerce with women until, having won his spurs, he can triumphantly take Katharine as his prize for having achieved manhood. She is the spoils of war, obliged to marry him in accordance with an English–French treaty. The woman is handed to Henry on a plate.

It is as though, in his English history plays, Shakespeare deliberately chooses a very different way from that of the comedies of thinking about the maturation of the young male. In Shakespeare's historical world, women are so little a part of Prince Hal's life because he has his mind on other things. He needs to discover who he is, what sort of son he can be to his father, and what sorts of male companions he can find to offer alternative visions of male achievement than those proposed by his father. Before he can be a man and a king, Hal needs to sort out his relationship to his father, to Falstaff, and to his great rival, Hotspur.

His father, King Henry IV, is a troubling figure. In the play of *Richard II*, with which Shakespeare began what was to become a four-play sequence, Henry Bolingbroke, son of the Duke of Lancaster, takes the throne away from his royal first cousin, Richard, and is crowned as Henry IV. This usurpation is the culmination of a series of actions, none of which at first seems consciously aimed at assuming the kingship. When Richard banishes Bolingbroke over a quarrel that threatens to expose Richard's own complicity in the assassination of their youngest uncle, Thomas of Woodstock, and then confiscates Bolingbroke's titles and property left to him by the recently deceased Duke of Lancaster, Bolingbroke protests and strikes back. He has considerable support among the nobility, who rightly view Richard's seizure of Bolingbroke's inheritance as legally unjustifiable and potentially an assault on their own baronial independence. If the King can confiscate property like this simply by edict, then no nobleman is safe. Supported by such outrage at an autocratic abuse of power, Bolingbroke returns from exile and soon has Richard militarily at his mercy.

What is Bolingbroke to do, however, with a defeated king? Bolingbroke insists that he has returned to reclaim his inheritance; having achieved that, he professes to acknowledge Richard as his king still. Yet Richard's fangs have been pulled to the extent that he is now only a paper tiger, or at any rate a fangless one. How can he rule, now that Bolingbroke has militarily forced him to concede? The result is an arranged abdication. Yet that event only presents Henry with another problem: what is he to do with a deposed king? Such a figure is sure to become the unceasing focus of rebellion against Henry IV's own rule.

'Have I no friend will rid me of this living fear?' Henry mutters, to himself but loud enough for others to hear, and a certain Sir Pierce of Exton takes him at his word. King Henry rebukes Exton for having carried out the execution – 'They love not poison that do poison need, / Nor do I thee,' he tells him – but the deed has been done. For all his attempts to shift the blame on to Exton, King Henry knows in his heart that he is another Cain having slain his brother Abel. He actually tries to pin the label of 'Cain' on Exton, but we see all too plainly that the resemblance fits far better the man who has countenanced the death of one who, if not literally his brother, was his first cousin and king. Henry admits as much when he resolves on a crusade to the Holy Land 'To wash this blood off from my guilty hand'.

King Henry's political problems do not disappear once he has become king and has entered into the phase of his kingship dramatized in *1 Henry IV*. Determined to rule with a firm hand, he soon quarrels with the very men who have done most to place him in power: the Percy clan, of whom the Earl of Northumberland is chief. Together with his brother the Earl of Worcester, Northumberland chafes at the King's highhandedness. Having supported him in the first place because of their distress at Richard II's autocratic ways, they are not happy to find themselves with another monarch bent on curbing baronial power. Comfortably established in the north of England, on the Scottish border, the Percys have no use for a centralized royal authority. Northumberland's son, Harry Percy, or Hotspur as he is known for his fiery temperament, has been fighting the Scots on behalf of King Henry, but readily joins his father and uncle in secret talk of treasonous opposition.

Henry has partly driven the Percys into rebellion by his hauteur and his suspicions of them, but he also is right to worry about them. Edmund Mortimer, nominally fighting for Henry against the Welsh in the west of England, has married the daughter of the very man he is supposed to be attacking, Owen Glendower. More dangerously still, this Mortimer can lay claim to the throne by virtue of the fact that he was proclaimed by the deposed King Richard II as his heir to the crown. Moreover, Mortimer is in league with the Percys; his sister is married to Hotspur. (Shakespeare conflates a number of Mortimers from English history in order to make the dynastic threat as vivid as possible; he also changes the name of Hotspur's wife from Elizabeth to Kate.)

Henry is thus faced with the daunting spectre of civil war, set in motion by his own usurpation of the English throne and the dynastic ambiguities that are sure to follow upon such a disturbance of the hallowed custom of primogeniture. Shakespeare presents a partly sympathetic view of both sides. Henry wants to rule well, having come to power with the support of the Percys; they, for their own part, are genuinely alarmed by his moves toward consolidation of authority. Civil war is in prospect not because the participants are spoiling for a fight; these are intelligent, powerful men driven apart by misunderstanding that feeds on itself. Most ironic of all in this impending conflict is the fact that King Henry greatly admires Hotspur. He admires his spirit and would like to have him as a kind of son – a better son, in fact, than the King's own wayward heir. Yet Hotspur wants no father figure intent on lecturing the young man in the duties of obedience. Thus the polarities feed on one another and gain momentum.

Although Prince Hal does not appear in person in *Richard II*, he is referred to by his disappointed father as an 'unthrifty son' (5.3). Three months have passed since last the King saw him. 'If any plague hang over us, 'tis he,' Henry laments. Reports confirm that the Prince frequents taverns, consorting with and actively supporting a dissolute crew of 'unrestrainèd loose companions' who assault the night watch and rob wayfarers. The essential plot of Hal's wild companionship with Falstaff is thus adumbrated in *Richard II*, even though Shakespeare appears not to have thought it through entirely; Falstaff is not named, and the whole business is merely the concern of a passing moment as Henry prepares to deal with the more immediate dangers of opposition to his regime.

Shakespeare knew the story of Hal's wild youth, of course; it was notorious, even if it was probably not historically true. It had been the basis of a boisterous, undisciplined historical play called *The Famous Victories of Henry the Fifth* which, at some point in the late 1580s, had breathlessly narrated in a single play the career of Prince Hal all the way from his tavern days through his 'famous victory' over the French at Agincourt in 1415. Legends had begun to accumulate around Henry V not long after his death; he was such a hero that he needed a fictional youth, preferably one in which, as a Prodigal Son, he could enjoy the heady pleasures of a wild youth and then be suddenly transformed into a great king who still remembers the ways of the common people with whom he has caroused.

Hal does not know what to make of his father, or how to be his son. A good part of what strikes others as his irresponsibility we can attribute to his hesitancy to be like his father – powerful but cold, baleful, disapproving. When Hal is obliged to go to court and face his father's wrath, the tongue-lashing is enough to daunt any prince. The lecture commences as follows:

> I know not whether God will have it so
> For some displeasing service I have done,
> That in His secret doom out of my blood
> He'll breed revengement and a scourge for me;
> But thou dost in thy passages of life
> Make me believe that thou art only marked
> For the hot vengeance and the rod of heaven
> To punish my mistreadings.
>
> (*1 Henry IV*, 3.2.4–11)

King Henry does not begin by asking his son if the rumours about him are true. He scarcely affords an opportunity for the Prince to justify himself. Instead, he wonders aloud if this son is a scourge, a punishment sent by heaven for the King's own sins. Henry must be thinking still of his culpability in the death of Richard II. Is this son heaven's way of settling the score? If so, is not the son himself in a fair way to be damned for his own wayward behaviour? Why have the heavens given Henry this source of open shame and embarrassment? Why could he not have a son like the valiant Hotspur?

These are not sentiments calculated to make a son feel loved by his parent. Part of Hal's intense rivalry with Hotspur grows out of his awareness that the father prefers Hotspur. Though they are not brothers in blood, they are half-brothers in the King's distressed imagination, and as such they partake of the rivalry we explored in Chapter 2. (Shakespeare changes the age of Hotspur to intensify the conflict; historically, Henry Percy was the age of Hal's father.) The rivalry in all such cases is at least in part a competition for parental love and approval. Hal attempts to reconcile himself to his father by promising that 'in the closing of some glorious day' he will 'Be bold to tell you that I am your son'. The desire to do so bespeaks Hal's wish to find a way to fulfill his potential as Prince of Wales and son of the King; it is also a plea to the father in intensely personal terms, to remember that the speaker is 'your son'.

Faced with such a denying father, and caught in a fierce rivalry with a young man his age whom his father would like to call 'son', Hal does what any young man might be expected to do: he indulges in the exaggerated irresponsibility of youth and chooses as his companion a raffish old hedonist who seems utterly devoted to him. Hal has other acquaintances, to be sure, such as Ned Poins, with whom he plans escapades. Still, Hal needs someone who will supply the very things that his father most denies: comradeship, fondness, approval, merriment, and above all *joie de vivre*.

At first glance, Falstaff would seem to be an odd and unsatisfactory choice for a companion. Falstaff is 'inclining to threescore' in age, nearly sixty (or perhaps older; Falstaff is, to use his own phrase, 'given to lying'), whereas Hal is perhaps twenty. Falstaff is a moocher, a highwayman, a heavy drinker, and grossly overweight; Hal is too wealthy to need to beg or steal, and he is in fighting trim, even if he does sometimes tipple with Falstaff and the under-skinkers or bartenders who inhabit the tavern. Falstaff is a commoner, even if he has somehow managed in his checkered past to be knighted; Hal is the Prince of Wales, the once and future king. What is more, the relationship of the two seems abusive, even uneasy; their habitual mode of dialogue is the trading of colourful insults. They are incessantly sparring with one another.

When we first see them together (1.2), they are debating a favourite subject: Falstaff's disreputable ways of stealing purses by night and then sleeping till noon. Is such a way of life to be defended? 'Let not us that are squires of the night's body be called thieves of the day's beauty,' argues Falstaff. 'Let men say we be men of good government, being governed, as the sea is, by our noble and chaste mistress the moon, under whose countenance we steal.' This is all said in fun, apparently, and yet a real topic is engaged: is Falstaff to be allowed to continue as a highwayman because of his friendship with the Prince of Wales? Or should he be hanged as a thief? 'I prithee, sweet wag', Falstaff asks Hal, 'shall there be gallows standing in England when thou art king? And resolution thus fubbed as it is with the rusty curb of old father Antic the law?' The Prince does not answer directly; instead, he plays with language, as Falstaff does too. When Falstaff puts the proposition to him straight, 'Do not thou, when thou art king, hang a thief,' Hal has his ready answer: 'No, thou shalt'. He elaborates: 'thou shalt have the hanging of the thieves, and so become a rare hangman'. This could be interpreted as meaning that Hal will appoint Falstaff as his Lord Chief Justice and thereby assure that thieves in England will only rarely be hanged. Yet Hal's ambiguous wording has a potentially opposite meaning as well: thou shalt hang a thief, thou shalt hang *as* a thief, and thus become a splendid ('rare') example of a man who is hanged. Beneath the playfulness of the word games, Hal and Falstaff are continually fencing for position as to whether Hal will continue to befriend Falstaff when Hal is king.

The issue is so serious in its playfulness that it quickly takes on a religious dimension. One of Falstaff's amusing mannerisms is his mimicry of pious Puritan talk. 'But Hal, I prithee, trouble me no more with vanity,' he croons. 'Thou hast done much harm upon me, Hal, God forgive thee for it. Before I knew thee, Hal, I knew nothing; and now am I, if a man should speak truly, little better than one of the wicked.' Is Hal indeed the tempter of Falstaff, rather than vice versa? The proposition is comically outrageous, and shows us Falstaff on the comic offensive, as he usually is. At the same time, the two men seem to concede that they encourage each other's bad habits. The offered alternative is repentance. 'I must give over this life, and I will give it over,' sighs Falstaff in mock remorse. 'I'll be damned for never a king's son in Christendom.' The words 'devil' and 'damned' appear repeatedly in the conversation, acknowledging that the issue has rapidly become one of salvation or damnation. Does Falstaff really mean that he will repent? The very question is greeted by Hal with a mirthful jeer: 'I see a good amendment of life in thee – from praying to purse taking'. Falstaff is incorrigible. They both know it; it is part of his endearing charm.

When this scene of brilliant badinage has ended with Hal's agreeing to go on one of Falstaff's highway robberies for once, his friend Poins having persuaded him privately that they can use the occasion to play a practical joke on Falstaff, the Prince is left alone in soliloquy. This much-discussed soliloquy is needed for a number of pressing reasons. The Prince of Wales is about to commit a serious crime, in the company of an endearing rogue who is nonetheless beyond reclamation. Part of Shakespeare's dramatic motive in his placement of this soliloquy, then, is to assure us that Hal is himself not beyond reclamation. He informs us as audience that he is on to Falstaff and his crew. He plans to play along with the 'unyoked humour' of their 'idleness' for a time in order that he may, at the propitious moment, burst forth in unexpected glory like the sun emerging from behind a dark cloud. He will be all the more admired for 'breaking through the foul and ugly mists / Of vapours that did seem to strangle him'. He will shine like bright metal set off against a sullen background.

These comparisons are hardly flattering in their implied judgement of Falstaff, and in saying so Hal even approaches a certain heartlessness. Is he really using Falstaff and his companions for a time merely as foils to his future greatness? If so, the calculation is somewhat dehumanizing. At the same time, one can read the soliloquy in quite a different sense: Hal is stalling for time, wanting to enjoy the irresponsible pleasures of the tavern and highway while he still can, before he must face his responsibilities as an adult and eventual king. Is he whistling in the dark, or is he planning every step of his career as Prince Hal, the future monarch with the common touch? Our uncertainty adds greatly to our interest in this young man. Recent stage productions have run the gamut, from Richard Burton's steely certainty in knowing exactly what temporary use he can make of Falstaff (Stratford-upon-Avon, 1951) to Gerard Murphy's clinging emotional dependency on a genial old man who is so unlike Hal's austere father (directed by Trevor Nunn at the Barbican Theatre in 1982).

The highway robbery, and its aftermath of revelry at the Tavern (2.2 and 2.4), show us what is so richly captivating in the competitive sport of wit that Hal and Falstaff play with each other. Like many a fat comedian coupled in a vaudeville routine with a thin straight man (Art Carney and Jackie Gleason, Abbott and Costello, Laurel and Hardy) Falstaff knows how to play his own fatness for laughter. He waddles grotesquely at Gad's Hill, the appointed location for the robbery, because Poins and Hal have taken away his horse. 'Eight yards of uneven ground is threescore-and-ten miles afoot with me, and the stony-hearted villains know it well enough,' he grumbles – loudly enough for his tormenters to hear, for he is aware that he is expected to put on a show. When Hal proposes that Falstaff lay his ear close to the ground to hear the tread of travellers, Falstaff knows how to play this for a laugh at his own expense: 'Have you any levers to lift me up again, being down?' Falstaff knows that by being funny he can endear himself to the Prince. Like many a stout person who discovers that he can gain a kind of popularity by inviting laughter at his avoirdupois weight for which he would otherwise be scorned, Falstaff begs to be loved as the comic fatman.

In the tavern after the robbery (2.4) Falstaff plays a remarkable number of roles. Indeed, his versatility as a mimic is part of his appeal. He acts out the role of the valiant hero deserted by his friends. 'A plague of all cowards, I say, and a vengeance too!' This is intended for Hal and Poins, who unexpectedly did not take part in the actual robbery when the time came. Next, Falstaff assumes the role of the adroit swordsman, taking on two combatants at once, 'two rogues in buckram suits', who, as he varnishes his tale, become four, then seven, then nine, and finally eleven. His best role is that of the teller of tall tales.

Falstaff's inventive lying is part of the fun, part of the charm with which he appeals to Hal for affection. At the same time, it is an essential ingredient in their contest of wits. Hal's practical joke, executed in concert with Poins, has been to don disguises and rob the robbers after the Gad's Hill escapade in order to see how Falstaff will lie about his exploits. They will catch him out in a monstrous lie. This is their plan from the start: as Poins explained it to Hal in proposing the caper, 'The virtue of this jest will be the incomprehensible lies that this same fat rogue will tell us when we meet at supper – how thirty at least he fought with, what wards, what blows, what extremities he endured; and in the reproof of this lives the jest'. In the tavern, Hal and Poins both egg Falstaff on, waiting with barely stifled mirth for the exposé. Falstaff, needless to say, does not disappoint. His story is monstrous, and his discomfiture is of epic size. 'What trick, what device, what starting-hole canst thou now find out to hide thee from this open and apparent shame?' concludes the Prince, as he and Poins await Falstaff's answer.

Who wins this contest of wits, however? The ever resourceful Falstaff, presumably after a theatrical pause that depends on skilled comic timing, comes up with the perfect and outrageously funny answer: he knew Hal through his disguise all the time, not consciously but by instinct. 'Was it for me to kill the heir apparent?' Instinct has saved the day. 'Instinct is a great matter; I was now a coward on instinct.' He manages to turn this into a sly joke at the Prince's expense, by suggesting that instinct has thus confirmed what might be otherwise doubted: that Hal is in fact 'a true prince'. Hal and Poins are presumably delighted. Not only have they caught out Falstaff in a monstrous lie, they have heard him invent an excuse extempore that is funnier than they could have imagined.

But wait a minute. Have they really caught Falstaff out in a lie, or has he allowed himself to be caught out in a lie? Consider the following. Falstaff knows that Hal and Poins agreed to ride with them on this robbing expedition. Hal and Poins then unexpectedly were not there when the robbery actually took place. A short time later, two athletic young men in Kendall Green descended on Falstaff and his robbing companions as they were dividing the loot and took it away from them. It wouldn't take a genius to figure out the math in this equation of two and two. Falstaff hints at his comprehending the situation even as he delivers his artfully constructed lie: 'I have peppered two of them. Two I am sure I have paid, two rogues in buckram suits.' He challenges Hal to catch him out in his lie. The lie itself is so splendidly self-contradictory that no one could be expected to believe it for a minute: two opponents turned into eleven, at a time when it was so dark one couldn't see one's own hand. Falstaff is, to be sure, a confirmed liar, but he is also, and supremely, an artist of the magnificent lie. He has his audience, and he knows what his audience wants.

A parallel tavern scene in *2 Henry IV* (2.4) seems to confirm this interpretation of Falstaff's awareness of what he is doing in Part 1. The Prince, no longer in touch with Falstaff on a daily basis, pays a visit to the tavern for old time's sake, and is dismayed to see how disreputable and sodden Falstaff has become. Trying to recover the ebullient spirit of those former days, Hal and Poins disguise themselves as tapsters (barkeeps) in order to be close to Falstaff and hear what he is talking about. The conversation is not edifying; Falstaff is as capable as ever of inventively insulting comparisons, but employs them abusively in this case. He is not engaging in wit-combat; he is unaware of their presence. When the Prince and Hal identify themselves, in a replay of the exposure of the lying in *1 Henry IV*, Falstaff is at a loss for words. The Prince rallies him by suggesting that 'you knew me, as you did when you ran away by Gad's Hill. You knew I was at your back, and spoke it on purpose to try my patience.' Hal seems almost to be pleading with Falstaff: please tell us that the insults you were uttering behind my back just now were part of our charade, spoken to amuse me by their adroit cheekiness. But it will not do. Falstaff can only stammer, 'No, no, no, not so, I did not think thou wast within hearing'. This time Hal has caught Falstaff out indeed. Yet he seems to understand now that Falstaff got the better of him in the Gad's Hill business. Shakespeare was certainly aware, as he wrote the second play, that one could interpret the scene in *1 Henry IV* as a demonstration of Falstaff's having been one step ahead of Prince Hal all the way.

If so – and we need to remember that the scene is funny in *1 Henry IV* if played 'straight' as the exposure of a comic liar – then we can perhaps sympathize with Falstaff, not only for winning the game of wits but for not taking credit for his victory. More important for him is to please his prince. If that requires making himself out to be a coward and a liar, so be it. Falstaff sees that his destined role is to be the butt, the scapegoat. He plays the role consummately, though perhaps a bit anxiously. Hal's comic rebuttals constantly remind Falstaff that he is on trial.

The defence of Falstaff as comic fatman comes to a head in the play-acting that he and Hal devise as a way of rehearsing Hal's upcoming interview with his father (Part I, 2.4). Both are superb actors and mimics; we gather that they have put on entertainments many times before, and are good at improvising comic dialogue. Falstaff first assumes the role of the ageing king, cross-examining Hal on how he is wasting his time, but then venturing to suggest that Hal appears to have one virtuous friend. Who might that be? asks Hal, knowing perfectly well what the answer will be. 'A goodly portly man, i'faith, and a corpulent', is Falstaff's reply. 'Of a cheerful look, a pleasing eye, and a most noble carriage.' His age is fifty 'or, by'r Lady, inclining to threescore'; Falstaff catches himself, realizing that his audience will not buy the absurd claim that he is only fifty. 'His name is Falstaff. . . . There is virtue in that Falstaff. Him keep with, the rest banish.'

Where did this note of banishment come from? Hal has said nothing on the subject. Yet it becomes the theme of their ensuing conversation. Hal takes over as king at this point, in a move that is symbolically suggestive; he is trying on his father's identity, if only in play, perhaps too with a hint of eventually supplanting that father on the throne. That is what play is for, after all. Hal jests in his role, castigating his interlocutor – which is to say his other self, the friend who is now impersonating Hal – for his association with a 'devil' that haunts Hal in the likeness of an old man, a 'bolting-hutch of beastliness', a 'stuffed cloak-bag of guts', a 'father ruffian' and 'vanity in years', and much more. This is the stuff of their old game, the bedazzling catalogue of colourful insults, and it is perhaps as amusing as Falstaff's deadpan answer to this description: 'I would Your Grace would take me with you. Whom means Your Grace?'

Falstaff knows of course that it is he who is under investigation, and he takes the opportunity to offer the best defence of Falstaff in the play. 'If to be old and merry be a sin, then many an old host that I know is damned.' Who would not prefer to be merry, to laugh as they all are laughing now? Can Hal even think of giving up this pleasure, simply because he has to go and face his father in the morning? Falstaff's plea that Hal banish anyone other than Falstaff himself becomes a kind of litany in which the tone of pleading turns suddenly serious. 'Banish not him thy Harry's company,' Falstaff urges in his peroration. 'Banish plump Jack, and banish all the world.' The Prince is suddenly quiet, serious too. 'I do, I will.' That is all he says in reply. Is this pronounced with some regret, some awareness of what a sacrifice it will be to give up Falstaff, even if that sacrifice now appears to be necessary and imminent? The Prince has a lot to think about.

If Falstaff's lying can perhaps be seen as a gambit on his part to endear himself to Hal, so too with his supposed cowardice. His reputation for cowardice is part of the legend about Falstaff, and as such, it is part of his act. Hal and Poins know what to expect at Gad's Hill. His companions are 'as true-bred cowards as ever turned back', Poins assures Hal as they prepare for the robbing escapade. As for Falstaff, 'if he fight longer than he sees reason, I'll forswear arms'. 'Longer than he sees reason.' What does 'reason' mean? At Gad's Hill, in point of fact, when the disguised Hal and Poins descend on the robbers, '*They all run away*', while Falstaff, '*after a blow or two, runs away too*'. This stage direction (2.2.102) carefully distinguishes between Falstaff and the others. They run 'on instinct', if you like; Falstaff runs when he sees that he faces two well-trained young adversaries. A man could get killed that way. Falstaff is a coward not 'on instinct', despite his joking about it, but as a matter of common sense. A man could get killed fighting one on two, especially if the one is old and fat.

This same reasonable approach to cowardice and honour sustains Falstaff in the battle sequences that end the play. When he suddenly finds himself in hand-to-hand combat with the Douglas, known as the most fearsome warrior of them all, Falstaff does the only thing that will save his skin: he '*falls down as if he were dead*'. The tactic is hardly glorious, but it achieves its purpose: Falstaff survives to live another day. One of his philosophical principles is that one has so few options when one is dead.

Earlier, too (5.1), Falstaff has made plain to us in soliloquy that when it comes to choosing between honour and death, he has little hesitation in knowing which to take. He catechises himself. 'What is honour? A word. What is in that word "honour"? What is that "honour"? Air. A trim reckoning! Who hath it? He that died o' Wednesday.' Honour has no skill in surgery, and is insensible to those that have it, since they are dead. If such is the case, Falstaff will have nothing to do with honour. His position is, by definition, dishonourable, and indeed he is capable of behaving cravenly, as when he hands Hal a whisky bottle instead of a pistol in the heat of battle or stabs the dead Hotspur in the groin in order to claim Hotspur as his prize. Yet Falstaff's disquisition on honour is also a probing, sceptical challenge to the very idea of war. Civil conflict has erupted because men of principle could not work out their differences and so have taken to butchering one another. Falstaff's is the chief voice in the play to question the premises of honour, and he does so with telling ironic insight.

By the time he reaches the field of battle in act five, Hal has many options to choose among. He can strive to win his father's belated admiration. This he does by rescuing his father in the heat of battle, thus demonstrating that he cares deeply about his father's life – something that the King has sadly doubted. Hal can cling to some of Falstaff's *joie de vivre* and his ironic questionings, even while distancing himself from Falstaff's self-interested claims on Hal's friendship. Most of all, Hal needs to come to terms with Hotspur, both as a rival in the pursuit of honour and as a competitor for King Henry's affection. Hal must show, through his vanquishing of Hotspur, that Hal is indeed his father's true son.

Hal invests this deed with a kind of commercial value. Honour exists for him in a limited, definable quantity: if Hotspur has it, Hal cannot. As he explains to his father on the occasion of their long interview (3.2), Henry Percy is merely Hal's 'factor' to 'engross up glorious deeds on my behalf' – that is, Hotspur is the agent who amasses glory for himself, but with the ironic ultimate result that Hal can gain more honour for himself by taking it away from Hotspur. Hal returns to this idea of their fighting over a limited supply of honour when they meet at Shrewsbury Field. 'Think not, Percy, / To share with me in glory any more. / Two stars keep not their motion in one sphere.' Hal can achieve greatness only at the expense of Hotspur.

The rivalry is all the more intense because they are so close in age, and have the same name. Yet that very similarity calls attention to a profound difference. When Hotspur addresses Hal as 'Harry Monmouth', after Hal's birthplace, and identifies himself as 'Harry Percy', the balance seems symmetrical. It is not so for Hal. He sees in Hotspur 'a very valiant rebel of the name', while Hal himself is 'Prince of Wales'. That is, he lays claim to a legitimacy through birth and legal sanctions of birthright; he has a valid claim to the throne. Never mind for the moment that Hal's father stole the crown from Richard II; Hal is his father's son, and his father is king. Percy is valiant, but he is a rebel. He is seeking an illegitimate pathway to power, and also to manhood. Hal will become king by becoming his father; Hotspur cannot do that. The very security of England's dynastic future lies in the family structure of fathers and sons. This is why, as Hal triumphantly proclaims, England cannot 'brook a double reign / Of Harry Percy and the Prince of Wales' (5.4).

Hal now must believe that the saga of his rise to glory is over, and that it has run exactly according to the script he fashioned for it. He has redeemed himself and has redeemed time itself, as he promised he would in act one. He is the Prodigal Son welcomed home by a grateful father whose very life he has saved in battle. His problem with Falstaff is solved, for Falstaff now lies dead beside Hotspur. Hal eulogizes both, saving his best words for a worthy opponent; about Falstaff he says only, condescendingly, 'I could have better spared a better man'. End of story. Exit the Prince.

Or so it seems, until Falstaff rises up off the stage, winking at the audience and explaining brilliantly how 'The better part of valour is discretion, in the which better part I have saved my life'. Falstaff is not dead after all. He has gone beyond the bounds of dramatic fiction, in fact, because he has violated an unspoken 'rule' of theatrical illusion. When an actor falls down 'dead' onstage, we stipulate that he is dead for the purposes of the play; we know that the actor will get up afterwards and live to play another day. Falstaff is an 'actor' in another sense. He refuses to abide by theatrical convention; he tricks us by insisting on coming back to life in the play where he is supposed to be dead. In this sense he occupies a greater sphere in our imagination than does Hal. Falstaff is larger than art; he comes close to being larger than life. Hal may reject him in time, but Falstaff will not go away. He is immortal.

Falstaff lives on in *2 Henry IV*, a diminished thing, largely because both Shakespeare and Hal have a problem with him. Shakespeare has made Falstaff so winsome that any rejection of him by Hal will seem heartless and callow. Hal is aware of the problem; that is part of the reason why he is dispirited in much of this play, complaining to Poins of being weary and bored. He knows that he is supposed to be reconciled with his father, and is certainly more distant from Falstaff, but he also knows that if he were to express regret for the King's sudden illness he would be accounted 'a most princely hypocrite'. Everyone expects him to rejoice at his father's death and institute a rule of lawless riot. That is why Hal must be so public about his rejection of Falstaff, in fact. Falstaff's behaviour has grown more and more menacing, from Hal's point of view. He hobnobs with garrulous old Justices of the Peace in the countryside whom he hopes to bring to London and reward for their generosity to him by putting them on the gravy train. He squanders his time with colourful rowdies like Pistol and whores like Doll Tearsheet. Hal's brothers and the Lord Chief Justice have little doubt but that Hal will appoint Falstaff in the Lord Chief

Justice's stead, if for no other reason than that the Lord Chief Justice has had the temerity to rebuke Hal and even incarcerate him briefly for irresponsible misconduct. Once he is king, Hal makes it his first order of business to confront the Lord Chief Justice on this matter. 'What? Rate, rebuke, and roughly send to prison / Th'immediate heir of England?' When the Lord Chief Justice explains that he did so because Hal had offended justice itself by striking the chief magistrate, the new King Henry reveals his purpose in asking the question. He will deliver full authority into the hands of the Chief Justice. Having lost his own father, Hal will embrace this pillar of justice as his new father: 'you, father, shall have foremost hand' (5.2). The public rejection of Falstaff is necessary, if distasteful, because only such a symbolic gesture can signal the new king's devotion to honour and law.

Hal at once proves himself a master at the symbolic use of public gestures. This is possibly the most important thing he has learned from his father. The dying king, reconciled after one last epic quarrel with a son whom he has mistrusted right down to this moment, has a few things to say to his son and heir. One is to confess that he, Henry, obtained the crown by 'bypaths and indirect crook'd ways', and that the rebellions he has had to deal with were incurred by that profound irregularity of usurpation (4.5). Perhaps, he hopes, the kingdom can now pass to the young man because that son will have inherited power from his father in a direct line of descent. Legitimacy can be fashioned out of the relationship of father and son.

Even more to the point, King Henry wishes to impress on his son the first principle of successful kingship: 'Be it thy course to busy giddy minds / With foreign quarrels'. That is, make war on some foreign country with the primary intent of uniting Englishmen in the name of a patriotic cause. The English will forget their quarrels among themselves when called upon to defeat the hated French. This advice is cynical; it is what we would call machiavellian. It is also politically pragmatic, and it is precisely what Hal proceeds to do in *Henry V*.

Henry IV has long wished to conduct a crusade to the Holy Land in order to unite the English nation and, simultaneously, to atone personally for the murder of Richard II. Now it will be Henry V's chance to do as his father has advised. With consummate skill he orchestrates a war against the French, garnering the enthusiastic support of his counsellors and the church. He also conceives of the war as a personal quarrel with the French Dauphin, the arrogant son of a weak-spirited French king –

young King Henry's counterpart and opposite number, and a replacement, if you like, for Hotspur.

Hal of course wins the battle of Agincourt, putting to shame the Dauphin. He prays on the night before the encounter that God will choose to forget, for the moment, the crime that Hal's father committed: 'Not today, O Lord, / Oh, not today, think upon the fault / My father made in compassing the crown!' Hal pleadingly insists that he has already re-interred Richard II's body and has endowed two chantries so that priests can sing masses in perpetuity for Richard's soul (4.1). His penance, and the fact that the crime was not his own, appear to be sufficient, for Henry wins gloriously. He has taken his father's advice, but he has also enriched it immeasurably by learning to be approachable and popular among his own people and leaders, so that he creates the illusion of ruling by consent even when the goals he pursues are intensely his own. Hal has come into his inheritance. He is his father's son and then some. He is, in terms of the central thesis of this chapter, a success as an adult male because he has matured the way a person should, coming to terms with his father, learning to understand his father's severe limitations in such a way as to love that father compassionately. The parricidal implications that have hovered over Hal's rebellious youth, and that have consciously erupted in the father's repeated fears that the son has indeed wished the father dead, are now assuaged and seen to be illusory. Hal has incorporated his father's image and has replaced his father through that man's death, and yet has done all this by a process that is seen as psychologically legitimate. In his wake he has left behind those like Hotspur and Falstaff from whom he has learned much but who somehow lacked his sagacity and judgement to mature fully. Whether we like him or not, Hal is the success story of this saga.

As we saw earlier, this same completion of a process of maturation has brought Hal to the point when he can and must marry. Being fully a man, he is now ready to take to him a wife. He does so as his due, his prize, his possession. Yet even here Shakespeare does not forget what he has been learning about mutuality from his writing of romantic comedies. *Henry V* ends as a comedy. Even though Katharine has no choice but to marry King Henry V as his spoils of war and as the most important pawn in a treaty negotiation between two nations, Shakespeare gives her the spirit to declare herself Henry's equal in wit, poise, and graciousness. As played by Emma Thompson to Kenneth Branagh in the Branagh film of 1989, and to no less a degree by Renee Asherson playing Katharine to

Laurence Olivier in his film of 1944, she is adroit at parrying his opportunistic ploys as a wooer and demure in a seeming capitulation once she has exacted from him certain conditions of equality in marriage. Henry's successful arrival at manhood is made to coincide with his success as a wooer.

Other father–son pairings in Shakespeare's later plays revisit the tensions of the maturing process that we see in the Henriad. Hamlet's need to avenge his father's death is also a crusade to be worthy of his father's heritage, unlike Claudius, who balefully illustrates how not to become a king. *Macbeth* is filled with images of sons and fathers, as though in mockery of Macbeth himself and his childless condition; Banquo is murdered, but he is to be succeeded, we know, by his son whom Macbeth attempts in vain to destroy. 'Thou shalt get kings, though thou be none,' the Weird Sisters tell Banquo, and indeed when Macbeth visits the Weird Sisters for a last time he is shown, by an apparition, a line of many kings stretching from Banquo down to the very time of the performance of the play before King James I, who took pride in his descent from Banquo. Gloucester's two sons in *King Lear*, Edgar and Edmund, demonstrate, like Hamlet and Claudius or Prince Hal and Hotspur, the right and wrong way to go about being the son of one's father; and, though in *King Lear* Edmund goes frighteningly far on the proposition that nature itself encourages competition without conscience, the play ultimately redresses the balance by demanding the death of Edmund at the very hands of the brother whose birthright he has attempted to supplant. Arviragus and Guiderius, in *Cymbeline*, are vindicated after long exile as the true sons and heirs of the King, whereas Cloten, their loathsome step-brother and unworthy claimant of the throne, dies in infamy. Prince Florizel in *The Winter's Tale* must endure the wrath of his father for having entered into what appears to be a socially unequal marriage with Perdita, but eventually is restored to his rightful place as crown prince of Bohemia.

As a last and crucial consideration in this chapter on fathers and sons, we need to examine what Shakespeare wrote about the deaths of sons and the impact of such deaths on the fathers. Shakespeare himself suffered such a terrible blow when his only son, Hamnet, born as a twin to Judith in February of 1585, died in August of 1596 at the age of eleven. What must it have been like for Shakespeare to lose his only son and heir, and how did the event manifest itself, if it did so at all, in his stage fictions? We can intuit the immense importance to him of progeny when we read his sonnets on the vital necessity of a man's marrying and fathering children, especially males, who will bear his name, and when we learn that he instituted proceedings in that same year (1596) to acquire from the Herald's College of London the right for him and his father John Shakespeare to bear arms and thus be entitled to the rank of gentleman. What do we learn from the plays he wrote in the months and years after August of 1596?

As Richard Wheeler points out, in a searching article on the subject,[1] the critical problem of connecting art to life is here particularly vexed. The tragic death of sons was not a new topic for Shakespeare in 1596: the death of young John Talbot in the arms of his father in *1 Henry VI* (4.5–7) is the poignant highpoint of that play, and is followed in other early history plays with the ritual slaughters of young Rutland and then of his griefstricken father, Richard, Duke of York, in *3 Henry VI* (1.3–4), the pitiable spectacle of a son that has killed his own father and a father that has killed his own son in the same play (2.5), and the murder of the two princes (Edward and Richard) in the Tower by order of Richard of Gloucester in *Richard III* (4.3). These depictions cannot have been written in response to the death of Hamnet. At the same time, the plays that Shakespeare did write in the years following Hamnet's death in 1596 include Shakespeare's most festive comedies, reaching a triumphant culmination in *As You Like It* and *Twelfth Night*. The problem has thus eluded critics who have looked for simple answers. If one were to suppose that Shakespeare's great tragic period was ushered in by personal misfortune, how are we to account for the delay between Hamnet's death in 1596 and that of the similarly named Hamlet in 1601 or thereabouts?

Yet to observe that Shakespeare wrote with intensity of feeling about the deaths of sons prior to 1596 need hardly suggest that his interest in the topic was dispassionately historical and objective; it could suggest instead his deep sensitivity to this aspect of human suffering, and, in even more personal terms, the abiding anxiety of a father living apart from his family and having only one son as a hostage to fortune. Manifestly, the Shakespeare of the early years thought a lot about the crucial importance of having a male heir. When tragedy did in fact strike, he may not have been with his family, since he spent most of his time in London and may have learned of the illness of Hamnet too late. We cannot be sure of such things. Nor can we know for certain if he wrote *King John* before or after the death of Hamnet. If afterwards, the lament of young Arthur's mother resonates with painful eloquence: 'Grief fills the room up of my absent child, / Lies in his bed, walks up and down with me' (3.4.93–4). Arthur is not yet dead when this lament is spoken, but his days are numbered; and his sad end is finally the result of neglectful caring for him by the fatherly Hubert who has attempted to spare his life but who is not with Arthur when he is most needed. This story of fatherly guilt over the death of a son can be read plausibly as having been written before or after Hamnet's death. The subject was one that had been much on Shakespeare's mind.

At all events, as Wheeler argues, the later history plays about Prince Hal who is to become King Henry V, written in the years 1596 or so to 1599, contain at least one important instance of guilt-ridden anxiety on the part of a father whose absence from the field of battle amounts to his having signed a death warrant for his only son and heir. Old Northumberland, in *1 Henry IV*, fails to show up at the Battle of Shrewsbury where Hotspur meets his end. This absent father is pointedly contrasted with King Henry IV, who has quarreled with his son Prince Hal but is reconciled with him at the battlefield by the son's brave rescue of the father. This son, who thus receives his father's blessing, goes on to triumph over the rebel son, Hotspur, whose father is not there. The desertion is bitterly remembered in *2 Henry IV* by Hotspur's widow, who reminds the father how he 'broke' his 'word' to his son in such a way that Hotspur 'did long in vain' to see his father's approach (2.3.10–14). Wheeler invites us to wonder if, as he wrote these words, Shakespeare considered how he too may have deserved reproach for not being present at the death of his son.

The festive comedies of those same years offer a more difficult problem of interpretation. Even so, *Twelfth Night* makes wonderful sense in Wheeler's interpretation as a play about the recovery of a lost male twin. Viola, the plucky heroine who is shipwrecked on the shores of Illyria and who believes her brother to have drowned, takes on two identities, as Viola and as her own male counterpart: she becomes the embodiment of twins. Because she resembles her supposedly dead brother to such a remarkable degree, she can vicariously enact the roles that will lead to the play's happy marital solution, with a partner for Orsino and another for Olivia. All that the spirit of comedy need do, in the way of dream-work, is to bring back the lost brother, giving him life through his twin sister by declaring the death to have been illusory. Any family that has lost a child (my wife Peggy and I lost our dear son Philip at the age of 14) knows how insistently one's dreams do exactly this, bringing the dead child back to life as if by miracle; the dream mellows as the years pass, but never goes away. (When my dear and only brother, also named Philip, became paraplegic in a car accident in his mid-twenties, I had and still have the same sort of recurring dream enabling him to walk again.) *Twelfth Night* restores, through fictive wish fulfillment, the dead male twin that Shakespeare's family had lost in 1596.

Once *Twelfth Night* can be understood in these terms, earlier romantic comedies of the years 1596 to 1601 reveal a similar pattern. Portia, in *The Merchant of Venice*, is both the desirable and rich heiress of Belmont and the enterprising young lawyer named Balthasar who saves the life of Bassanio's dearest friend, Antonio. Rosalind, in *As You Like It*, prompts those who know her only in her male disguise of Ganymede to imagine her to be some long-lost son of Duke Senior; as Orlando says to the Duke, 'My lord, the first time that I ever saw him [Ganymede], / Methought he was a brother to your daughter'. The Duke himself is reminded, by Ganymede, of 'Some lively touches of my daughter's favour' (5.4.27–9). Rosalind's transformation back into a woman at the end of the play, like that of Viola, restores the broken family by embodying in herself the twin siblings who then materialize as separate persons in the play's wish-fulfillment ending. As if by magic, Rosalind's transformation satisfies the longings of a father for his long-lost daughter, Orlando for a companion in marriage, the shepherd Silvius for a loyal wife, and the shepherdess Phoebe for a man she can genuinely love.

The tragedies help point the ways in which this repeated motif of a recoverable loss can evolve toward a darker vision, one that embodies both the stark horror of death and a sense that the tragic loss of a son must be accepted when it cannot be avoided. 'What's done cannot be undone.' In *Macbeth*, particularly, the tragic protagonist and his queen are doomed to have no progeny, while Banquo learns that he will beget kings though he will be none himself. Macbeth strives frantically to stamp out this rival lineage, but manages only to achieve the death of Banquo, while Fleance escapes. The gruesome evil of Macbeth's crime (killing a king and a father figure) is underscored by his ordering the butchery of Macduff's wife and children; what we are shown onstage, in unrelieved violence, is the death of the son (4.2). Macduff is tortured by the guilt of having deserted his family, even though he believes that he has done so in response to the presumably higher calling of his duty to Scotland. Old Siward, in the concluding military action at Dunsinane, also must come to terms with the death of his son, but he does so without the guilt of having deserted his family responsibilities. Assured by witnesses that his son had 'his hurts before', that is, facing the tyrant Macbeth who has slain him in a last desperate assault on fruitful progeny, old Siward accepts his son's death as a soldier's dues and as Lord Talbot had done at the time of his son's death in *1 Henry VI*. 'Why then, God's soldier be he!" exclaims old Siward. 'Had I as many sons as I have hairs / I would not wish them to a fairer death' (5.8.47–9). The pun on 'hairs' and 'heirs', indistinguishable one from the other in the spoken language of the theatre, underscores by its playfulness the assuredness of old Siward's faith in the goodness of the cause his family's sacrifice has served. There are times when the death of a son is a sad necessity.

In his late plays, when Shakespeare returns from the writing of tragedy to romance, the vision of the lost son continues, but now with varying conclusions of the story: the son is either recovered through the miraculous dream-work of romantic comedy, or is truly lost forever, or is recovered to the father as a son-in-law rather than as a direct male heir. *Pericles*, interestingly, writes the son out of the story entirely in order to tell a narration of father and daughter and absent wife, to which we will return in Chapter 8. In *Cymbeline*, somewhat as in *Twelfth Night*, a resourceful heroine in disguise as a young man manages to find and restore to their father her two brothers, Arviragus and Guiderius, whom the banished Belarius has raised in a mountain cave far from civilization; the king is given a second and undeserved chance to enjoy the happiness of progeny that he had angrily discarded. The son who dies in this play is Cloten, son of the wicked Queen by a former marriage, so that he is not at all related by blood to Cymbeline or to Imogen and her brothers; he is instead the scapegoat or antichrist figure, defining by his boorishness everything that true progeny is not.

In *The Winter's Tale*, conversely, King Leontes of Sicilia must pay the frightful price of his groundless suspicions against his wife by learning of the death of Prince Mamillius. Though the exact age of Mamillius is not disclosed, he is, like Hamnet, still young and tender, a pre-adolescent 'boy' tended by ladies-in-waiting whom he entertains with tales of 'sprites and goblins' (2.1.26). And he is truly, irrecoverably, dead. The father is so burdened with devastating guilt over this death and the seeming demise of the boy's mother that he is still inconsolable sixteen years later and is resolved not to remarry until given authorization to do so by his dour voice of conscience, the lady Paulina. Eventually, Leontes is restored to his wife and to a long-lost daughter, Perdita (again, the subject of Chapter 8 below), but the significant fact here is that Mamillius is gone forever.

In terms of dream-work, the story appears to acknowledge the necessity of coming to terms with irrecoverable loss. *The Winter's Tale* finds its hope and recovery in the daughter. She is no longer able, like Viola, to bring a twin brother back to life; instead, she herself must be the consolation.

In these terms, *The Tempest*, which brings dramatic closure to so many ideas that have fascinated Shakespeare throughout his writing career, offers a new compromise: the son-in-law. Miranda has no brother, though she does have a kind of playmate in Caliban whose sexual advances, when they materialize, are offensive to her, and he is of course no blood descendant of Prospero; that magician figure can do many remarkable things, but he cannot produce a son. Alonso, to be sure, does see his presumably drowned son restored to him, as though the dream fantasy of bringing a dead son back to life still lingers on in the poet's imagination; but Alonso is a guilt-ridden father, like Leontes, and one does not sense the author's identification with him as in the case of Prospero. Prospero's best hope, at all events, is in finding a son-in-law who will love him as a father and be a kind husband to Miranda, and who will also enable Prospero to reunite the kingdoms of Naples and Sicily that fell apart many years ago when Prospero was banished from his dukedom. Now he and his daughter and his son-in-law will return to a reunited Italy, and their children will be his progeny. The descent will not be through the male line, but it will continue the heritage as best it may. Shakespeare perhaps took similar comfort in the marriage of his elder daughter Susanna in 1607 to John Hall, a successful physician in Stratford-upon-Avon; he bought for them one of the finest houses in town, now known as Hall's Croft, and he may have felt that he had found a son-in-law to his liking. (Judith's later marriage to Thomas Quiney, in 1616, shortly before Shakespeare died, may not have been as pleasing to the father; he had quarreled with Quiney, though he did make provision for this marriage in his will.) Shakespeare could not know, of course, that his line of descent through his daughters would dwindle and disappear, so that no descendants of his are alive today. Still, he may well have hoped that he would succeed brilliantly in his other bid for immortality: the writing of his plays and poems.

CHAPTER FIVE

◆

Jealous in Honour

Love and Friendship in Crisis

Most friendship is feigning, most loving mere folly.
As You Like It, *2.7*

This chapter focuses on a striking development in Shakespeare's dramaturgy around the year 1600, roughly halfway through his writing career. It was about this time that he wrote *Hamlet* and *Troilus and Cressida*. These and other of the so-called 'problem' plays written soon afterwards – *All's Well That Ends Well, Measure for Measure* – turn in a number of new directions. They explore new dimensions of genre: comedy is no longer as comic and delightful as before. The endings of these plays are notoriously problematic; *All's Well* and *Measure for Measure* end with marriages, as is the custom in romantic comedy, but the marriages themselves are doubtful and perplexed. The heroines are no longer heroines in the vein of Rosalind and Viola, offering patient sustenance to their unselfknowing young men; they are more apt to be cunningly resourceful and willing to avail themselves of ethically dubious means of achieving their ends.

Most troubling of all is the spectre of womanly infidelity. Cressida leaves Troilus for another lover. The Dark Lady of the Sonnets, perhaps a creation of this same period in Shakespeare's career, cheats on the poet with the poet's best friend. And in *Hamlet*, Queen Gertrude is in her son's eyes the very emblem of womanly inconstancy: 'Frailty, thy name is woman!' *Hamlet* is a tragedy, a genre opening up possibilities for exploring the darker side of human existence, including sexual infidelity. It seems significant that Shakespeare begins writing tragedies in earnest during these years around 1600.

As we have seen, Shakespeare devoted himself primarily, in the 1590s, to the writing of English historical plays in which he could explore themes of male maturation, and, at the same time, to the writing of romantic comedies interested in courtship. He wrote few tragedies as such. *Titus Andronicus* was indeed a tragedy, an early experiment (*c.* 1589–92) in the genre of the revenge tragedy, but Shakespeare seems not to have wanted to follow up on this. *Romeo and Juliet,* around 1594–6, is in many ways closer in spirit to his romantic comedies than to the genre of tragedy; Juliet is much like Rosalind and Viola as a heroine, and the first part of the play is often as delightfully funny as anything Shakespeare wrote. The play's chief characters are more typical of comedy than of classical tragedy: they come from bourgeois families rather than the aristocracy, and they are quite ordinary except for the memorable passion of their unhappy story. Comedy traditionally chooses protagonists who are like us, and whom we can look at on our own level rather than looking up to.

Some of Shakespeare's English history plays during the 1590s have tragic elements in them, and are even called tragedies on their quarto title pages, such as *The Tragedy of King Richard the Third* and *The Tragedy of Richard the Second.* Yet generically these plays are chronicle plays rather than tragedies. *Richard III* ends with the accession to power of Henry VII, founder of the Tudor dynasty and grandfather of Queen Elizabeth, under whose rule Shakespeare lived much of his life. *Richard II* similarly ends with the death of Richard but also the coming to the throne of Henry IV. History is open-ended in these plays, as suggested in the inclusive title of another of them, *The Life and Death of King John.* Some of Shakespeare's histories were actually classified as comedies by his contemporaries, especially the *Henry IV* plays and *Henry V.*[1]

Shakespeare did not engage deeply with tragedy as a genre in the 1590s, then. Perhaps the extant models for tragedy were not as clear or as inspiring to him as for comedy and history. Or perhaps he was waiting for the right time to focus on tragedy, when he was a bit older and more experienced, and when the social and personal problems he wanted next to dramatize were more intractable and challenging.

With women like Cressida, Gertrude, and the Dark Lady of the Sonnets, the jinnee is out of the bottle. The dark fantasies that men have tortured themselves with about women, the usually groundless fears of cuckoldry, now turn out to have a basis in reality. Tragedy at this point becomes appropriate and necessary.

Plate 3 The 'Armada' portrait of Elizabeth I, by George Gower, 1588. Reproduced by kind permission of His Grace the Duke of Bedford and the Trustees of the Bedford Estates.

Much Ado about Nothing (1598–9) aptly illustrates where Shakespeare was coming from. Paired with its delightful comic plot of Benedick and Beatrice, in which the lovers eventually find their way through the hazards of their own emotional defences to something approaching true mutuality, this play delves into a darker plot of slander and the appearance of death. Claudio and Hero, the protagonists of this second plot, are the counterparts of Benedick and Beatrice, but are strikingly unlike those two. Claudio is Benedick's best friend and Hero is Beatrice's cousin, but at this point the resemblances end. Claudio and Hero are as conventional as the other two are unconventional. And it is their conventionality that makes Claudio and Hero so vulnerable to the insinuations of the play's villain, Don John.

Claudio and Hero have met briefly before Claudio went off to war, but they scarcely know each other. On his return, having earned his spurs and thereby achieved manhood in his own estimation, Claudio now finds himself ready to woo and wed. He knows that he was attracted before to Hero, and finds himself even more attracted now, though they do not exchange a word so far as we know. Claudio is in love with the idea of marrying Hero. Like a dutiful young man, he goes to his commanding officer, Don Pedro, and asks that gentleman to assist him. Don Pedro does so, by speaking to Hero's father Leonato about the match and then wooing the lady on Claudio's behalf at the masked ball planned for that evening. Claudio is the socially correct young wooer. The questions he asks of Don Pedro about Hero deal with her financial expectations: 'Hath Leonato any son, my lord?' Don Pedro amusedly understands at once the purport of the question: 'No child but Hero; she's his only heir'.

Matters thus arranged by the elders, the marriage might be expected to go forward without a hitch, were it not that Don John sees occasion to breed mischief. At the masked ball, he speaks in confidence to the disguised Claudio as though addressing Benedick, warning him that Don Pedro seems romantically interested in the young lady for himself. This is not true, of course, but the ruse works. Claudio at once assumes the worst. Here he speaks in soliloquy when Don John has left him:

> 'Tis certain so. The Prince woos for himself.
> Friendship is constant in all other things
> Save in the office and affairs of love;
> Therefore all hearts in love use their own tongues.
> Let every eye negotiate for itself
> And trust no agent; for beauty is a witch
> Against whose charms faith melteth into blood.
> This is an accident of hourly proof,
> Which I mistrusted not. Farewell therefore Hero!
> (2.1.168–76)

Claudio's disappointment is understandable, but the cynicism is surprising. So is his instant resolution to have no more to do with Hero. Why is he so suddenly persuaded that Hero has been false to him, solely on the testimonial of a man known for his deviousness? To be sure, Don John has used the clever stratagem of telling this 'news' as though speaking to Benedick, but even so the collapse of Claudio's faith in Hero is dismaying. He is a young man all too ready to believe the worst of women. His bitter generalizations embrace the whole sex, indeed both sexes: beauty is witchcraft and so friendship is not to be trusted in affairs of the heart. These clichés lead him into a certitude that he has been betrayed by the woman he loves and by his friend and mentor, like the poet in the Sonnets.

Only a little practical reassurance is needed to persuade Claudio that he was mistaken; Hero is brought to him as his intended bride, having never wavered in her affections. The marriage is back on track. Yet Claudio has not learned his lesson. When Don John plays on him essentially the same trick a second time, by insinuating to him (and Don Pedro) that Hero has been false on the night before her intended wedding, Claudio is again convinced that he has been betrayed.

We must grant that Don John does his work cleverly. He arranges an apparent tryst at Hero's window involving Hero's lady-in-waiting, Margaret, and a henchman of Don John's, Borachio, with whom Margaret is besottedly in love. Led by her heart rather than her good sense, Margaret agrees to appear at Hero's window in the guise of Hero and receive the attentions below of Borachio masquerading as Claudio. Don Pedro and Claudio, watching from 'afar off in the orchard', are persuaded of the infidelity. Hero is publicly exposed at the wedding ceremony and sent off in disgrace. Later she is reported to be dead.

Claudio's culpability in losing faith in Hero, who is of course innocent, is extenuated by the fact that the estimable Don Pedro also believes the cleverly constructed lie, and that Hero's father too collapses in grief at the wedding because he is sure the accusation must be true. Claudio is not alone. This is only to say, however, that the men collectively bear a heavy burden of responsibility for what happens to Hero. They are all too apt to believe the testimony of a man, any man, even the acknowledged villain Don John, rather than listen to a woman. Hero is not even asked by Claudio and Don Pedro if the accusation is true. When she is belatedly asked the question, by the friar who has come to marry her to Claudio, she professes complete innocence. Her father rallies at last to her support. Benedick, deeply perplexed by what he has heard, has the good sense to listen to Hero, and to Beatrice, who never loses faith in her cousin and is furious about the slander. She even asks Benedick to avenge the wrong by killing Claudio. The matter need not come to that dire pass, because the contretemps is cleared up by the inept watch that has stumbled on the truth by arresting Borachio.

Much Ado is a romantic comedy in its genre, and thus resolves the difficulty by comic means. Yet the picture it presents of men in love is troublesome. Men such as Claudio are woefully dependent on the opinions of other men and too prone to believe the worst of women. This proneness arises out of the men's own vulnerability. They are overly dependent on women for their happiness and sense of male achievement. The threat of cuckoldry is intolerable; it represents a loss of face among one's male companions. Men such as Claudio need women to bolster their own egos as males, but by the same token they fear women for their imagined inclination to be faithless. This is essentially why Claudio is putty in the hands of Don John. The comic world of *Much Ado* can reclaim Claudio by showing him that his fears were unfounded, and by forgiving his loss of faith through the extraordinary generosity of the young woman he has wronged. Given a less happy turn, however, this story could quickly become the tragedy of Othello and Desdemona. And indeed in Edmund Spenser's telling of the story of the maiden falsely accused (*The Faerie Queene*, 2.4, based on Ariosto's *Orlando Furioso*), the outcome is unrelievedly tragic. Shakespeare is on the verge of his serious encounter with tragedy.

Troilus and Cressida is not a tragedy in the normal sense, though it does end with the death of Hector at the hands of Achilles and with the dissolution of the love affair between Troilus and Cressida. It chronicles events of the Trojan war, and yet it is not a regular history play like Shakespeare's English histories. It is not like his earlier comedies, either, though in ways it reads like a bitterly satirical black comedy. *Troilus and Cressida* is a hybrid, quite unlike anything Shakespeare had attempted before. The editors of Shakespeare's plays after his death, dividing the great folio edition of 1623 into comedies, histories, and tragedies, did not know how to categorize this play. They evidently obtained permission to include it only late in the printing process, for it was printed with atypical page signatures and almost entirely without page numbers. The editors finally inserted it between the histories and the tragedies. It is an authentically unique creation.

Part of what makes it so is the unconventionality of the love story. Troilus and Cressida were famous and legendary lovers. They are not part of Homer's *Iliad*, though Troilus does appear there in battle as one of

Priam's many sons. A kind of analogue to Cressida can be found in the captured Trojan woman named Chryseis, daughter of Chryses, a priest of Apollo, whom the seer Calchas urges the Greeks to return to her father as a means of ending the plague sent by Apollo; when the Greeks do so, obliging Agamemnon to give her up, that general takes instead the captive slave-girl Briseis from Achilles, thereby setting in motion the great quarrel with which the *Iliad* begins. The love story of Troilus and Cressida, based on such slender hints, is a post-Homeric tradition that grew in importance and complexity in successive versions of the saga of Troy.

The account of Cressida's abandoning Troilus when she is sent back from Troy to her Greek father Calchas, where she takes up with the Grecian Diomedes, proved to be immensely distressing to readers of Shakespeare. The play was rewritten by John Dryden in 1679 to make her innocently misunderstood; only in this sanitized version could it appear on the Restoration stage. Otherwise the play disappeared from the theatre until the twentieth century, since when it has belatedly become a great favourite because of its bitter view of love and war. Even before Shakespeare wrote his play, Cressida's name had become a byword for womanly inconstancy. In some versions she was punished by becoming a leper.[2] Chaucer, to be sure, had presented her with remarkable sympathy and insight in his *Troilus and Criseyde*, but generally she was seen as a fallen woman. Shakespeare took on the story knowing of her deeply tarnished reputation. Infidelity is evidently something he wanted to look at closely.

Cressida is indeed a woman unlike the romantic heroines of the earlier comedies. When we first encounter her (1.2), she is being mercilessly witty at the expense of Troilus and of her uncle, Pandarus, who is trying to promote the match. She is wary, caustic, fully aware of what Pandarus and Troilus want from her, determined to control her own destiny. She is interested in Troilus, but sees every reason not to capitulate too soon. 'Yet hold I off', she confides in soliloquy. 'Women are angels, wooing; / Things won are done, joy's soul lies in the doing.' Once Troilus achieves her, she knows, she will be less attractive to him, and her own freedom will be diminished. She is not heartlessly playing with him, however; she has genuine reasons for being cautious. She considers giving up her autonomy, but only if dependence on Troilus can be counted on to bring her stability and happiness. The Trojans and the Greeks are at war, and she is living at present in Troy, separated by the war from her father. Uncertainties surround her. Ought she to surrender to Troilus?

For his part, Troilus is importunate, lovesick, utterly reliant on Pandarus to help him with the affair. When at last the moment of her surrender is at hand, Troilus is giddy with expectation, fearful only that his physical ability to make love to her cannot match the infinite reach of his will and appetite. She is fearful for other reasons: if men have 'the voice of lions and the act of hares', can Troilus's vows be trusted? He sees himself as the very embodiment of loyal, manly devotion, whose name will be remembered for all time in the phrase 'As true as Troilus'. She is more sceptically attuned to the possibility that her name will be registered in fame by the phrase 'As false as Cressid', not because she plans to be false to him but because she is more of a realist. Pandarus is content with the prospect that, if the lovers ever prove false one to another, his name will be forever equated with the go-between, the pander. Because we know that these predictions will come to pass, we are weighted down by the melancholy of the occasion; historical determinacy insists that the story will take its inevitable course. Shakespeare seems as fascinated with this idea of history and reputation as he is with the subject of womanly infidelity.

What happens in the immediate wake of the consummation of this love affair is thus what history demands: Cressida learns the next day that she is to be returned to her father in exchange for a valuable prisoner the Trojans want back, Antenor. The responses of Troilus and Cressida to this devastating news are tellingly unlike. Troilus, receiving the news from his brother Aeneas, accepts the inevitability of it. 'Is it so concluded?' he asks, and then, simply, 'How my achievements mock me!' He consents to the arrangement. After all, his brothers are all agreed on the military necessity of the exchange; Antenor is a linchpin in their endeavours, whereas Cressida is only a very pretty girl. Troilus is having an affair with her, but – too bad. Troilus himself accedes to the logic of this. He puts the war and the male-dominated concerns of his family and country ahead of his love for Cressida.

She cannot understand this. She has trouble even grasping what Troilus is saying to her when he explains how she will have to go back to the Greek side. How can he possibly mean this? She has surrendered to him, after months of delay in which she wanted to make sure he loved her sufficiently to warrant the risk. What she feared all along now turns out to be true. In her set of priorities, her leaving Troilus is absolutely unthinkable, but now she sees that to him the matter is quite otherwise. Is this because he has enjoyed her sexually and now is not driven by quite the same itch of desire? Was she right to argue with herself that surrender would bring with it loss of control over the man's insistence on having his way?

Such questionings require that we ask of ourselves who deserts whom. Troilus sends her back to the Greeks. He intends to keep seeing her, to be sure, by secret visitings of the Greek camp at night, but how often will he be able to do that, and how long will he really want to? She feels deserted, as well she might. The sad way in which her deepest fears of loss of control have been realized goes a long way toward explaining why she takes up with Diomedes in the Greek camp. He is an abrupt, arrogant man, utterly cynical about both men and women, but he wants her and she needs the protection of a male. The sex-starved Greek officers start ogling her the moment she arrives, and they are accustomed to taking captive women as their mistresses; can she hope to escape that fate? Her father leaves her to her own devices. Who has deserted whom?

Cressida is not proud of her disloyalty to Troilus. She firmly believes that women are weak. 'Ah, poor our sex!' she laments to herself. 'This fault in us I find: / The error of our eye directs our mind.' Men are weak, too, in their way, but in Cressida's own eyes that does not excuse her infidelity. The ending of her story is anticlimactic. The play comes to its close with the war going on and Troilus manically determined to fight to the death; Cressida is no longer heard from. She is the faithless woman of legendary history. Yet Shakespeare presents her as admirable in many ways, victimized by war and male importunity, a survivor like Brecht's Mother Courage. Infidelity turns out to be a morally complex issue, as complex as other aspects of human behaviour.

Measure for Measure (1603–4) is experimental in a different way. Though nominally a comedy ending in marriage, it earns its sobriquet of 'problem play' (a term invented in the late nineteenth century) by plunging us into a *demi-monde* of vice and squalor that tests the moral fortitude of its most upright citizens. Vienna, at the start of this play, is rife with sexual corruption. Houses of prostitution openly solicit customers; men boast of their conquests. The list of characters includes Mistress Overdone, a bawd; Pompey, her pimp; Froth, a gentleman customer; Lucio, a rake; and various prisoners. A significant portion of the action takes place inside the prison. Vienna has strict statutes against fornication and adultery, but those statutes have been allowed to atrophy 'like an o'ergrown lion in a cave / That goes not out to prey'. A strange place in which to set a comedy, one might say.

The characters who inhabit this strange world are also oddly fitted to comedy. The Duke of Vienna, Vincentio, resolves to address Vienna's social problems by absconding. Leaving his deputy, Angelo, in charge, the Duke adopts the disguise of a friar and simply disappears from public view. His reasons are difficult to piece out. He knows that he has been too lenient toward sexual licentiousness; he agrees that harsh laws are needed to stamp it out or at least control it, but has been unwilling to enforce those laws. Aware that threats from him would now be ignored because he has been overly permissive, he turns the matter over to a deputy with a reputation for severity.

Yet is Angelo the person to whom this responsibility should be assigned? We learn later that the Duke is aware of Angelo's having reneged on a promise of marriage to a certain Mariana when her dowry settlement vanished owing to the sudden death of her brother. The disguised Duke wishes to test Angelo to determine, as he says, 'If power change purpose, what our seemers be'. Is Lord Angelo a champion of strict and impartial justice or is he a 'seemer'? The goal of determining this state of things is laudable, perhaps, but the secretive means of doing so by the use of disguise smacks of snooping, and is certain to cause trouble in Vienna if Angelo turns out to be dangerous. The Duke's personal plan for investigating the soundness of Angelo's professed severity would seem to be at odds with the public good. The Duke is something of an enigma.

Angelo takes on his new responsibility with alacrity; indeed, one can imagine that he has been itching for the chance to do what the Duke has failed so abysmally to do. Angelo need pass no new laws. The statutes against sexual indiscretions are draconian: they demand the death of first-time offenders. No 'three strikes and you're out' in Vienna; one fornication can cost you your head. Angelo sees no reason not to enforce the letter of the law.

With an irony that seems almost inevitable, given the stringency of this legislation, Angelo's first culprit is a person as technically innocent as one could hope to find anywhere: a young gentleman who has impregnated the lady he loves and hopes to marry. Claudio and Juliet would have been married by this time, were it not for a hold-up in a dowry settlement. 'She is fast my wife', explains Claudio to his friend Lucio as he is being led off to prison, 'Save that we do the denunciation lack / Of outward order.' They are in fact married according to custom and law in Elizabethan England. Although they have not been to church, they evidently have exchanged vows in the presence of a witness or witnesses, and that is enough to bind them for life. Shakespeare may himself have been involved in just such a premarital contract when he impregnated Anne Hathaway; certainly his marriage to her already three months pregnant gave him reason to be sympathetic with the case of Claudio and Juliet.

Interestingly, Juliet takes primary responsibility for the pregnancy, and the heavier sense of sin; as the desired object in the love match, she had the responsibility to deny sex to her lover until marriage. Yet her life is to be spared, since she is a woman and since she bears another life within her womb. Claudio is to be executed.

Angelo is not hesitant to defend his course of action, even if Claudio is a decent young man with well-connected friends who plead for clemency. Angelo's legal argument is for deterrence. Chop off enough heads of fornicators and you will see how quickly fornication will diminish as a social problem. Too bad it had to be Claudio, but his death can set a sobering example as well as that of the next fornicator. Angelo's theory of deterrence is set in debate with other milder approaches, notably that of equity (adjusting the law to individual circumstances) advocated by Lord Escalus, but Angelo's ideas are never refuted as such. The approach is absolutist and inflexible, but might work in its way if given a chance. The law he seeks to enforce is in fact the law of the land, not of his own devising. The trouble is not with the law but with Angelo himself. He turns out to be a hypocrite. And no one is as surprised at this as Angelo.

The shock forcefully presents itself to him when he is asked to hear the petition of one Isabella, a novice about to become a nun, on behalf of her condemned brother Claudio. Isabella dislikes having to ask the deputy to pardon Claudio for what she, as a would-be nun, regards as a primary human weakness: unlawful carnal desire. Their first interview is fraught with ironies. Part of Isabella is prepared to argue against her own petition, and yet she loves her brother. Angelo, finding himself face to face with a lovely young woman of such animation and intellectual acumen, begins to realize to his dismay that he is seized with desire for Isabella – with a would-be nun who is begging him to save the life of a condemned man! Part of what appalls him is his realization that both he and Isabella are involving themselves in a kind of bribery: she is asked to bribe him with the gift of her body, while he will bribe her to have sex by agreeing to spare Claudio. Angelo has never bribed anyone, or accepted a bribe; he prides himself on his absolute integrity. What is more, he has not been inclined toward sexual indulgence in his private life. The scandal-mongering Lucio reports that ice water is said to run in Angelo's veins and that even his urine is congealed ice.

The discovery is devastating. Angelo's speeches in soliloquy read like tragic utterances. He is tortured by his loss of self control, by the sheer nastiness of what his lusting body is proposing for him. Why has he lost control? The seeming answer is that he realizes that for the first time no one is watching over him. With the Duke having disappeared from the scene (though we know that the Duke is in fact watching), Angelo thinks he is free to do whatever he wants. No one can stop him. The terrifying consequence of this realization is that he now knows what his body really wants, if unchecked by law and social control: it wants to 'raze the sanc-tuary'. Isabella's very sanctity is part of what appeals so perversely to his rampant sexuality:

> Never could the strumpet,
> With all her double vigour – art and nature –
> Once stir my temper; but this virtuous maid
> Subdues me quite. Ever till now,
> When men were fond, I smiled and wondered how.
> (2.2.190–4)

Angelo knows for the first time that, being a man, he is a sexual monster. The marauding lecher that he has wished to restrain and punish with the full rigour of the law turns out to be himself.

Isabella, faced with her own nightmare in this confrontation, also has things to learn about herself. In an odd way, she and Angelo are alike. They have both responded repressively to the dismal pageant of sexual licentiousness in Vienna. He has sought the authority of the law to stamp it out; she has turned to the life of the novitiate as a way of distancing herself from men and from all forms of sexuality. She embraces strictness. When asked by a sister of the order she is joining if the scant privileges afforded them in their sequestered life will be enough for her (for example, they may speak with men only in the presence of the prioress, and may not both speak and show their faces at the same time), Isabella eagerly agrees to the lack of freedom: 'I speak not as desiring more, / But rather wishing a more strict restraint / Upon the sisterhood, the votarists of Saint Clare'. We should not question the sincerity of her sense of calling, but we certainly note that absolute escape from sexual com-mitment is a part of what appeals to her.

For such a woman, to be bribed into laying down her body in exchange for her brother's life is an appalling prospect. In her unhappy uncertainty, she turns for solace and advice to the one male she hopes she can trust: her brother Claudio. She must ask his help in refusing this unconscionable offer by agreeing to die in order that she might preserve her virginal integrity. Their confrontation on this issue (3.1) is searing to them both. Her fear is that Claudio will not hold true. When at first he agrees to die bravely for her, her gratitude takes the form of thanking him for playing the role that their dead father can no longer play, of intervening on her behalf. 'There spake my brother!' she exclaims. 'There my father's grave / Did utter forth a voice.' A young woman needs protection, needs a father, and her brother must now be that father.[3] She honestly insists that she would lay down her life for Claudio; what she is asking is that he help her preserve that which is far more precious in her scale of values, her virginity. Claudio starts to weaken on this very point. Is he to die for her virginity? Is lechery not the least and last of the Seven Deadly Sins? Would not her transgression be exculpated by her charitable motive in saving his life?

Claudio no doubt has a point, but his motives are craven. We see him break at this point, if only for a brief time. He likes to think of himself as brave, as ready to encounter the darkness of death 'as a bride / And hug it in mine arms'. He relishes the role of the strong male defending the innocent female. Yet he now hears himself pleading with his sister for life. His fear of death is real, after all. Who would wish 'to die, and go we know not where, / To lie in cold obstruction and to rot'?

The fact that Claudio has just received a sermon on renunciation of life's vanities by the disguised Duke, and has embraced the Duke's argument as a reason to welcome death and thereby enter into a better eternal life, underscores the momentary moral confusion of a young man staring death in the eye. So long as death appears inevitable, he can face it; now that he is offered a chance to live, however shamefully, he discovers that he has not the willpower to say no. This is a sad moment; fortunately it is brief. The Duke, intervening in his disguise, assures Claudio that the death warrant is already signed and that Angelo was only testing Isabella with no intent of sparing Claudio. The Duke knows this to be untrue, but says it in order to persuade Claudio to give up his hope of living through Isabella's shame, and the young man bows once more to the inevitable. Doubtless ashamed of his failure of spirit, he is eventually restored to his sister and is forgiven by her. Claudio is a good young man;

he simply did not know his own capacity for moral weakness under duress. In that he is strangely like Angelo. The discovery of that weakness is ultimately healthful for them both.

Isabella too fails in this searing encounter with her condemned brother. She has the strength of will to ask that he do the brave thing on her behalf. What she may not be prepared for is to discover the hatred she is capable of when he proves to be like other men instead of her imagined father. 'Take my defiance!' she screams at him. 'Die, perish! Might but my bending down / Reprieve thee from thy fate, it should proceed. / I'll pray a thousand prayers for thy death, / No word to save thee.' She has every reason to be angry and disappointed, of course, but this momentary desire that Claudio actually die is a terrible failure of charity, and charity is among the chiefest of the holy virtues to which she has been intending to devote her life. Her refusal to imagine any way in which she would save his life amounts to her own sentencing of her brother to die.

From such a failure the road to recovery will not be easy. Nevertheless, in the play's finale (5.1) Isabella rises to the challenge. The Duke, having resumed his full ducal identity in order to bring all parties to justice, makes it as difficult as possible for Isabella to forgive Angelo. Still the master of playful manipulations, the Duke allows Isabella to think that Claudio has been executed; indeed, everyone thinks so too except the Duke, the Provost who saved Claudio's life by providing a substitute dead man's head, and us as audience. Can Isabella forgive Angelo, who is now on public trial, for Claudio's death? The Duke rubs it in: he is merely offering her 'measure for measure', 'An Angelo for Claudio, death for death'. He even insists that he will carry out the execution of Angelo whether she agrees or not.

What persuades Isabella to kneel for Angelo's pardon, and thus act out in physical gesture the very kneeling that she insisted earlier she would not do to save Claudio's life, is partly her own recovered instincts for charity, and, as she explains, her realization that Angelo did not actually manage to carry out his sexual intent because of the substitution of Mariana for Isabella in his bed. No less importantly, though, she asks pardon for Angelo because Mariana has turned to her and begged her to kneel. Mariana loves Angelo, however badly he has behaved. She is prepared to forgive him and claim him as her husband. Arguably, Angelo has been deeply chastened by his own failure and is perhaps grateful in a way to have been caught and thereby released from the terrifying prospect of being able to go on with his budding career as seducer, rapist, and murderer. Who is to stop him? Now that the Duke has returned, there is, thank goodness, an answer. Rescued from his own deeply perverse criminality, Angelo can try to be a husband to Mariana.[4] Isabella saves the life of Angelo in the hope that something can still be found to redeem that beleaguered institution, marriage.

Isabella too marries at the end of the play, or at least she is presumed to do so in traditional interpretations. The script gives her no lines, and in recent decades actresses and directors have opted to allow her to refuse the Duke's offer of marriage, or think it over.[5] The feminist issue of a woman's choice nicely underscores the problematic nature of marriage in the play. One position in the ongoing debate is that marriage is, despite undeniable difficulties, a necessary conclusion in this play, for Isabella as much as for Mariana. Isabella has had to learn much about her own human frailty, as well as about that of men. Perhaps marriage is meant to signify the best available compromise – the only game in town, if you like. Isabella, viewed in this light, no longer sees the necessity of withdrawing from the world as a nun. Marriage is the alternative that can accept the fact of our human fallen condition and say, in effect, let us make the best of it. The romantic idealism of Shakespeare's early comedies fades into a nostalgic dream. *Measure for Measure* tries to be more realistic about men and women in love.

All's Well That Ends Well is similarly wry and perplexing. It features as its protagonist a young man who shies away from marriage, especially when it is foisted upon him by royal edict and when his bride-to-be is of considerably lower social station than himself; he is now Count of Rossillion after the recent death of his father, whereas she is the daughter of his family's physician who has saved the life of the French king and thereby won Bertram as her reward. We can understand his reluctance to marry Helena under these forced conditions, but we are distinctly less sympathetic when he chases after another non-patrician young woman, Diana, with a view to seducing her. Bertram wants sexual pleasure without the constraints of marriage. His warm friendship with Parolles makes plain that, for companionship, he prefers men of his own age and military inclination. The indications are that Bertram has yet to grow up.

Helena eventually brings home her wayward husband by a trick couched as a riddle. When he has abandoned her bed for the wars, Bertram offers her conditions of a sort about his return, but in such a way as to make the fulfillment of the conditions seem impossible. 'When thou canst get the ring upon my finger, which never shall come off', he writes, 'and show me a child begotten of thy body that I am father to, then call me husband; but in such a "then" I write a "never." ' How can she manage to do these things?

Helena is an attractive young woman who is also something of a worry, at least to many men. She is plucky, resourceful, even jaunty in her determination to find and recover Bertram. She leaves the family home to do so, travelling as an unprotected woman, and finds allies in Florence. At the same time, she admits to herself that she has been pushy about trapping Bertram into marrying her. She is aware too of ethical dubieties in what she finally decides to do. Bertram is courting Diana, the daughter of the Widow of Florence with whom Helena happens to be staying. What if Helena herself were to take Diana's place in Bertram's bed for the desired assignation? This is much the same trick, in fact, that Isabella consented to in *Measure for Measure*, though she did not think up the stratagem; Angelo's once-intended fiancée, Mariana, secretly replaces Isabella in the assignation that Angelo has so fervently sought. Meantime, in *All's Well*, Diana has managed to obtain Bertram's ring in return for her promise to sleep with him.

Since the seemingly impossible conditions that Bertram specified in his riddle have now been fulfilled, he accepts his destiny of being a husband to Helena and the father of their child. We have another strange marriage. Whether Bertram is truly contrite we cannot be sure, for he says little, but we can hope that he has learned something about himself. Men are carnal beings; so too, in their way, are women. Carnal desire often has its consequences in the birth of a child. If men are to be fully mature, they must accept the consequences of their own physical importunities. They must also be wary of friendships of the sort that encourage emotional immaturity. Parolles turns out to be a blowhard and coward who tries to get credit for an intrepid military action (recovering a drum from the enemy) that he has no intention of actually doing. His scenes are the funniest in the play, and we have to admit there is something endearing about this braggart soldier, this 'bubble', but he is not the kind of friend Bertram needs. Bertram's truly worthy colleagues in the army deplore his friendship with Parolles and are determined to expose Parolles for what he is. They also grieve at Bertram's skirt-chasing as a stain on his family's honourable scutcheon. In both of these matters, Bertram seems to learn his lesson. He certainly sees the necessity of his giving up Parolles.

'The web of our life is of a mingled yarn, good and ill together', comments one of Bertram's fellow officers. 'Our virtues would be proud if our faults whipped them not, and our crimes would despair if they were not cherished by our virtues' (4.3.70–3). This sentiment captures much of the bittersweet tone of *All's Well* as a perplexing study in the human instinct for love and sex that manages to remain a comedy despite, or perhaps because of, its moral ambiguities. The idea finds a saving grace even in our weaknesses, since they remind us of our frailty and our need for forgiveness. The idea has a spiritual dimension as well: we would despair of our corrupted natures if we did not also possess some glimmer of virtue prompting us to strive to find a better self. Such urging that we find a virtuous accommodation with our fallen natures, rather than surrendering helplessly to the promptings of carnal desire, is in keeping also with the closing cadences of *Measure for Measure*.

In the tragic world of *Hamlet*, sexuality is presented in very dark colours. Claudius has killed his brother, Hamlet senior, for the Danish crown and for Gertrude, Claudius's own sister-in-law. Young Hamlet is contemptuous of his uncle's seizure of power and resentful of having been excluded from the throne himself, but we never sense that Hamlet is really itching to be king. What burdens his imagination is the thought of his uncle and his mother as sexual partners. 'Nay, but to live / In the rank sweat of an enseamèd bed, / Stewed in corruption, honeying and making love / Over the nasty sty!' he arraigns his mother in his earnest undertaking to force her to consider what she is doing (3.4). Under no circumstances, he insists, is she to 'Let the bloat king tempt you again to bed, / Pinch wanton on your cheek, call you his mouse'. She must not let him wheedle compliance out of her 'for a pair of reechy kisses', or 'paddling in your neck with his damned fingers'. Hamlet is obsessed with graphic imaginings of their sexual coupling.

Toward his uncle he feels fury and contempt; toward his mother he feels regret and deep disappointment. Boys and young men generally find it uncomfortable to think of their parents engaging in sexual intercourse. How much more intolerable, then, to dwell on the prospect of one's mother having sex with some other man – worst of all, with one's father's brother! Hamlet cannot stop thinking of his mother as coupling with a monster. Her disloyalty to his father oppresses him. Hamlet senior was, as Hamlet remembers and no doubt idealizes him, 'Hyperion', a sun-god, in contrast to Claudius, 'a satyr' – that lecherous creature of classical mythology depicted as half-human adorned with the legs, tail, ears, and horns of a goat. How could she desert the one for the other? Her affection to Hamlet senior seemed so strong:

> Why, she would hang on him
> As if increase of appetite had grown
> By what it fed on, and yet within a month –
> Let me not think on't; frailty, thy name is woman! –
> A little month, or ere those shoes were old
> With which she followed my poor father's body,
> Like Niobe, all tears, why she, even she –
> Oh, God, a beast, that wants discourse of reason,
> Would have mourned longer – married with my uncle,
> My father's brother, but no more like my father
> Than I to Hercules.
>
> (1.2.143–53)

Hamlet's first problem is how to understand this 'wicked speed', this posting 'With such dexterity to incestuous sheets'. Is there something he should do about it? He must seek revenge on Claudius for his father's death; can he also recover his mother from her loathsome carnality?

The play called 'The Murder of Gonzago' that he commissions the travelling players to perform in the presence of Claudius, Gertrude, and the court is intended to 'catch the conscience of the King', putting Claudius's innocence or guilt to the test by showing him an image of his purported crime. The device works; Hamlet, together with his dear friend Horatio, is persuaded that Claudius is guilty as charged. Yet 'The Murder of Gonzago' seems oddly directed also toward Gertrude. Why does the Player Queen go on at such lengths in her insistence to her husband that she will never remarry? 'In second husband let me be accurst! / None wed the second but who killed the first.' Why does the play-within-the-play characterize her husband as so loving and at the same time so wise, willing to accept the earnestness of her protestations that she will never remarry while seeing also that human beings soon forget their resolutions of this sort? Why is the King portrayed as not only wise but forgiving, in his striving to let his queen understand that she probably will remarry after his death and that it is all right if she does?

One interesting speculation is that Hamlet wrote these lines himself. He did, after all, ask the lead player if his company could 'study a speech of some dozen or sixteen lines which I would set down and insert in't', and the lead player readily agreed. The dialogue of King and Queen in 'The Murder of Gonzago' reads like an attempt on Hamlet's part to reconstruct imaginatively what his own father and mother might have talked about before Hamlet senior's death.

This part of the play-within-the-play is certainly also designed to 'catch the conscience of the Queen', to rephrase Hamlet's stated mission. Hamlet interjects his own wry comments, most of all when the Player Queen has just mouthed her pious vows of eternal loyalty. 'Wormwood, wormwood!'[6] is his first interjection, and then, 'If she should break it now!' To his mother he poses a direct question between scenes, before the murder has occurred: 'Madam, how like you this play?' Her answer acknowledges that Hamlet is asking about her response to the dramatic representation of herself that she has just witnessed. 'The lady doth protest too much, methinks,' she answers. The mirror in which she has been asked to see herself has made her distinctly uncomfortable.

The idea that Hamlet has staged 'The Murder of Gonzago' as much for her as for Claudius is borne out by what he does next. Informed by Rosencrantz and Guildenstern that the Queen has sent for him, Hamlet responds with alacrity. He must talk with her in order to learn what it has meant to her to see a representation of her husband's murder. Yet with what intent? Is he to accuse her, to quarrel, to condemn? He remembers what his father's ghost has said to him: he is to revenge the 'foul and most unnatural murder' of Hamlet senior, but he is to spare his mother:

> But howsoever thou pursues this act,
> Taint not thy mind nor let thy soul contrive
> Against thy mother aught. Leave her to heaven
> And to those thorns that in her bosom lodge,
> To prick and sting her.
>
> (1.5.85–9)

It is in this spirit, presumably, that Hamlet warns himself not to let 'the soul of Nero' enter his bosom as he confronts his mother. 'Let me be cruel, not unnatural; / I will speak daggers to her, but use none.' Hamlet seems prepared to follow the dictates of his ghostly father.

Even if Hamlet has ruled out violence toward his mother, she can hardly be blamed for not feeling safe on that score. He parries her attempts to chastise him with accusations of his own:

> QUEEN: Hamlet, thou hast thy father much offended.
> HAMLET: Mother, you have my father much offended.
> QUEEN: Come come, you answer with an idle tongue.
> HAMLET: Go to, you question with a wicked tongue.
>
> (3.4.10–13)

In a passage that brilliantly demonstrates the rhetorical devices we saw earlier in Shakespeare's poetry, such as stichomythia, antithesis, parison, and isocolon (see Chapter 1), Hamlet makes plain that he is on the offensive. Gertrude is alarmed: 'What wilt thou do? Thou wilt not murder me? / Help, ho!' The cry for help elicits a response from behind the curtains of her private chamber; Hamlet stabs, thinking he has found the perfect occasion to kill Claudius when he is 'in th' incestuous pleasure of his bed'; and Polonius lies dead on the floor in a pool of his own blood.

The ghost of Hamlet senior is not sure, either, that Hamlet is not out of control. The ghost makes himself visible to Hamlet (though not to Gertrude; what can the ghost possibly have to say to her at this point?) in order to 'whet thy almost blunted purpose'. Why is Hamlet bearing down on Gertrude instead of getting on with the revenge? This is a pertinent question, one that Hamlet acknowledges to be such: he freely admits that he deserves chiding because he 'lets go by / Th'important acting' of the ghost's 'dread command'. Yet he does have a purpose in confronting Gertrude with her guilt. If he is to 'leave her to heaven' and the stinging of her conscience, he can at least awaken the remorse that she needs to feel. Hamlet has good reason to think that Gertrude simply cannot face what it is that she has done.

What is it, in fact, that she has done? That question will help determine whether or not she is recoverable through the prick of conscience. Was she partner in the crime of murdering Hamlet senior? Briefly, Hamlet charges her with this degree of culpability to see how she will answer. When she cries out, in response to Polonius's sudden death, 'Oh, what a rash and bloody deed is this!' Hamlet parries with a suggestive parallel: 'A bloody deed – almost as bad, good mother, / As kill a king, and marry with his brother'. This statement equates killing a king with marrying Claudius; the implied agent in both is Gertrude. Yet it is not put as a direct interrogation: 'Did you kill Hamlet senior in order to marry Claudius, or did you at least consent to the plan?' And Gertrude's response – 'As kill a king!' – appears to satisfy Hamlet that she did not do that or know of it. Gertrude is not a skilled player of a false role; Hamlet knows how to 'read' her. He passes on to other matters that are not so quickly dismissed.

The extent of Gertrude's guilt is a matter of interpretation, in the theatre or as we read. Hamlet, however, is not content with much uncertainty here. Just how guilty was she? Perhaps she knew nothing of the plan to murder Hamlet senior before it happened, but has it dawned on

her that her first husband's sudden death was perhaps not naturally caused
and that she herself may have been the desired object for which a murder
was committed? Hamlet can see that Gertrude is very uneasy. She admits,
implicitly at least, that she has disappointed her son – abandoned him,
really, despite her attempts to reconcile Hamlet to his new stepfather. Part
of her knows that Hamlet is right in chiding her for unseemly haste; that
is why she was so uncomfortable watching the play-within-the-play. She
bristles at first, and tries to guard herself with appeals to the truisms of
motherhood and filial duty: how dare her son speak to her like this? Yet
Hamlet's relentless bearing down on her does have the salient effect
of drawing from her a confession of deep unhappiness with her own
behaviour:

> Oh, Hamlet, speak no more!
> Thou turn'st mine eyes into my very soul,
> And there I see such black and grainèd spots
> As will not leave their tinct.
>
> (3.4.90–3)

This is a first big step toward remorse, but, again, what is she admitting? Is it only that she has disappointed her son and proved herself guilty
of a short memory of her first husband? Perhaps, more importantly,
Hamlet and Gertrude can together consider the great likelihood that
Claudius did what he did knowing that he could have Gertrude as his
reward. He did not speak to her of his plan, but he knew her temperament to be a yielding one and he sensed that she did not dislike him.
Kenneth Branagh's 1995 film shows a flashback in which we see Gertrude
and Claudius, on some past occasion while Hamlet senior still lived, enjoying one another's company in some innocent pastime.[7] This interpretation seems plausible. Claudius is a man who would not have made his
move had he not known that he could have what he craved from it: the
crown and the lady. Claudius knew that Polonius and other likeminded
counsellors could readily be persuaded to 'elect' him as their new king,
and he knew that Gertrude would come around despite her fears of alienating young Hamlet. Gertrude, he knew, would feel herself to be in a vulnerable position as dowager queen, in need of a man to shelter and cherish
her.

Hamlet and his mother do not spell all this out; to do so would be
tactless and unnecessary. What Hamlet needs is a mutely understood sce-

nario regarding the Queen's degree of culpability, one that will allow her to repent and Hamlet to forgive her. He could hardly forgive her active participation in the murder, but he need not consider this now, and the ghost's admonition to leave her to the workings of her conscience plainly implies that the ghost too thinks she is reclaimable. What is that reclamation to be like?

Hamlet's method of proceeding, once he has elicited from her a confession of perceiving 'black and grainèd spots' in her very soul, is to help her find the path to contrition and repentance. He delivers to her what amounts to an admonitory sermon:

> Confess yourself to heaven,
> Repent what's past, avoid what is to come,
> And do not spread the compost on the weeds
> To make them ranker.
>
> (3.4.156–9)

Hamlet is a Christian. He believes, as a fundamental of his faith, that heaven rejoices in the penitence of a sinner. Heaven can help; indeed, there is no other way. Yet the individual must make a terrific effort to be worthy of that offered help by doing what he or she can to live a better life. When his mother cries out that Hamlet has cleft her heart in twain, he has a ready answer: 'Oh, throw away the worser part of it, / And live the purer with the other half'. Recovery to spiritual health is possible if one will devote one's entire will to the project.

Hamlet's advice about implementation of a desire for reform is immediately practical, and is concerned first and foremost with Gertrude's sexual behaviour. 'Go not to my uncle's bed,' he admonishes her. 'Assume a virtue, if you have it not.' Hamlet is a student of psychology. He believes, as did William James of a later century, that inward states of mind and heart can be shaped by a conscious effort to change one's outward behaviour. The process is not easy; it is like breaking a bad habit, and we all know that bad habits are much easier to fall into than to crawl out of. Hamlet puts it more elegantly than that: habit is a devil, he says, and yet habit can be an angel too in this, 'That to the use of actions fair and good / He likewise gives a frock or livery / That aptly is put on'. In practical terms, this means something very concrete for Gertrude: she is to stay out of Claudius's bed one night, then try two, then three. She will find in this process 'a kind of easiness / To the next abstinence; the next more easy'. A deliberate changing of habit can almost alter 'the stamp of nature' itself. Hamlet's guarded optimism about the human chance for happiness rests on this hope that self-reform is possible with the help of heaven.

The evidence of the play is that Hamlet succeeds. He bids Gertrude not to give away his secret that his madness is a mere pretence, and he bids her see less of Claudius, especially in bed. In the very next scene, after Hamlet has left, dragging offstage the lifeless corpse of Polonius, we see Gertrude with her husband, explaining the death of Polonius as a consequence of Hamlet's insanity. She has lied to Claudius. He is taken in: he informs Rosencrantz and Guildenstern that 'Hamlet in madness hath Polonius slain'. Thereafter, husband and wife are seen less often together until the final scene of catastrophe: Claudius confides not in his wife but in Laertes, with whom he concocts, out of Gertrude's hearing, a scheme to kill Hamlet with poisoned sword or poisoned cup. Her ignorance of this plot proves fatal to Gertrude, for she drinks the poisoned cup in the play's denouement. Some stage productions imply that she figures out that the cup is poisoned, and by whom, and drinks it as expiation for what she has done. Other productions portray her as the unknowing victim of her husband's villainy, in a wonderfully ironic demonstration of how carefully laid plans can go awry: the queen for whom Claudius killed his brother now dies from the poisoned cup that he helped prepare for her son. In either case, Gertrude has disobeyed her husband by drinking the wine when he ordered her not to do so, seemingly as a demonstration of her love for Hamlet. She and her son appear to be reconciled. She has done what he asked of her to the best of her ability. Her death is an atonement, and her son is ready now to join her in death.

Hamlet's searing if vicarious experience with sexuality, both male and female, colours his other relationships as well. His love for Ophelia seems doomed from the start. She is as frail in her way as Gertrude, as much swayed by male importunity. She hearkens to the counsel of her father and brother when they warn her that she must not open her 'chaste treasure' to Hamlet's 'unmastered importunity'. This advice is sensible in the main, but gratuitous so far as we can tell in the present instance. Hamlet does not act like a would-be seducer. He is hurt and saddened by her returning to him the gifts that he has sent her. Even though he is perceptive enough to see that her father and brother are abetting her reticence, he blames the whole female sex as well, generalizing his deep misogyny into an indictment of universal human perversity. 'Get thee to a nunnery!' he exclaims to Ophelia, alluding to the defamatory linking of nunneries and whorehouses in Renaissance misogynistic and anti-Catholic lore. 'Why wouldst thou be a breeder of sinners?' He throws down a challenge to Claudius, whom he suspects hiding behind a curtain to overhear his interview with Ophelia, by shouting 'We will have no more marriage'. From the start, he is persuaded that 'Frailty, thy name is woman'.

Even though Hamlet discovers at last how to come to terms with and forgive the weaknesses of Ophelia and Gertrude, his pervasive misogyny has darkened the prospect of heterosexual union in this tragedy. The marriage of Claudius and Gertrude is a guilty and offensive one, all the more so because it is contrasted with the affectionate pairing of Hamlet Senior and Gertrude as remembered, and no doubt idealized, by Hamlet and the play-within-the play. The love of Hamlet and Ophelia ends in disappointment and perhaps a suicide. Instead of a parade to the altar at the play's end we witness a scene of universal carnage. What, if anything, takes the place of romantic love in *Hamlet*?

One important answer is friendship. That human relationship too is under strain in this play: Rosencrantz and Guildenstern disappoint Hamlet no less than does Ophelia, showing as they do that friendship can mean making the right political connections. Polonius's worldly advice to his son Laertes is that he cherish one or two friends, but not others; friendship is too often shallow and treacherous. On the other hand, Hamlet's friendship with Horatio is extraordinary. They have their differences, but those differences are of philosophical persuasion. One can imagine them at Wittenberg, arguing long into the night. Horatio is a sceptic. He refuses to believe the appearance of the ghost 'Without the sensible and true avouch / Of mine own eyes'. At the play's end, what he remembers and wants to describe is a tale 'Of carnal, bloody, and unnatural acts, / Of accidental judgements, casual slaughters'. As a historian, he believes in telling the unvarnished, deglamorized truth. He is, moreover, a stoic in the classical Roman mould, attuned to secular interpretations of human history. Hamlet is religious. At the end of the play he praisingly accepts the role of Providence in his life, as having provided a more satisfactory answer to his dilemmas than he could have devised for himself. He exults in showing to Horatio the limits of Horatio's secular and sceptical view: 'There are more things in heaven and earth, Horatio, / Than are dreamt of in your philosophy'. By 'your philosophy' Hamlet means all secular learning that rational men try to acquire.

These differences do not offend Hamlet. To the contrary, they delight him. Horatio, in his openness, candour, and loyalty, is a man Hamlet can trust. He knows that Horatio has nothing to gain from him by flattery. He greatly admires Horatio's stoicism. The stoical view may be argued with on philosophical grounds, but as a basis for personal integrity it enables Horatio, in Hamlet's view, to suffer 'Fortune's buffets and rewards' with 'equal thanks' – which is to say, to be equally indifferent to bad luck or good luck. Such rising above vicissitude enables Horatio not to be 'a pipe for Fortune's finger / To sound what stop she please'. Passionate feeling and good judgement are 'commeddled' in him, so that he is not 'passion's slave'. Hamlet loves this in Horatio because it embodies a principle of personal virtue. Hamlet longs to be like that himself. The calm, the equanimity, the decency – how does one find those qualities for one's own use? Hamlet's openness to Horatio arises from a deep sense of sharing values and commitments, even if they sometimes agree to disagree about philosophical matters.

To say that Hamlet loves Horatio is not to misrepresent the case. In the absence of other rewarding human relationships, Hamlet clings to Horatio for all he is worth. He dies in Horatio's arms, bidding that friend to live to tell his story and thus ensure that posterity will not be misled by Claudius's insinuations. Hamlet also refuses to give up on his relationship with his mother, but Horatio is the one who matters most. It is with Horatio that Hamlet visits Ophelia's graveyard, where they can debate on the vanity of human wishes and the meaning of death. Again, they disagree: Horatio protests, perhaps amusedly, that ' 'Twere to consider too curiously to consider so,' when Hamlet's freewheeling imagination has set before them the image of Alexander's mouldering body serving to stop a bunghole. No matter; friends need to argue in order to learn from each other and to share experiences. Friendship is one redeeming factor in the fallen world of *Hamlet*.

This opposition of erotic love and friendly love extends into the great tragedies that follow *Hamlet*. A notable example is *King Lear*, where, once again, carnal love is portrayed very darkly. Other than the marriage of Cordelia and the King of France, which disappears almost entirely from view once the first scene has concluded, the marriages of this play are fearsome to behold. Goneril despises her husband Albany as a milksop and goes about cuckolding him with someone she considers a real man, Edmund. 'Oh, the difference of man and man!' she murmurs, as Edmund leaves her to go on an important mission. 'To thee a woman's services are due; / My fool usurps my body' (4.2.26–8). Her sister Regan gets along well enough with her husband, the Duke of Cornwall, since they see eye to eye about such things as banishing old Lear into the storm or torturing the Earl of Gloucester for his supposed treason, but the portrait of married bliss here is scarcely edifying. A sexual rivalry over Edmund leads finally to the death of both sisters: Goneril poisons Regan lest she enjoy Edmund, and then slays herself.

King Lear's mad indictment of human sexuality, especially in women, is all the more gripping and persuasive because he is mad. What prompts this outburst? He has no cause to be sexually jealous, since he is old and a widower; his wife, so far as we know, was true to his bed. Yet he is right, in his madness, to see that the sex act has led to unforeseen and horrendous consequences. 'Let copulation thrive!' he raves. 'For Gloucester's bastard son / Was kinder to his father than my daughters / Got 'tween the lawful sheets.' Lear has the details importantly wrong, not knowing that Edmund is a villain, but he understands the larger issue of carnality and its disastrous consequences. Women, in his tortured imagination, are only creatures of unbridled appetite:

> Down from the waist they're centaurs,
> Though women all above.
> But to the girdle do the gods inherit;
> Beneath is all the fiends'.
> There's hell, there's darkness, there is the sulfurous pit, burning, scalding,
> stench, consumption. Fie, fie, fie! Pah, pah! Give me an ounce of civet, good
> apothecary, sweeten my imagination.
>
> (4.6.124–31)

The conventional misogynistic image of the woman's sexual body as the portal of hell's gates is made devastating and personal because of Lear's dreadful mistakes and because of what he has suffered from his ungrateful daughters.

As in *Hamlet*, the only relationships that can begin to compensate for this universal horror of sexuality are ones in which carnal desire plays no part. A daughter like Cordelia and a son like Edgar can redress in some measure the sordid concupiscence of their siblings. The child–parent relationship offers more hope than the marriage bed. Then, too, the Fool is a kind of son to Lear, offering consolation and wry perspective as a good child can hope to do. Kent, banished by Lear, self-effacingly returns in disguise to serve his master with loving duty. The servant–master relationship offers some hope, then; Kent and the Fool do much to compensate for the perverted and self-interested kind of service we see in Oswald. In the apocalyptic devastation that ends this terrifying play, the devotion of friends, caring children, and loyal followers, together with the sad wisdom that comes from proper knowing of oneself, are all that they, or we, can cling to.

CHAPTER SIX

◆

Wise Saws

Political and Social Disillusionment, Humankind's Relationship to the Divine, and Philosophical Scepticism

> *Placed in this isthmus of a middle state,*
> *A being darkly wise and rudely great,*
> *With too much knowledge for the Sceptic side,*
> *With too much weakness for the Stoic's pride,*
> *He hangs between; in doubt to act or rest,*
> *In doubt to deem himself a god or beast,*
>
> .   .   .   .
>
> *Created half to rise and half to fall,*
> *Great lord of all things, yet a prey to all;*
> *Sole judge of truth, in endless error hurled:*
> *The glory, jest, and riddle of the world.*
> *Alexander Pope,* An Essay on Man, *2.3–18*

Along with his probing of disillusionment about human sexuality and friendship, Shakespeare, in the years around 1600, explores with new intensity a number of vexed issues about governance in human society and humankind's relationship to the divine. The large and nearly incomprehensible questions of human existence now seem increasingly to demand his attention as a writer especially of tragedies: what is the role of divine providence in our lives? What choices have we in shaping our destinies? Why are suffering and evil so manifest in human experience, and how are we to understand the reasons for the persistence of evil? Do our struggles have meaning? How should we attempt to govern ourselves, both personally and as a society?

At about the same time that he began writing tragedies in earnest, Shakespeare also discovered the immense value of the ancient classical world as one in which to explore questions of the sort just outlined. The ancient world of Rome and, secondarily, of Greece was the only prior civilization of which Western Europe had any substantial knowledge. For the English, in particular, Rome was their ancestry, their roots: legend had it that Aeneas's grandson, following the burning of Troy and the founding of Rome by Aeneas, had sailed through the straits of Gibraltar and around to England, where he founded a neo-Roman culture. London was familiarly known as Troynovant, the new Troy. Moreover, the classical civilization of the ancient world was highly literate, culturally sophisticated, and pagan. Within its precincts, Shakespeare could ask questions not posited on a providential belief in the Christian God, and could investigate political systems that bore no necessary resemblance to late feudal monarchy. He began this study with *Julius Caesar*, written in 1599 for performance in his acting company's new theatre, the Globe, on the Bankside south of the Thames River.

Shakespeare had chosen a Roman setting much earlier, in about 1589–92, for his earliest tragedy, *Titus Andronicus*, but there the history is fictionalized and composite, so that it is much more a revenge tragedy than a study of Roman culture.[1] *Julius Caesar*, on the other hand, takes up one of the most famous events of ancient Rome: the assassination of Julius Caesar by Brutus and his fellow-conspirators in 44 BCE, and the aftermath of civil war between that party and the defenders of Caesar's memory, with the defeat of Brutus and Cassius at Philippi two years later.

Politically, the Rome of *Julius Caesar* is worlds apart from that of *Henry V*, written at about the same time in 1599. The conflict in Rome is between the so-called Republican party, headed by Brutus and dedicated to protecting Rome's ancient liberties of senatorial authority, and Julius Caesar, the brilliant general who believes in strong-man single rule and who appears to be tempted by the offer of a kingship. Republicanism is not like any form of government that England had ever known. Analogies to England are therefore imprecise and not very helpful. Instead, the Roman setting allows Shakespeare to look at political strife in a distinctly non-English context.[2]

In the absence of Christian ideology, moreover, the moral imperatives underlying political choices and actions are non-English. No doctrine of the divine right of kings can hope to underpin Caesar's claim to single rule. Nor can the Republicans claim biblical or clerical authority for their

Plate 4   De Witt drawing of the Swan Theatre, executed by Van Buchell, *c.* 1596.
Utrecht, University Library.

cause of senatorial governance. The church hardly exists as an ideological
force in the Rome of this play. Soothsayers are consulted, and the movements of birds are interpreted as oracles, but an English audience is hard
put to hear the voice of God in all this. Instead, men must work out their
destinies in a pagan universe that seems to provide little guidance for
human action.

How do humans behave in a world so different from that of
Elizabethan England, and how do they justify their actions? Brutus is a
thoughtful man, generous among friends and family, proud of the Republican tradition he heads. His motive in joining a conspiracy to assassinate

Caesar seems to be public-spirited: he is appalled at the prospect of Rome's destinies being in the hands of one man only. Caesar, for his part, also thinks about the welfare of his country: he is convinced that the centralizing of power will provide more efficient and intelligent governance. Confident of his being the right man at the right time, he seizes power to improve Rome's lot while simultaneously solidifying his own political authority.

Oddly, ironically, Brutus and Caesar are much alike. They both believe that they have the right answer and that forthright, ruthless action is necessary on their part to prevent disaster. They both regard themselves as persons of impeccable integrity, well armed against flattery and insinuation. Yet both succumb to flattery, and march to their tragic destinies because of this. Brutus hearkens to Cassius's arguments that only he, Brutus, can lead the Republican cause in its time of crisis; only he can head up a plot to kill Caesar. For his part, Caesar ignores the warning of his wife's ominous dreams and goes to the Capitol on the fateful Ides of March because one of the conspirators has persuaded him that if he stays home out of fear he will be laughed at. Caesar scoffs at superstition and yet listens to the soothsayers. He prides himself on being like the North Star, the one fixed star in the firmament, and yet he is deaf in one ear and physically unable to keep up with Cassius in a bout of swimming. Caesar is, it seems, a mere mortal after all.

The ironies continue to pursue Caesar and Brutus. Caesar dies having just pronounced his godlike quality of being 'unassailable' and 'Unshaked of motion'. Brutus's unwarranted confidence in his own speaking ability leads him to allow Mark Antony to address the people of Rome about the assassination after Brutus has spoken. Antony exploits the occasion by unleashing chaos. In the ensuing civil strife, Brutus unwisely insists on being first among the Republican generals; it is his choice to fight Antony and young Octavius Caesar at Philippi, when the older and more experienced Cassius counsels against the decision.

The irony is that a humane, decent man like Brutus, willing to devote his very life to his city, cannot command a revolution. The events he and Cassius set in motion by the assassination overwhelm them. The cause for which they have fought and killed – senatorial liberty – has only been attenuated by their striving. Their own weaknesses return to haunt them, just as Caesar contributes to his own death by his monomania. Character is fate; our destinies are a product of who we are. An idea of tragic justice can be seen to dwell in this prospect, but it is not an idea of justice that seems to be presided over by any intelligent deity. History is a series of ups and downs: certain men and ideas prevail for a time and then are supplanted by new movements of history. Civilizations come and go. Where, in this secular view of the historical process, is there a role for belief in the divine?

Again and again, in *Julius Caesar*, men turn to the heavens for some kind of assistance or guidance, only to be perplexed by an enigmatic silence. The fearful storm on the night preceding Caesar's assassination would seem to prognosticate some terrible event about to occur: a lioness is reported to have whelped in the streets and a slave's hand has been set aflame without consuming the flesh. Yet what do these signs mean? Cassius, for his part, takes the opportunity to dare the heavens to strike him with lightning; he does not believe in any nonsense about the gods punishing presumption. Casca, another of the conspirators and ordinarily a pretty cynical fellow, is scared out of his wits by the omens. Brutus, self-absorbed and reflective, notices merely, as though observing some kind of scientific curiosity, that the night sky is so lit up with 'exhalations whizzing in the air' that he is able to read without a candle. Cicero's comment on the strange night is perhaps the most wise of all:

> Indeed, it is a strange-disposèd time.
> But men may construe things after their fashion,
> Clean from the purpose of the things themselves.
> (1.3.33–5)

Like Socrates, Cicero is aware that our best hope in trying to be wise is to realize that we know nothing, that all is uncertain, and that we humans stumble about seeking blindly for answers in a universe that will not tell us who we are. That is the nature of our tragic destiny in this play.

Cassius, the great sceptic as the play begins and even villain-like in his temptation of Brutus to join the conspiracy, is ultimately seen as a very thoughtful person. He accedes to Brutus's misguided generalship again and again because their friendship to him is precious. Brutus, too, the great stoic of the play, whose need to be calmly indifferent to hostile fortune prompts him to treat the news of his wife Portia's suicide as though it were something to take in his stride, is also moved by that friendship. Together they face disaster brought about by their own personal failures with resolution and something like resignation. Cassius even changes the very fundamentals of his beliefs: no longer arrogantly certain of his Epicurean persuasion that the gods are indifferent to human affairs, he confesses that he now must 'partly credit things that do presage'. The personal decency of these men, and their difficult striving to make sense out of human failure, redeem a historical account that might otherwise seem bleak and meaningless.

The lessons of history in *Troilus and Cressida* are much the same. Concepts of good and evil are not well suited to describe the political and military conflict of this play. The Trojans are, on the whole, a more attractive people than the Greeks (since England legendarily regarded herself as of Trojan and Roman stock), and yet they will lose the war. Hector, the greatest Trojan of them all, lies dead on the battlefield at the play's end, having been unfairly massacred by Achilles and his Myrmidons. One can hardly say that justice has been served. The gods are rather abstractly referred to at times ('Well, the gods are above') but seem to play no part in the war or in the love affair.

As a tragic figure in a satiric black comedy, Hector is not unlike Brutus. He is the most decent and wise of all his brethren, and lectures them with devastating logic on the folly of their fighting the Greeks just to keep Helen in Paris's bed and away from her husband, Menelaus; and yet he backs down at a crucial point in the argument, agreeing that 'honour and renown' oblige them to fight on. He is a devoted family man, and yet when his wife Andromache pleads with him not to go to battle on a certain day because of omens and dreams, he orders her to be silent. He will fight because 'the gods have heard me swear'. Like Caesar and Brutus, he ignores his wife's counsel with fatal consequences. In all these cases, the women are right, whereas the men are stubbornly unwilling to listen to a woman's advice. Hector's character is his fate. What is wise and unwise in him is inextricably woven; his failings are the obverse of his virtues. His death in battle is destined, partly because the story of Troy is so well known that Shakespeare is constrained from having things turn out differently, but also because Hector's temperament determines how he will act. He has free choice: the fateful decision to go into battle that day is his. Yet we also sense that he could not have chosen otherwise.

Achilles's fate is to slaughter Hector. Again, we see him choosing to do something that we know he must do, and at immeasurable personal cost. Hector chooses to go to battle and thus marches to his death; Achilles chooses to murder Hector, and thereby earns for himself a reputation throughout all time as a savage bully. This is ironic, since Shakespeare (like Homer) reveals him to be a man of substance. He is a great warrior, and he understands well enough what Ulysses tells him about time. Time waits for no man; opportunity must be seized. Reputations tarnish quickly if not made to shine anew by fresh deeds of valour and renown. The pity is that Achilles hears this lesson with the ears of one who has grown desperate for renown. He is eaten by envy of those who win fame in battle, most of all Hector; he confesses that he is 'sick' with desire, smitten with 'a woman's longing', to behold this great adversary. Thus, under the pressure of anxiety about fame, Achilles takes the moral shortcut of ganging up on Hector when Hector is unarmed and badly outnumbered. Achilles's reward is to be jeered at by history. Shakespeare is fascinated with this narrative of the decay of great reputations. Once again, he sees history as a process of change, of undulation, not something that has teleological meaning. Instead of being directed toward some purposeful end, history appears to be governed by mechanical causes and ironic failures. Human beings are too often their own worst enemies.

The tawdriness and senselessness of the greatest war in history are brought home to us in scabrous language by the play's leering chorus, Thersites. Shakespeare magnifies the part of this loathsome but engaging rascal (taken from Book II of Homer's *Iliad*) to make the connection between violence and sex: 'Lechery, lechery, still wars and lechery; nothing else holds fashion'. Choric utterances like these incessantly deflate all pretensions of heroism and greatness. The war is, after all, about a woman, about Helen. Her one scene onstage, with Paris, shows them both to have become perfectly vapid in their well-publicized tryst. Is Helen worth fighting over? Diomedes, for one, is implacably bitter:

> For every false drop in her bawdy veins
> A Grecian's life hath sunk; for every scruple
> Of her contaminated carrion weight
> A Trojan hath been slain.
>   (4.1.71–4)

Human strivings after heroism dwindle into absurd posturings when seen from this devastating point of view. The illusion of meaningful choice is overwhelmed by the seemingly uncontrollable and relentless oscillations of history.

Lest we conclude from this that Shakespeare has himself turned sceptic, however, let us consider the political and metaphysical worlds of *Hamlet* – a play that is nearly contemporaneous with *Julius Caesar* and *Troilus and Cressida*. *Hamlet* is set in Christian Denmark. Claudius is a cunning murderer and astute politician; he is also a sinner. He knows this all too well. 'Oh, my offence is rank! It smells to heaven!' he cries out in agonized soliloquy, when he has seen 'The Murder of Gonzago' and has had to confront anew his guilt in having slain his own brother. He even knows, as one who has been schooled in the teachings of the church, what he must do to save his imperilled soul: he must experience remorse and penance. He makes a desperate attempt at prayer. Why will his prayers not ascend to heaven? He knows the answer well enough: it is because he is unwilling to give up those things for which he committed the crime, his crown and his queen. 'May one be pardoned and retain th'offence?' he asks rhetorically, only to answer his own question. One can get away sometimes with hypocrisy in this corrupted world, but 'There is no shuffling' when one must face God in His awesome tribunal above. Claudius knows that he is doomed because he cannot turn to God in true contrition.

Claudius's acknowledged sinfulness postulates a world in which we are asked to distinguish good from evil. To Hamlet and his father's ghost, Claudius is a heinous sinner, one who has tempted Gertrude to his lewd lust and 'damnèd incest'. True virtue is an essence that can never be moved, says the ghost, 'Though lewdness court it in a shape of heaven', whereas lust, 'though to a radiant angel linked, / Will sate itself in a celestial bed / And prey on garbage'. The polarities of good and evil shape the language of the play at every turn. Hamlet senior and Claudius are like 'Hyperion to a satyr'. 'Things rank and gross in nature' possess the unweeded garden of the world in which Hamlet finds himself.

How are we to account for this massive and unbridgeable gulf in human nature between the celestial and the bestial? No question is more troubling to Hamlet.

> What a piece of work is a man! [he marvels]. How noble in reason, how infinite in faculties, in form and moving how express and admirable, in action how like an angel, in apprehension how like a god! The beauty of the world, the paragon of animals! And yet, to me, what is this quintessence of dust?
>
> (2.2.304–9)

The world itself to him is nothing but a 'pestilent congregation of vapours'. His disappointment in humankind poses the play's most intense philosophical challenge.

Hamlet does not exclude himself from his indictment of the human race. Here is what he says to Ophelia when she returns his love tokens to him:

> Get thee to a nunnery. Why wouldst thou be a breeder of sinners? I am myself indifferent honest, but yet I could accuse me of such things that it were better my mother had not borne me: I am very proud, revengeful, ambitious, with more offences at my beck than I have thoughts to put them in, imagination to give them shape, or time to act them in. What should such fellows as I do crawling between earth and heaven? We are arrant knaves all; believe none of us.
>
> (3.1.122–30)

Hamlet's view of fallen human nature derives from medieval-Renaissance theology hearkening back to the teachings of Saint Paul and Saint Augustine. Hamlet recognizes in himself the Deadly Sins of Pride, Wrath, Envy, and Covetousness that beset humanity from every side. We commit these sins daily, even the most well-intentioned of us. Because Hamlet senior died unexpectedly and was sent to his final reckoning 'With all my imperfections on my head', he has had to endure the unimaginable torments of Purgatory until the 'foul crimes done in my days of nature / Are burnt and purged away'. Hamlet senior, like his son, was a better man than most, and yet he has had to suffer in this way because his sins had not been atoned for through penance and last rites; he died 'unhousled', without having received the Sacrament. The emphasis on Purgatory is Roman Catholic; the reformed Anglican church in England had rejected such dogmas, but it retained the essential Augustinian idea of the inherent depravity of humankind. Hamlet's acquaintance with that teaching has been deepened by his own perceptions about himself and about the stunning contrast between Claudius and Hamlet senior.

The resulting view of humanity, as seen through Hamlet's eyes, is that though we are all fallen creatures, we may still hope for grace. That key word in Protestant theology resonates in Hamlet's consciousness. 'Angels and ministers of grace defend us!' he exclaims on seeing his father's ghost for the first time. He adjures his companions on the battlements to keep his secret by swearing, 'So grace and mercy at your most need help you'. He pleads with his mother 'for love of grace' not to betray the secret of his pretended madness. Calvinism had made a great impact in the England of Shakespeare's generation, with its emphasis on total human depravity and yet at the same time the irresistibility of grace, in a process of pre-destined election presided over by God with absolute power to choose those whom He wishes to save and whom to condemn. Hamlet, having studied at Wittenberg, is attuned to Calvinist thought.

This training prepares Hamlet to distinguish between Claudius and Gertrude. He need not be concerned about the welfare of the soul of Claudius, that unredeemable sinner and reprobate; to the contrary, Hamlet hopes to send Claudius's soul to hell, if only to pay back for what Hamlet's father has suffered in Purgatory. Gertrude is another matter; she is a sinner who can, he hopes, be recovered by the prick of conscience. His father thinks so too. Hamlet's course of action regarding Gertrude, as we have seen, appears to be reasonably clear: coax her into penitence. With Claudius, on the other hand, Hamlet faces a philosophical dilemma. Claudius's crime calls for vengeance, and a part of Hamlet responds with alacrity to that call. 'Haste me to know't', he urges his father, 'that I, with wings as swift / As meditation or the thoughts of love / May sweep to my revenge.' On the other hand, Hamlet's mind is filled with scruples. Is the ghost to be believed, or may Hamlet have seen a devil tempting his susceptible mind toward self-destructive violence? 'The spirit I have seen / May be the devil', he reflects. 'The devil hath power / T'assume a pleas-ing shape.' If the ghost he saw was in fact the devil, would it not be damnable to pursue the act urged on him by that apparition?

Hamlet's dilemma is in seeking to know the moral basis of what action he should take. Two great systems of thought and theology bear down on him: revenge, which contains its own consistent ethic of an eye for an eye, and the Christian ideology to which he was born. Denmark, posi-tioned geographically between the austere north of Norway and the more civilized Europe of Wittenberg and Paris, nicely symbolizes Hamlet's dilemma. So do Shakespeare's varied sources in writing *Hamlet*: the ancient story of Amlethus the Dane is a revenge epic in which moral scru-ples about killing play no part, whereas Shakespeare's own more humane sensibilities call for a wholesale re-evaluation of a code of savagery.

Given this disparity in world views, how is Hamlet to understand the ghost's command? The order to 'revenge my foul and most unnatural murder' seems clear enough, and yet one must ask, by what sort of author-ity does the ghost speak? He has come back from the world of the dead, from Catholic Purgatory, in fact. Does this mean that he returns by sufferance of the Supreme Deity? Is the revenge sanctioned by divine command? If so, Hamlet's way would indeed lie clear, but surely that cannot be the case; in Elizabethan England, church and state alike insisted that personal vengeance was forbidden by divine command ('Vengeance is mine, saith the Lord'). More likely, the ghost is speaking out of his own deep personal hatred for Claudius. His feelings are those of revenge, not Christian thought.

If that is the case, how can Hamlet hope to find a moral sanction for revenge that is consistent with a providential view of human action? He could simply ignore the problem, but he is too thoughtful a person for that. The puzzle is essentially insoluble. And, as is so often true of insoluble difficulties, the answer comes to him in the form of a paradox: he finds the way to avenge his father's death only when he no longer has a plan and has instead put himself in the hands of Providence.

This realization dawns on him after he has been sent to England and has had plenty of time to think things over. Perhaps he should wait for Providence to lay opportunity in his way. In retrospect, he sees that something just like this has happened on his trip to England, escorted by Rosencrantz and Guildenstern. Afforded no opportunity on that journey to kill Claudius, he discovers an unexpected occasion to make use of what he calls rashness:

> Rashly,
> And praised be rashness for it – let us know
> Our indiscretion sometime serves us well
> When our deep plots do pall, and that should learn us
> There's a divinity that shapes our ends,
> Rough-hew them how we will.
>
> (5.2.6–10)

It is in this accepting mood that Hamlet prepares for his own finale without having a clue what it will be, or what he is to do; he knows only that he must be ready.

Hamlet's persuasion that 'what must be, shall be'[3] only deepens as his sense of impending finality intensifies. 'We defy augury', he admonishes Horatio when that dear friend urges him to call off the proposed duelling contest with Laertes if he is uneasy about it.

> There is special providence in the fall of a sparrow. If it be now, 'tis not to come; if it be not to come, it will be now; if it be not now, yet it will come. The readiness is all.
>
> (5.2.217–20)

'Special providence' – a Calvinist catch-phrase. Hamlet cannot doubt that Providence will provide for him, and that he will be its instrument in some way. And so it proves. The ending is the perfect resolution of his dilemma, for it brings about the killing of Claudius without Hamlet's having to commit premeditated murder, and it provides for the death that Hamlet has longed for without his having to offend God by committing suicide. Perfect. The Comedy of Hamlet.

Hamlet is gracious enough not to see his dilemma, in retrospect, as some kind of cosmic dark joke. If the answer all along was that he should let Providence work out the plan for him to kill Claudius, how was he to know this? Why was he encouraged to flail about in search of an answer, castigating himself for delay and yet never finding the right moment? Was his killing of Polonius a wrongful act, even if he had every reason to think that the man's voice heard behind the arras in his mother's room was that of Claudius? Yes, Hamlet concludes, that was a wrongful act for which he must be held to account before the highest tribunal of all. Yet that event too, he sees, was an essential part of the plan that he did not plan. His killing of Polonius brings about the madness of Ophelia and the return of Laertes, seeking revenge; hence the duel, the poisoned sword, the poisoned cup, everything. It all falls into place; it all reveals the dark and mysterious ways by which Providence guides us even as we stumble about in ignorance.

Hamlet's is an enlightened reading of his own story; it also provides an astute reading of the play in which he appears. *Hamlet* is masterfully constructed in much these same terms, and in ways that Aristotelian critics of tragedy most admire: the parts fit together, events proceed forward by cause and effect, and deaths are justly dealt out to those who deserve them. 'I am justly killed with mine own treachery,' confesses the dying Laertes. To the extent that tragedy is an attempt to find meaning in human suffering and greatness in the characters who search most honestly for such meaning, then *Hamlet* does these things admirably. Hamlet is a tragic hero not merely because he suffers terribly but because he cannot be satisfied until he thinks he understands why that suffering has happened and what he was supposed to do about it.

Yet this darkly providential reading of human tragedy in *Hamlet* may be too neat. Shakespeare ends the play as though he were aware of the problem, for he counters Hamlet's providential reading of history with one that is profoundly sceptical. To Horatio, as he grieves over his friend's dead body, the story is one of 'purposes mistook / Fall'n on th'inventors' heads'. Horatio may be taking his cue from what the dying Laertes has just said: Laertes is 'as a woodcock to mine own springe'. This motif of a kind of ironic reciprocity, in which human beings unknowingly go about planning their own undoing, runs through the play. Hamlet wryly observes of Rosencrantz and Guildenstern, whose knavery he utterly mistrusts, that ' 'Tis the sport to have the enginer / Hoist with his own petard,' that is, to have the deviser of military mining operations blown up by his own explosives. We see a pattern of cause and effect in this, of course, but it is scarcely providential. Instead, it reminds us of the ironies of *Julius Caesar* or *Troilus and Cressida*. History, for the humanist and stoic Horatio, is apt to be a chronicle of 'carnal, bloody, and unnatural acts'. Shakespeare ends the play by encouraging an unresolved debate as to what the tragedy of Hamlet *did* mean.

Hamlet is famously a mystery, and the central character in it is a mystery most of all. Hamlet positively revels in unknowability. 'Why, look you now, how unworthy a thing you make of me!' he exults in his conversation with Rosencrantz and Guildenstern. 'You would play upon me, you would seem to know my stops, you would pluck out the heart of my mystery, you would sound me from my lowest note to the top of my compass, and there is much music, excellent voice, in this little organ, yet cannot you make it speak.' His ire is apt, for they are guilty of trying to figure him out and think they have the answer: frustration at being cut out of his inheritance as Prince of Denmark. The answer is tediously oversimplified, and tells more about them and their political ambitions than about Hamlet.

So too with Hamlet's other would-be interpreters. Polonius fatuously concludes that Hamlet is suffering from love-madness (since Polonius knew that malady in his youth, too). Claudius, with his secret knowledge of the crime he has committed, suspects that Hamlet's unhinged behaviour stems from a jealous, revengeful rage. Gertrude sees the matter through her own eyes: the cause of Hamlet's supposed madness, she proposes to her husband, is simply 'his father's death and our o'erhasty marriage'. All these diagnoses contain significant elements of truth, but each is woefully insufficient by itself, and even together they cannot tell the whole story. Hamlet cherishes his uniqueness. He speaks for us; we all know that there is no one quite like us, and that no one can ever fully appreciate the complexity of who we are. This view has rich potential for tragedy: the tragedy of misunderstanding. We see here one of many reasons why we become so involved with Hamlet as a character.

Shakespeare's most devastating exploration of scepticism is in *King Lear*. Throughout the play, those who suffer plead with the heavens to intervene on their behalf against the practices of villainy. 'O heavens', implores King Lear, 'If you do love old men, if your sweet sway / Allow obedience, if you yourselves are old, / Make it your cause; send down and take my part.' He is asking for divine assistance against Goneril and Regan, who have just joined forces to deny him his followers and then to drive him out into the storm (2.4). Lear appeals to the gods' pity: 'You see me here, you gods, a poor old man, / As full of grief as age, wretched in both'. Are the gods collaborating in the cruelty of Lear's daughters? 'If it be you that stirs these daughters' hearts / Against their father, fool me not so much / To bear it tamely.' In the storm, as he begins to lose his wits, Lear madly proclaims that divine justice is at hand: 'Let the great gods, / That keep this dreadful pother o'er our heads, / Find out their enemies now' (3.2). Lear's prediction that his persecutors will be punished is indeed a sign that he is losing his sanity, since the gods in whom he believes are nowhere to be found. The storm, whether or not heaven-sent, afflicts him and his companions, while his tormenters are safe inside Gloucester's house.

Edmund believes in quite another deity. He owes his services to goddess Nature. This is his way of announcing his creed, that Nature sanctions ruthless competition in which the race goes to the swiftest. Conventions of morality are, in his eyes, social constructions designed by a culture to protect vested interests against innovation and competition. How else can one explain a legal tradition that gives all property rights to the owner's eldest son upon the owner's death, and denies any rights of inheritance to a son who happens to be (as Edmund is) illegitimate and younger? Any notion that primogeniture and exclusion of bastards from inheritance are divinely ordained is a myth, self-interestedly nurtured by the elite and privileged to ensure themselves against loss of control of wealth and property.

This is a bracing creed. It has a distinctly 'modern' flavour. It shows intellectual daring and unconventionality. Edmund's ideas are apt to make us uncomfortable today, because he is a villain and yet he is so clear-sighted about the mythologies through which a culture invents and perpetuates itself. He sees traditional religious belief as superstition. This argument too has the unsettling appeal of sceptical insight. Edmund's father, the Earl of Gloucester, cannot think beyond the received opinion of those who believe in astrology. Here is his analysis of the supernatural causes lying behind the troubles that England currently finds itself in:

> These late eclipses in the sun and moon portend no good to us. Though the wisdom of nature can reason it thus and thus, yet nature finds itself scourged by the sequent effects. Love cools, friendship falls off, brothers divide; in cities, mutinies; in countries, discord; in palaces, treason; and the bond cracked twixt son and father. This villain of mine [Edgar] comes under the prediction: there's son against father. The King falls from bias of nature: there's father against child.
>
> (1.2.106–15)

Gloucester's thinking here is a ripe example of what is often called the 'Elizabethan world picture',[4] that is, a philosophical view of all of creation as linked in a Great Chain of Being, so that hierarchies in heaven serve as the models for hierarchies on earth. The motions of the heavens determine human fate because all is coherently designed and presided over by a divine majesty. Structures like monarchy and the family are divinely ordained and immutable; disorder in the cosmos signals disorder in the kingdom and in the family.

The Elizabethan world picture is a construct of great beauty and harmony. Shakespeare's characters often appeal to it as a wonderful idea, especially in his early plays, as in *The Merchant of Venice*, when Lorenzo, in the quiet of the night in Belmont, looks up at the stars and sees a heavenly design in them:

> Look how the floor of heaven
> Is thick inlaid with patens of bright gold.
> There's not the smallest orb which thou behold'st
> But in his motion like an angel sings,
> Still choiring to the young-eyed cherubins.
> Such harmony is in immortal souls,
> But whilst this muddy vesture of decay
> Doth grossly close it in, we cannot hear it.
>
> (5.1.58–66)

What could be more beautiful? Yet the physical evidence for this great picture of cosmic order is hard to come by, and as a way of thinking about nature it sounds – for better and for worse – old-fashioned.

Edmund will have none of it. Here is his scornful dissection, when he is alone onstage, of his father's gabble about eclipses and their 'sequent effects':

> This is the excellent foppery of the world, that when we are sick in fortune
> – often the surfeits of our own behaviour – we make guilty of our disasters
> the sun, the moon, and stars, as if we were villains on necessity, fools by
> heavenly compulsion, knaves, thieves, and treachers by spherical predomi-
> nance, drunkards, liars, and adulterers by an enforced obedience of plane-
> tary influence, and all that we are evil in, by a divine thrusting on. An
> admirable evasion of whoremaster man, to lay his goatish disposition on
> the charge of a star! My father compounded with my mother under the
> Dragon's tail and my nativity was under Ursa Major, so that it follows I am
> rough and lecherous. Fut, I should have been that I am, had the maiden-
> liest star in the firmament twinkled on my bastardizing.
>
> (1.2.121–36)

Edmund's critique is devastating because it is so candid and so apt. His call for the right and power of the individual person to shape his or her destiny is a creed of intellectual freedom. Edmund's idea of the self-made man has a distinctly modern ring, at least outwardly akin to Ralph Waldo Emerson's glorification of self-reliance. Edmund is, par excellence, the self-made man. He is proud to be beholden to no one other than himself and his own wits, though he does understandably resent the out-of-date social structures that have left him no alternative.

The great problem with Edmund is that he chooses to be a villain. Self-reliance and intellectual candour need not lead one to villainous behav-iour, but Shakespeare fashions a logical connection in Edmund's case. If the gods are mere constructs of the human imagination, Edmund reasons, then morality and conscience are also fabrications that one can choose to ignore. Since in his view one is not being watched by some deity, one can act with impunity against anyone standing in one's way. Indeed, one has a decisive advantage over persons who think morally, for they will be con-strained by conscience and morality whereas one need not be so con-strained oneself. This is a frightening syllogism, because there appears to be no logical flaw in it.

The play of *King Lear* tests this terrifying proposition to its limit, that conscience-less men and women enjoy the upper hand in the competition for self-aggrandizement and can do anything they want since the gods, if they exist at all, will not intervene. Consider the evidence of the

Edmund–Edgar–Gloucester plot. Edmund persuades his father, through a clever lie, that Edmund's older and legitimate brother Edgar is plotting Gloucester's death. Edgar is driven into banishment, with a price on his head. Edmund meanwhile ingratiates himself with the Duke of Cornwall by turning over to that powerful lord information of Gloucester's secret communications with King Lear and the French forces that have landed in England to help the old king; since this is technically treason, Gloucester's eyes are put out. Edmund, now given the title of Earl of Gloucester in place of his condemned father, ingratiates himself also with Cornwall's wife, Regan, and is ready to marry her and become the Duke of Cornwall in her name once Cornwall has died in a scuffle with a servant. Edmund is also the adulterous lover of Regan's sister, Goneril, and clearly is aiming at the life of her husband, the Duke of Albany. Edmund and Albany find themselves in an uncertain rivalry as joint military commanders against the French invasion. If Edmund could kill Albany or topple him from power, Edmund would become king. He is narrowly prevented from becoming so only at the last minute. Edmund comes very close to proving his thesis that a person can achieve anything if he does away with conscience and morality. Goneril and Regan, till the last minute, succeed to no less an extent.

This devastating challenge to order distresses well-meaning observers in the play, as well it might. Will the heavens pay no heed to the sufferings of Gloucester, or of Lear at the hands of his daughters? 'If that the heavens do not their visible spirits / Send quickly down to tame these vile offences', warns the Duke of Albany, 'It will come, / Humanity must perforce prey on itself, / Like monsters of the deep' (4.2).[5]

Unnamed servants, whose anonymity gives them an especially chorus-like character, are appalled at what they see. In a passage found in the quarto text only, following the blinding of Gloucester, the servants who are ordered to thrust the old man out of doors see that blinding as a supreme test as to whether morality has any meaning or not. 'I'll never care what wickedness I do, / If this man come to good,' declares one, referring to the Duke of Cornwall, who performed the actual blinding. His comrade applies the same testing standard to what Regan has just done in countenancing and assisting the deed: 'If she live long, / And in the end meet the old course of death, / Women will all turn monsters'. These commoners flirt with Edmund's credo: if the gods do not exist or do not seem to care about human misdeeds, then one might as well become a villain and prosper like Edmund or Cornwall or Regan. Having said this in their shock and dismay, the servants proceed to do what they would rather do: they help poor old Gloucester (at risk to themselves, by disobeying Cornwall's orders) by bandaging his desecrated face and by enabling him to find further assistance. This is only a small moment in the play, and it is one that Shakespeare may have decided to excise when he rewrote the play or cut it for performance, but it does suggest that some ordinary people are revolted by iniquity and are willing to act in the name of compassion and pity against narrowly self-preservative instincts. Perhaps they behave with human decency simply because they have been culturally conditioned to believe in the virtue of generosity, but at any rate they practise charity as something that is deeply a part of themselves.

Edgar is a counterpart to his brother Edmund in every way. As such he is crucial to our understanding of the intellectual and sceptical challenge that Edmund and the other villainous characters present to traditional ideas of moral and religious order. Edmund is cunning and inventively deceitful; Edgar is trusting, innocent, and therefore easy prey to Edmund's insinuations. Edmund has no difficulty persuading his father that Edgar is plotting against his life, for Edgar has unguardedly said something about how ageing fathers need to put themselves and their revenue in the custody of their sons – a statement which, maliciously misinterpreted, gives the appearance of parricidal intent. Edgar loves his father, and continues to do so forgivingly even when his father tries to hunt him down as a criminal. Yet, like his brother, Edgar sees his father's ideas about the gods as anthropomorphic and antiquated. Edgar is charitably tolerant of his father's beliefs, but sceptical. At the same time, he does not embrace that scepticism as an invitation to become a villain. Quite the opposite.

Edgar is a sceptic because he is a realist. He does not reject belief in a divine presence in the universe; he simply wants to reject any easy answers as to the gods' presumed intervention in human affairs on behalf of good people. The evidence suggests to him (and, overwhelmingly in this play, to us) that the gods act very belatedly if at all. What Edgar wants to learn is how to live charitably and compassionately in a world that offers no divine assistance of any practical sort. Above all, he sees the need to banish the illusion that things are bound to turn out all right sooner or later. When, at the start of act four, he sees himself as a hunted man with no worldly possessions, friends, or family, his first instinct is to say that at least things cannot get any worse. 'To be worst, / The lowest and most dejected thing of fortune, / Stands still in esperance, lives not in fear.'

The one good thing about being at the very bottom of the turning of fortune's wheel is that one can begin to hope for better; one need not fear even worse luck. He does not yet know, however, when he says this, that his father, Gloucester, has just been blinded. When that pitiable old wreck is thrust forth from his own house to encounter Edgar as a crazy beggar, Edgar's immediate response is to castigate himself for assuming that things would now have to take a turn for the better. In his self-concern he was forgetting his father. Things are now worse. Edgar does not miss the implication of this: we are fooling ourselves when we hope for anything good to happen to us, anything at all. If we think we are entitled to some good luck after a run of bad luck, we are deceived. Edgar puts this with unsparing honesty: 'The worst is not / So long as we can say, "This is the worst"'. As long as we are able to put sentences together, the one thing we can count on is that things may get worse.

Nature to Edgar is not unlike Edmund's goddess Nature: she or it is simply indifferent to human happiness or suffering. Yet Edgar does not embrace this as a cue for villainy. Instead, he sees it as demonstrating the need for stoic philosophical calm. Stoicism, with its persuasive argument that one must be equally unaffected by good fortune or bad, offers the only way to withstand the vicissitudes of a fallen world. If one suffers misfortune with equanimity, then fortune can have no power over one's happiness. Conversely, if one is proof against the desire for wealth and power, one has discovered the perfect way to ward off disappointment when prosperity disappears. Stoicism offers the key to a contented life in an existential universe. It constructs no mythology of beneficent gods; it posits no harmonious world order. It protects against the insidious danger of assuming an entitlement that is sure to be rebuffed by hostile fortune. If one expects nothing, one cannot be let down.

Edgar's kindly and stoical scepticism is most manifest in his care for the ageing, blinded father who had once put a price on Edgar's head. Gloucester's needs are more than merely physical; he is in despair. The injustice that he has suffered has shattered his belief in a coherent cosmic view. He adopts instead a contrary thesis, that the gods are malicious. 'As flies to wanton boys are we to th'gods', he avers. 'They kill us for their sport.' This often-quoted passage is not a key to *King Lear* as a whole, as it is sometimes read. It is, on the other hand, a key to understanding Gloucester's despair. It enables him to hold on to his habitual belief in the gods while at the same time accounting for massive human injustice. We are the playthings of the gods.

Such a despairing doctrine can lead to thoughts of suicide, and indeed Gloucester longs to die at his own hands. Not only will suicide end his wretched existence; it will perhaps atone for the terrible thing Gloucester has done to his son Edgar. The old man suffers not only a disillusionment about the gods; closer to home, he finds that he is unable to forgive himself. A great redeeming fact about this poor old man is that when he belatedly learns of Edmund's perfidy toward himself and Edgar, and that Edmund was the real villain after all, Gloucester's first and only response is to lament what he had done to his good son: 'Oh, my follies! Then Edgar was abused. / Kind gods, forgive me that, and prosper him!' Now, deserted and blind, accompanied by a seeming beggar, Gloucester sees no alternative other than to end his pitiable existence.

Edgar, with all the fibre of his being, wants to do something about his father's philosophical and personal despair. That despair is inimical to Edgar's stoical approach to understanding the existential nature of human life; one must endure, one must come to terms with the world as it really exists, one must not give up. As Samuel Beckett so eloquently puts the idea, centuries later: 'I can't go on, I'll go on'. But how is Edgar to help his father find something approaching this great truth? Gloucester is an old dog, and Edgar knows what you can and cannot teach an old dog.

Edgar's answer is to invent an entire cosmic mythology for his father. Guiding him to a place where the blind father believes that he can throw himself down a cliff to his death (4.6), Edgar allows the 'suicide' to proceed. Actually, Gloucester is nowhere near the edge of a cliff; he is on some flat terrain, or, in theatrical terms, he is in the middle of the Elizabethan stage. He throws himself forward and lands on his face. Edgar, adopting a new accent and a new character, fictionalizes what has just happened. The old man, he says, has somehow managed to survive a huge fall; his life is 'a miracle'. Some monstrous creature at the top of the cliff, a creature whose eyes are 'two full moons' and whose face possesses 'a thousand noses, / Horns whelked and waved like the enridgèd sea,' has encouraged Gloucester to jump. Edgar pronounces his verdict: 'It was some fiend'. The father accepts all this and concludes, with Edgar's help, that he has been miraculously preserved because the gods have protected him and wish him to live until nature reclaims him in a natural death. Gloucester accedes to this wisdom: 'Henceforth I'll bear / Affliction till it do cry out itself / "Enough, enough" and die'.

Edgar has fashioned an elaborate lie for his father. The lie is not even very convincing to us, with its laughable exaggerations of a thousand noses and such. We see what Edgar is doing: he is playing god. He is inventing gods and devils to people Gloucester's imagination with a psychologically necessary if entirely bogus mythology. Like the compassionate doctor in Henrick Ibsen's *The Wild Duck*, Edgar knows that some emotionally crippled individuals need stories to live by, even if they are absurd. Most of us, in fact, need a crutch, a mythology, a dream to keep us going. Because Edgar wants his father to see his suicide attempt as impious in the largest sense, not as an offence against suppositious gods but as an offence against life itself, he invents a poem, a lie, a religion. He does so compassionately because he wants his father to find resignation. To the extent that anyone could succeed at this, Edgar succeeds.

Edgar's strictures against the dangers of a feeling of entitlement apply tellingly to King Lear. His folly, from the start, is that he believes the world and the gods owe him a lot. His daughters owe him obedience and love because of all that he has done for them. Servants like Oswald owe him unquestioning fealty. The gods owe him their benison and support because, like them, he is old and a monarch. Lear is rather like a child, expecting all his needs to be met instantly. As king, Lear is especially prone to this sense of entitlement, for he has enjoyed absolute power all his life. Belief in self-entitlement is, for monarchs, an occupational hazard.

The Fool is wise enough to know this. Many if not most of his gnomic witticisms are directed at Lear for expecting kind treatment when he has given up the authority to be able to demand kindness. As the Fool says, by abdicating his throne Lear has 'banished two on's daughters' – that is, he has turned over authority to them, alienating them by giving them the capacity to be heartless. Lear resists the cruel teaching he does not want to hear. When Goneril turns against him, insisting that he disfurnish himself of most of his retinue of followers, Lear pins his hopes on Regan. The Fool knows what will come of this: Lear's other daughter is 'as like this as a crab's like an apple' – Regan is as like Goneril as two crab apples are like each other. Any fool can see what Lear cannot see.

Lear's blindness to harsh realities is a product of his reliance on a mythology like the one that fails the Earl of Gloucester. In Lear's traditional and patriarchal cosmos, the gods are old men like him. They care about order and degree; they punish insubordination. The trouble is, of course, that in this play nothing of the sort happens until, possibly, the end. How is Lear to learn this hard lesson? Can he learn, or is he too old and too stubborn? The Fool playfully engages with the problem, for he appears to love the old man. In the main, though, nothing can get through to Lear except the appalling misery to which he is subjected in the storm.

Experiencing the storm first brings rage and ranting – 'Blow, winds, and crack your cheeks!' – as though Lear's shouting could do anything to lessen the heartbreaking irony that he, rather than his enemies, is being beaten upon by the storm. When, on the other hand, the tempest in his mind overmasters his sanity, a remarkable thing begins to happen. For the first time, seeing that his companions are wet too, he feels sorry for them. He begins to learn compassion through his own suffering. In his madness, he expresses this idea in paradox: 'The art of our necessities is strange, / And can make vile things precious'. The paradoxes of this astonishing play, interchanging madness and sanity, blindness and seeing, all derive from Lear's experience in the storm. Only through suffering, it seems, can he begin to comprehend the condition of other mortals. Only thus, in madness, can he begin to know himself.

The precious wisdom thus gained at such a terrible price gains in intensity as Lear applies it to the large questions of justice. Lear sees that suffering is widespread and that he has been complacently neglectful – he, who as king could have done something about poverty and inequality. 'Oh, I have ta'en / Too little care of this!' he chides himself.

> Take physic, pomp;
> Expose thyself to feel what wretches feel,
> That thou mayst shake the superflux to them
> And show the heavens more just.
> (3.4.33–6)

Lear's vision here is both utopian and revolutionary. It proposes that kingship be administered a stiff dose of a purgative drug so that the wealth of the complacently rich may be wrested from them and distributed to the poor. Only thus can divine justice be shown to exist. The image is of wealth as excrement ('flux' here means a fluid discharge from the bowels), forced from the body politic by a violent emetic and thereby scattered where it may fertilize the human landscape.

The idea is at once immensely attractive and impossible. What could be more commonsense than to perceive that some privileged folk have more money than is good for them, since money corrupts the soul, whereas many other people are in dire need, so that the obvious solution is a redistribution of wealth? The Earl of Gloucester says something closely parallel when, as a broken and blinded old man intent on suicide, he gives his purse to the seeming beggar Edgar, and thereby, without realizing he is doing so, restores Edgar's birthright to him. Here is Gloucester's prayer as he gives the purse:

> That I am wretched
> Makes thee the happier. Heavens, deal so still!
> Let the superfluous and lust-dieted man,
> That slaves your ordinance, that will not see
> Because he does not feel, feel your pow'r quickly!
> So distribution should undo excess
> And each man have enough.
>
> (4.1.64–70)

Gloucester's utopian vision is essentially that of Lear: take money from those insolent mortals who abuse it through corrupted appetite and insensitivity to social injustice, and distribute it to the poor so that each person will have 'enough'. That ideal of moderation and sufficiency for all is the essence of all utopias. It mocks us because we know that it will never happen, despite the certainty that all humans would be the better for it.

In *King Lear*, this vision of a better world offers a critique of the world as it exists, even though little or nothing can be done to improve things. The virtuous characters keep hoping for a turn for the better that will show the gods to be caring after all. 'This shows you are above, / You justicers', Albany triumphantly apostrophizes the gods, 'that these our nether crimes / So speedily can venge!' He is celebrating the news of Cornwall's death as just retribution for his having blinded Gloucester. But what then of Gloucester's eyes? How can that injustice be explained? Each time that a character utters a hopeful statement, something intervenes to pull the rug out from under him.

Cordelia, silent, victimized, utterly decent and loyal, chooses not to express herself in terms of philosophical questioning. Yet the very fact of her being who she is offers a refutation to Edmund's cynical premise that an existential universe demands ruthless and unconscionable action. Cordelia is good because that is who she is. She forgives her father and helps him back to sanity, much as Edgar forgives his father and rescues him from his despair. Cordelia dies, unjustly, when even the villain (Edmund) who has ordered her execution relents and tries to save her life. Her death seems so gratuitous. Nonetheless, the play suggests a kind of tragic necessity in that terrible event. Having lost all the other titles and dignities to which he has long been accustomed, having lost his very sanity for a time, Lear belatedly discovers a precious truth: he is father to a daughter who appears to forgive him, unworthy as he sees himself of being forgiven. This discovery atones for everything: as he goes off to prison with Cordelia, Lear is happy for the first and only time in the play. Yet the existential world that Shakespeare has created around King Lear will not allow him to have Cordelia. This is not mere cruelty on the part of that world, which is simply indifferent to him rather than hostile. The reason that Lear is denied Cordelia at last is that he cherishes her too much, as his right to a belated bit of happiness. He stakes his very being on having her; she makes everything all right. Edgar could have told him the stark truth: to depend on something like that for one's happiness is to give hostages to fortune.

Much happens at the end of the play to support a hypothesis that crimes will eventually be punished. Cornwall, Goneril, Regan, Oswald, Edmund – they all come to seemingly instructive ends. One of the most tenacious myths of our culture is that evil will eventually undo itself, as plainly happens in Shakespeare's earlier *Richard III*. Does *King Lear* support such a reading of human history, however? The devastation encompasses most of the virtuous characters along with the villains. Only Albany and Edgar survive – Edgar perhaps especially because he has become so clear-sighted as to how to cope with existential nightmare. Whether any divine agency of retribution is at work in bringing about the eventual punishment of evil in *King Lear* is endlessly problematic. Yet certain human values are greatly prized in this play, as something by which to live or die as circumstances require. One can try to practise the compassion and loyalty of Edgar, Kent, and Cordelia because, in the play's terms, it is better to be like them than to be Goneril, Regan, Edmund, or Cornwall. The price of being good may be fearfully high, but one has a choice.

The play in which Shakespeare most intently puzzles out the great question of personal choice is *Macbeth*. Can we choose our destinies, or are the essential features of our lives determined even before we act? The puzzle is a paradox, and, like all such paradoxes, dwells in the realm of absolute contradiction. We have free choice and we do not have free choice. What could be clearer than that? At some point, contradictions like this take on the character of a religious mystery, to be understood spiritually in a way that human reason cannot adequately formulate.

Indeed, paradox and riddle are at the heart of any religion worthy of the name. At its highest reach, religious truth deals in perceptions and spiritual states that go beyond ordinary human understanding.

Macbeth's puzzle is not unlike that of Oedipus in Sophocles' great play, who must try to understand how it is that, by fleeing from his homeland in an attempt to evade the terms of a prophecy declaring that he would kill his father and marry with his mother, Oedipus has managed to do exactly what the prophecy said he would do. He has made deliberate choices at every turn, and his choices turn out to be those required by fate. Character is fate: the way Oedipus thinks about problem-solving dictates how he will go about solving his own crime and punishing himself for it. Oedipus is the author of his own tragedy. His journey to someplace else brings him right back to where he began life. His quest for the man who murders his father and sleeps with his mother turns out to be a quest for his own identity. These puzzles can never really be explained, and Oedipus makes no attempt to explain them. His noblest quality, perhaps, it that he believes ultimately in the gods' justice and does not blame them for his tragedy, even though our logical minds keep asking if he was not framed.

Macbeth commits the terrible crime of killing a wise king who has been especially generous to Macbeth. The murderer is fully aware of the heinousness of his crime. King Duncan's virtues 'Will plead like angels, trumpet-tongued, against / The deep damnation of his taking-off' (1.7). Like Claudius in *Hamlet*, Macbeth knows that he is about to commit a crime that offends every idea of civilized decency: Duncan is king, is a good man, and is Macbeth's guest, so that the crime is at once a regicide, a murder, and a brutal violation of the sacred obligations of hospitality. 'He's here in double trust,' Macbeth acknowledges in soliloquy. 'First, as I am his kinsman and his subject, / Strong both against the deed; then, as his host, / Who should against his murderer shut the door, / Not bear the knife myself.' Raised in a Christian culture, Macbeth sees every reason not to do the deed. In favour of proceeding he can find no argument other than his own 'vaulting ambition', which he knows to be a kind of pride, the deadliest of the Deadly Sins. And yet he goes ahead and does it.

Something is compelling Macbeth to act against his better judgement. The pride of ambition dwells within him, of course, and is a facet of that fallen condition to which we all are heir since Adam and Eve, but it is also given exterior and objective form in the three Weird Sisters and in

Plate 5 Macbeth greeting the three sisters, from Holinshed's *The firste Volume of the Chronicles of England, Scotlande and Irelande*, 1577. The Bodleian Library, University of Oxford, Douce H. 240, Vol. I.

Macbeth's wife. As witches, the Weird Sisters appear to have some considerable control over the natural world. They can raise storms at sea in order to revenge themselves on sailors whose wives have ill-advisedly insulted the witches. One of them has collected the thumb of a shipwrecked victim. They can sail in a sieve. They pronounce ominous charms. In their cauldron they concoct a veritable witches' brew of disgusting things like eye of newt and toe of frog. They cannot actually bend a human heart to accede to something that it refuses to countenance, but they can mightily affect the circumstances in which human choices will be made.

Can the Weird Sisters also see the future, and can they determine it? There's the puzzle. When they first appear to Macbeth and Banquo upon the heath (1.3) and all-hail Macbeth as Thane of Glamis, Thane of Cawdor, and one 'that shalt be king hereafter', Banquo certainly is intrigued by their apparent ability to predict. 'If you can look into the seeds of time / And say which grain will grow and which will not', he bids them, 'Speak then to me.' They oblige by informing him, in a series of paradoxes, that he is 'Lesser than Macbeth, and greater' in that he will 'get kings', i.e., beget future monarchs, though he will not be a king himself. All this turns out to be true. Is their knowledge supernatural?

The answer has to be yes. Arguably, the Weird Sisters might have some way of knowing that Macbeth, the Thane of Glamis, has already been named to be Thane of Cawdor in the place of the gentleman who has just lost his head fighting treasonably against his king and country. This is not, strictly speaking, a prediction, since we know it has already happened even if Macbeth and Banquo do not. Conceivably, the Weird Sisters may know that their chances of tempting Macbeth to seize the throne by murder are good if they can lay this temptation in his way. They cannot, however, know that Banquo will not be king but that his children will be kings, unless they can read the future. And their ability to do so has grave consequences for the play, as in the case of *Oedipus*: what they have predicted must come true. The future is, by some means, already determined.

The hand of Providence in such a determined future is enigmatic at best. Providence seems not to intervene directly in human affairs, whereas the witches are allowed free licence to tempt Macbeth beyond the limits of his ability to withstand. Lady Macbeth is also instrumental in the temptation; her agency is human, theirs supernatural. Why is evil allowed such wide scope to tempt Macbeth? Why does Providence allow the murder of a virtuous king? John Milton might provide an answer, as set forth later in his *Paradise Lost, Paradise Regained*, and *Areopagitica*, that goodness remains a 'fugitive and cloistered virtue' unless it is tested, and that accordingly we are to understand the vicissitudes of temptation as practised by the devil with the sufferance of God; if Adam and Eve were not given freedom to choose between good and evil, their obedience to God would be involuntary and meaningless. *Macbeth* offers no such redeemingly cosmic explanation of the necessity of evil. That is one reason why *Macbeth* is such a dark play.

According to the teaching of the Christian church in medieval and early modern times, the devil is of course a potent and omnipresent tempter but cannot implant evil into a human heart without the willingness of that person to listen to insidious counsel. The devil must be summoned if he is to find an apt pupil. One thing we learn about Macbeth is that he and his wife have conversed about the idea of killing Duncan well before Macbeth encounters the Weird Sisters. When Macbeth makes his last attempt to persuade his wife that they should not proceed against a king who has shown them such favour, she cuts off his protestations with a reminder that the idea of the murder was his in the first place. 'What beast was't, then, / That made you break this enterprise to me?' she demands. 'When you durst do it, then you were a man.' 'Nor time nor place / Did then adhere, and yet you would make both. / They now have made themselves' (1.7). We are not told when or where this happened, but the circumstances are graphically detailed. Macbeth and his wife appear to have had a plan that he nearly acted on, except that the time and the place were not ideal.

If, as appears to be the case, Macbeth conceived of and plotted the murder of Duncan before the Weird Sisters spoke with him, then we can understand how they sensed that they had a ripe opportunity in him. The minor devil in C. S. Lewis's *The Screwtape Letters* knows this; the devil comes to us when we are being mean or vengeful or just catty. So does Mephistopheles in Christopher Marlowe's *Doctor Faustus,* who candidly explains to Doctor Faustus that he has come not because the doctor knew magically how to conjure him up but because the devil comes to anyone in spiritual difficulties. Summoning the devil, it turns out, is the easiest thing in the world.

What freedom of action did Macbeth have, then, to kill Duncan or not kill him? We hear him debating the issue as though his life depended on it, since in fact he knows that the life of his very soul is at stake. Can he make any other choice than to kill Duncan? The witches have known that it will happen. Is this simply because they know their man, know his inclination to commit a crime he has long contemplated? Need they do anything more than provide the vastly tempting circumstances of Duncan's having decided, at this critical moment, to pay a state visit to Dunsinane and sleep under Macbeth's roof?

Lady Macbeth knows nothing of the Weird Sisters. Yet she comes in uncannily on their side, at a critical point in the timing of Macbeth's temptation, and is indeed instrumental in shaping his final decision. How are we to understand this intervention as part of the process through which a predetermined action of murder will be taken? She is driven by her own very human desires for the power and social prominence that she hopes to gain through her husband's new royal rank. Clearly the motivations of both husband and wife are a product of their own personal inclinations and beliefs. They see themselves as able to choose. Yet the choices that they make are somehow a part of a supernatural plan. Or so it seems.

The working out of their lives after they have gained power through murder emphatically underscores a pattern of supernatural accountability. Macbeth knows all too well that justice will demand an account of regicides and murderers, both in this world and the next. Even if one were willing to 'jump the life to come', he reflects, 'in these cases / We still have judgement here, that we but teach / Bloody instructions, which, being taught, return / To plague th'inventor' (1.7). Killing a king teaches others how to do the same. He knows too that he will never sleep soundly again after murdering Duncan, that he cannot undo the crime once it is done, and that 'all great Neptune's ocean' cannot 'wash this blood / Clean from my hand'. His bloody hand will, instead, 'The multitudinous seas incarnadine, / Making the green one red'. The hyperbole is deliberate; Duncan's blood cannot literally turn the world's oceans red, but the blood will remain indelible in Macbeth's guilty imagination. His wife, conversely, sees this as not a problem: 'A little water clears us of this deed' (2.2). He is right about this and she is wrong. She will become a victim of her attempts to repress the horror, becoming a sleepwalker, unable to escape the nightmare of what she has done, compulsively attempting to cleanse her polluted hands: 'Out, damned spot!' (5.1). Macbeth retains his sanity in a way, though he becomes manic as Banquo's forces start to close in on Dunsinane Castle. He and his wife have drifted apart; he is not with her when she takes her own life.

Prophecy continues to haunt Macbeth with the spectre of seeming choice that turns out to be no real choice. Determined to know his fate, he goes one last time to the Weird Sisters and is shown a dismal pageant of three apparitions. The first warns him to 'beware Macduff'. The second bids him to 'be bloody, bold, and resolute', and laugh to scorn the power of his enemies, since he need fear 'none of woman born'. Macbeth exultingly draws from this what seems to be the logical conclusion, that he need not fear Macduff or anyone if he is bloody enough. The third apparition promises that he will never be vanquished until 'Great Birnam wood' comes 'to high Dunsinane Hill' against him. To be sure, the third apparition also shows him a line of monarchs descending from Banquo to James I rather than from Macbeth himself – a prospect of a distant future so devoid of hope for Macbeth that he is appalled and frightened. At least he knows what he must do in fulfillment of the second prophecy: surprise the castle of Macduff and slay his wife and children. Yet this atrocity ultimately backfires, by spurring on armed resistance to his tyranny. Macbeth persuades himself that he is safe for the moment, but we understand that his apparent choices aimed at self-preservation are all illusory.

The betrayal of his hopes through 'th' equivocation of the fiend', revealing at last that Macduff is technically not 'of woman born' since he was delivered through Caesarian section, and that Birnam Wood can indeed march against Dunsinane when Macduff's soldiers hew down

Plate 6 James I by John de Critz, before 1641. © National Maritime Museum, London.

boughs with which to camouflage themselves, recalls for us what Banquo knew from his and Macbeth's first meeting with the Weird Sisters:

> oftentimes to win us to our harm
> The instruments of darkness tell us truths,
> Win us with honest trifles, to betray's
> In deepest consequence.
>   (1.3.123–6)

Evil equivocates with Macbeth, and wins by tempting him with the prospect of a success that is, by its very nature, illusory, since it is won through foul means.

The play of *Macbeth* does offer some reassurance that evil, even if it can do its terrible work in the hearts of those who are somehow destined to fall prey to temptation, will ultimately go down to defeat. The utter desolation at the end of *King Lear* is not to be found in *Macbeth*. Political and moral order is brought back to Scotland; Macbeth will be reviled throughout history as a bloody tyrant. As Queen Isabella says in Marlowe's *Edward II*, 'Murder cannot be hid'. Duncan will be remembered as a good and kindly king; so too the English monarch who can miraculously cure the 'King's evil' with the touch of his hand, and who lends support to a moral crusade against tyranny in Scotland. Banquo nobly demonstrates for us how to resist insidious temptation: he is tempted, like Macbeth, and he is honest enough to know that as a human being he is frail and vulnerable, but he also knows his spiritual enemy and is on guard.

Yet despite these reassurances, the play is shatteringly disturbing. Macbeth and his wife are the major figures, and we are drawn to them despite the unsettling signs of moral and spiritual malaise. No one in the play speaks in more eloquent poetry than does Macbeth; no one understands the large issues of spiritual peril more keenly than he; no one is better able to predict the terrible consequences of acceding to temptation. Yet this thoughtful, intelligent man makes the choice that he knows will destroy him. The choice is inevitable since it is foreknown by the powers of darkness. How can we say that they do not choose for him? As Hamlet might have said, 'Ay, there's the rub'. There's the consideration that 'Must give us pause'.

CHAPTER SEVEN

◆

Modern Instances

*Misogyny, Jealousy, Pessimism,
and Midlife Crisis*

*Set me as a seal upon thine heart, as a seal upon thine arm: for love is
strong as death; jealousy is cruel as the grave.*

The Song of Solomon, 8.6

*Oh, beware, my lord, of jealousy.
It is the green-eyed monster, which doth mock
The meat it feeds on.*

Othello, 3.3

Not until the late stages of the human life cycle dramatized in Shakespeare's plays do we encounter the fullest consequences of human perversity. Shakespeare's romantic comedies of the 1590s found a way around human failure toward harmony and reconciliation; his history plays, though aware of the disastrous consequences of political and social failure, moved forward in the later 1590s toward an image of personal and political success in *Henry V*. Plays like *Measure for Measure, Hamlet, King Lear*, and *Macbeth*, on the other hand, engage with human failure in personal and cosmic terms and with an intensity not found in the earlier plays.

In *Othello* (*c.* 1603–4) and *Antony and Cleopatra* (1606–7), Shakespeare focuses on particular dilemmas of human sexuality, notably jealousy and midlife crisis. These dilemmas are especially acute in middle age, when men and women marry only to discover how immensely difficult it can be to sustain a mutual and trusting relationship. The earlier comedies look at courtship before marriage; only in his later years does Shakespeare take a hard look at marriage itself. Claudius and Gertrude are married in *Hamlet*, of course, as are Macbeth and Lady Macbeth, but these marriages are hardly calculated to reassure audiences about the sanctity of the institution, and in any event marital difficulty between the partners is not primarily at issue. In fact, Claudius and Gertrude get along quite well until Hamlet intervenes; and in *Macbeth*, husband and wife collaborate in murdering Duncan with an intimacy that comes of years of domesticity.

The phrase 'Oh, curse of marriage' is a leitmotif in *Othello*. It occurs at a critical point in Othello's new marriage with Desdemona. Heretofore untroubled by thoughts of jealousy, blissfully happy with her, Othello suddenly finds himself overwhelmed with doubt. Perhaps his attractive young wife is being unfaithful to him after all. What has brought on this attack of jealousy? In soliloquy, Othello analyzes what might be the ingredients of such an unhappy situation:

> Haply, for I am black
> And have not those soft parts of conversation
> That chamberers have, or for I am declined
> Into the vale of years – yet that's not much –
> She's gone. I am abused, and my relief
> Must be to loathe her. Oh, curse of marriage,
> That we can call these delicate creatures ours
> And not their appetites!
>
> (3.3.279–86)

As Othello reasons with the prospect, he considers his race and his age. Might Desdemona be disenchanted with him, after the first excitement of being in love with a person of a different race and colour? Might she long for a mate of her own social background? And might she prefer a lover nearer her own age? Othello sees himself as only somewhat advanced in age, but still older than, say, Cassio. Desdemona may not yet be twenty years old, though we are not told her exact age; he is an experienced warrior, a veteran. Is that the problem?

What is so dismaying about the soliloquy is that Othello is so certain of his newly discovered unhappiness. 'She's gone. I am abused.' It has happened. Yet nothing has in fact happened other than that Iago, Othello's resourceful ensign or junior officer, has warned Othello to cast a wary eye on his wife. Iago has presented no evidence, only a hypothesis. That hypothesis does indeed contain in it the elements that now worry

Othello, especially his being black and his wife a white woman. When Othello himself has raised the issue of miscegenation as a potentially inherent difficulty in his marriage, by pondering, 'And yet, how nature erring from itself –' Iago has been quick to follow up on this insidious line of reasoning:

> Ay, there's the point! As – to be bold with you –
> Not to affect many proposèd matches
> Of her own clime, complexion, and degree,
> Whereto we see in all things nature tends –
> Foh! One may smell in such a will most rank,
> Foul disproportion, thoughts unnatural.
>
> (3.3.244–9)

Iago has the evil genius to know that this imagined picture of Desdemona as 'unnatural' in choosing to marry a black man, when she might better have followed 'nature' by marrying her own kind, is sure to trouble Othello where he is most emotionally vulnerable.

Yet Othello has not struck us as emotionally vulnerable. In his dealings with Desdemona's father and the Venetian senate, Othello is the embodiment of calm, dignity, and gentle reasonableness. He has chosen Desdemona with eyes wide open, and, until Iago gets to work on him, Othello trusts his wife implicitly. Indeed, when Iago first raises the question of jealousy, when he introduces the term into their conversation ('Oh, beware, my lord, of jealousy'), Othello's defence of Desdemona and of his own choice of her is serenely confident:

> Exchange me for a goat
> When I shall turn the business of my soul
> To such exsufflicate and blown surmises
> Matching thy inference. 'Tis not to make me jealous
> To say my wife is fair, feeds well, loves company,
> Is free of speech, sings, plays, and dances well;
> Where virtue is, these are more virtuous.
>
> (3.3.194–200)

A special poignancy about *Othello* is that it is all about the destructive effects of sexual jealousy and yet it contains, in this speech, one of the most noble and eloquent descriptions of marital happiness to be found anywhere in the Shakespeare canon. Othello knows exactly why he is happy and why he need not fear marriage. He knows that Desdemona is attractive to other men; that attractiveness is part of what is so wonderful about her. Her love of dancing and vivacious company bespeaks the warm vitality that he cherishes in her. So long as she is virtuous – something he has no reason to doubt at this point – her *joie de vivre* is all the more commendable.

Othello seems to understand jealousy perfectly, and he will have nothing to do with it. Not for him are the fears experienced by too many husbands prompting them to guard their wives from the gaze of other males. Othello is proud of Desdemona's openness to others beside himself. Her physicality, her beauty, her love of pleasure do not awaken in him – not yet, at any rate – the anxiety that those qualities might be expended illicitly in an intimate relationship with some other man. Othello's male ego seems, in this speech, not so fragile as to worry that his own defects may drive Desdemona into the arms of another lover. He is happily married because he is at peace with her sexuality; it does not threaten him.

How is it possible that the confident Othello of this speech becomes the shattered, wife-loathing husband who can cry, 'Oh, curse of marriage' only some eighty lines later in the same scene? This, I take it, is the puzzle that Shakespeare sets before us in this play about marriage and jealousy. In order to come up with some tentative answers to such a baffling question, we need to look at Othello and Desdemona at the start of the play and ask what it is about their relationship, and especially about him, that might help explain why such a confident husband can turn out to be a jealous murderer.

Othello is an imposing, majestic, charismatic man. To be sure, the play begins with some terrible racist epithets at his expense, calculated to diminish his stature as someone scarcely human. Iago and his despicable sidekick Roderigo refer to Othello as 'the thick-lips', 'an old black ram' who is 'tupping' a 'white ewe' (that is to say, Brabantio's white daughter Desdemona), and a 'Barbary horse' whose animalistic coupling with Desdemona will beget a generation of creatures half human and half animal. Desdemona, in the language of these villainous men, has surrendered her virginity 'To the gross clasps of a lascivious Moor', and has made a 'gross revolt' by her elopement with Othello. These terrible defamations are the utterances of men we quickly learn to despise and mistrust; yet what they say is bound to leave its mark. The play's first description of the elopement is that it is unnatural, even sodomistic (in that it entails the coupling of animals and humans). Brabantio, the kindly old father of Desdemona, quickly agrees: 'This accident is not unlike my dream' (1.1). He arrests Othello for having practised damnable enchantment, since to Brabantio the prospect is unthinkable that his daughter would otherwise have run 'to the sooty bosom / Of such a thing as thou' (1.2).

Othello refutes these terrible insinuations, partly by simply being who he is and partly by the extraordinary power of his simple eloquence. His military career bears witness to great bravery and to endurance under harsh conditions. His description to the Venetian senate of his wooing of Desdemona (1.3) reveals him to have been an attractive and indeed amazing person whom Brabantio was eager to invite into his house so that the old man might listen to Othello's fabulous travel accounts. Desdemona was plainly fascinated, too; she kept coming into the room to 'Devour up' Othello's discourse 'with a greedy ear'. Having heard only parts of it, she asked Othello to recount his whole story to her in private. Her response showed unmistakably that she was drawn to Othello by his manliness, his courage, his greatness:

> My story being done,
> She gave me for my pains a world of sighs.
> She swore, in faith, 'twas strange, 'twas passing strange,
> 'Twas pitiful, 'twas wondrous pitiful.
> She wished she had not heard it, yet she wished
> That heaven had made her such a man. She thanked me,
> And bade me, if I had a friend that loved her,
> I should but teach him how to tell my story,
> And that would woo her.

Othello could not fail to hear in these words a tactful invitation that he proceed to matters of the heart:

> Upon this hint I spake.
> She loved me for the dangers I had passed,
> And I loved her that she did pity them.
> This only is the witchcraft I have used.
>   (1.3.160–72)

At the end of this remarkable narrative, the Duke of Venice is utterly convinced, as are we, that the interchange of vows was innocent of any wrongdoing. 'I think this tale would win my daughter too,' he affirms.

Only one aspect of this remarkable narration gives cause for concern, and even this does not trouble us until later on when the jealous infection has begun. Othello's reasons for being attracted to Desdemona are decidedly masculine. He was flattered by the attentions of a beautiful and well-born young woman. She provided an admirable audience. He came into her life as the man of action and experience, and she responded with fascination and an avid desire 'That heaven had made her such a man'. These words seem to invite a dual meaning: she wished that heaven had created a man like that whom she could cherish as her husband, and she wished that she could somehow have been a man like that herself. Both readings must have seemed intensely flattering to Othello: that she should wish to admire him so, and that his life so inspired her that she could hope to partake of his adventures. He sees in their marriage a chance for both things: he will tell her of his exploits to gain her lasting admiration, and he will take her with him to Cyprus. There he will show her what the soldier's life is like. He will call her 'my warrior'.

Othello sees their relationship as reciprocal along a sharply delineated line of gendered difference: as a male he will encounter dangers for her, and she as a woman will love and pity him for being a hero. 'She loved me for the dangers I had passed,' he says, 'And I loved her that she did pity them'. Men need the admiration of the women they cherish and protect; women love to admire the men who offer this protection. Othello loves Desdemona because she makes him feel wonderful about himself. It is the classic relationship of Mars and Venus as interpreted by many Renaissance authors: the soldier and the lady, the hero and his grateful, admiring dependant. His manliness shelters her; her beauty and soft graces adorn his life and give meaning to it. The male attitude in this, as expressed by Othello, is self-regarding. It also contains in it the potential for tragic failure: if the woman ceases to admire the man, or if the man simply ceases to believe that she loves him, then all is lost for him. As Othello later says, when he thinks this has happened, 'Othello's occupation's gone'. The world may be a man's world, but the men in it are extraordinarily vulnerable in their need for being admired. A woman has the power, real or imagined, to destroy a man's happiness simply by demonstrating to him that he is not loved and may therefore be unlovable.

You might think that this need for admiration is mutual in marriage, and no doubt it is to a significant extent, but Desdemona simply does not talk in these terms about her love for Othello. She never describes how

Othello has listened to her or admired her. Her reason for loving Othello is that she has come to admire him.

> My heart's subdued
> Even to the very quality of my lord.
> I saw Othello's visage in his mind,
> And to his honours and his valiant parts
> Did I my soul and fortunes consecrate.
>
> (1.3.253–7)

Othello was drawn to Desdemona initially because she admired him; she was drawn to Othello out of admiration for him. Yet the identity of situation is not at all an identity of motive or feeling. Both manifestations of feeling are directed from Desdemona and toward Othello.

Desdemona, in the passage just quoted, calls Othello her 'lord'. The term is significant. Like Portia in *The Merchant of Venice*, she bestows everything on her husband when she marries him: her love, her independence, and whatever fortune her heartbroken father will allow her; she has no other means to take with her, in any case. As she points out, 'That I did love the Moor to live with him, / My downright violence and storm of fortunes / May trumpet to the world'. Hers was no easy choice; she is fully aware of the hazards of social ostracism and, more importantly, rejection by her father. The choice was not easy for Othello, either; as he explains to Iago, 'But that I love the gentle Desdemona, / I would not my unhousèd free condition / Put into circumscription and confine / For the seas' worth'. Othello comes from a royal family ('I fetch my life and being / From men of royal siege', he tells Iago), and even if his elopement with a white patrician woman might seem presumptuous to some, in his view the marriage has required sacrifice and commitment on his part. Still, Desdemona's commitment brings with it a condition of willing self-subjection: Othello will henceforth be her 'lord'. She is accustomed to being dutiful to men: her father was heretofore her 'lord of duty', so that in elopement with Othello she has sought not freedom but a new obligation.

Othello and Desdemona seem overwhelmingly happy with each other as they arrive at Cyprus on separate vessels and are reunited. Othello is so much taken with her that he even loves her teasing and wheedling when she pleads with him to reinstate Cassio, who has been cashiered for drinking and fighting on watch. At the very moment when Iago is about to begin his temptation, Othello is still completely in love with Desdemona. 'Excellent wretch!' he exclaims as she leaves him alone with Iago. 'Perdition catch my soul / But I do love thee! And when I love thee not, / Chaos is come again' (3.3). Othello does not mean this as some kind of warning that things might fall apart in his marriage; he means simply that he cannot imagine an existence without her. He and Desdemona may be different in many ways, but the differences of male and female are complementary with them, as they ought to be. *Vive la différence!*

How then is Iago able to succeed in ruining a marriage that is so blissful? Iago is a driven man. He is jealous without cause in his own marriage, and is so, as his wife Emilia lucidly explains, because jealousy is a condition of his very existence. Men are 'jealous for they're jealous,' she tells Desdemona, and she has every reason to know. What is jealousy, after all? Shakespeare fascinates us with the question. It is 'the green-eyed monster which doth mock / The meat it feeds on', that is, it torments the heart of the person who suffers it and feeds on that person's innards. Jealousy can be rationally caused, of course, and is so in this play, as for instance when Bianca, Cassio's kept woman, is jealous that he may stray into other women's beds. Her fears are not unfounded; Cassio regards her as his chattel, attractive and useful during his tour of duty in Cyprus, but not a woman he would ever think of marrying. The idea is laughable to him. Other jealousies, however, can be pathological, arising generally in men out of irrational fears of a lack of male potency or attractiveness to women. This sort of jealousy is a helpless fear of being cuckolded because, in one's inmost heart, one knows that one deserves to be cuckolded. Such a man is Iago.

One of the symptoms of sick jealousy like this is that it craves company. The suffering jealous male needs to see other males in just his pitiable condition. By definition, such a man hates women. They are the ones who can reduce men to self-loathing and ridicule by cuckolding them. Women are frighteningly powerful, and must be destroyed. Men must take vengeance for what women have done to them. Feelings of this sort are obviously irrational and not often clearly enunciated or understood by the men who suffer these afflictions. That is why Emilia's definition seems so perfectly self-explanatory: men are jealous because they are jealous.

Something has happened, at the time *Othello* starts, to provoke Iago into a rage. Clearly he is a bitterly resentful man, and yet he has managed to function quite well on a social level. For some years he has served Othello, whom he hates, as his junior officer, biding his time. 'I follow him to serve my turn upon him', Iago confides to Roderigo. Whatever this ominous phrase means, it points toward some fearful vengeance, evidently as a payback for the insufferable indignity of having to take orders from a superior officer who is also black. Why does Iago lash out now? Two events suggest themselves, as we saw briefly in Chapter 2: first, Iago has been passed over for promotion in favour of Michael Cassio, and second, Othello has married Desdemona. Both events seem to have exacerbated Iago's jealousy past enduring.

That Iago should feel envy toward Cassio in being passed over for promotion is, at first, understandable as a plausible human response. Iago sees his failed case for promotion as a matter of cynical politics: Cassio has better friends in high places, and he has long enjoyed the friendship of Othello, so that the promotion is simply a matter of favouritism. Cassio is, moreover, good-looking, and he is a staff officer who knows how to please his commanding officer with his 'prattle', whereas Iago is a field officer, experienced in battle but not so adept at courtly shenanigans. Iago sees himself as a victim of the old game in which hardworking field officers are passed over for promotion in favour of men who practise courtliness. This is an understandable resentment, and is something we might properly call 'envy' rather than jealousy.

Yet we soon begin to suspect that Iago's feeling is one of jealousy as well. Iago is stung by demonstrations of Othello preferring Cassio to him, Iago. A kind of sibling rivalry is at work; the parental figure, in bestowing his favour on Cassio, is rejecting Iago. The fact that Iago hates Othello does not change this situation much. Iago still feels rejected. And the same feeling emerges in his response to the marriage. Why should the marriage mean anything to him? Why, increasingly in the play, does Iago want to kill Desdemona? What has she done to him? One possible answer is that she has married Othello. Once again, Iago has been left out. He has no intention of allowing this snub to go by unrevenged.

Iago's racist hatred for blacks gives him both a motivation for wanting to destroy Othello's happiness and a means of proceeding to do so. All that Iago need do is to insinuate to Othello that Desdemona hates him because he is too old for her, and because he is black. Iago, who hates blacks and hates Othello, must find a way of prompting Othello also to hate what is black in himself, since that blackness presumably would make him unlovable and dirty in Desdemona's eyes. One might suppose that such an undertaking would not be easy, since Othello is proud of his black heritage. Yet the play suggests that Othello is ready to hate himself when goaded to do so by the seeming evidence of his having lost the love of Desdemona.

The term 'Moor' used to describe Othello in the play's title and at various points in the text might seem to suggest that he is a Muslim and an Arab rather than belonging to the Negro race; the point is sometimes argued. Shakespeare may indeed have had a somewhat imprecise sense of the racial identity of people from the north of Africa, few if any of whom he had ever actually seen. Still, we should not be misled by these imprecisions. The term 'Moor' might be applied to Africans generally. Moors were commonly supposed in Shakespeare's time to have been mostly black or very swarthy (though the existence of 'white Moors' was also recognized). Hence the term 'Moor' was widely used as a synonym for 'Negro'. The title figure of Shakespeare's play is referred to as 'black Othello'. He himself uses the adjective to describe his skin colour. Various speakers describe him as having thick lips, staring eyes that roll menacingly, and a 'sooty bosom'. In any case, it is this blackness that Iago successfully turns against Othello by teaching him to think about blackness and racial difference as most Venetians think about these things.

Iago succeeds in part because he is such a brilliant and resourceful manipulator of language, and because he knows where Othello is vulnerable. His method is to use logic; his tool is the syllogism. He tries his logic out first on Roderigo. Beginning with a racist premise – that Moors are 'changeable in their wills' – Iago argues from this that Othello will soon tire of Desdemona. A relationship that began in violence cannot endure long. She for her part will also tire, because young women too by their very nature long for a partner their own age. 'She must change for youth; when she is sated with his body, she will find the error of her choice. She must have change, she must' (1.3). Nature itself 'will instruct her in it and compel her to some second choice'. Iago then moves on to his next logical step. 'Now, sir, this granted – as it is a most pregnant and unforced position – who stands so eminent in the degree of this fortune as Cassio does?' (2.1). Ergo, Desdemona must fall in love with Cassio.

There is nothing wrong with the syllogistic structure of Iago's argument, other than its low premise. This premise is that men and women have appetites. Desdemona is a woman; therefore she has appetites. 'Blessed fig's end!' Iago exclaims. 'The wine she drinks is made of grapes.' All is unassailably demonstrated except for two hidden assumptions: first, that 'appetite' must lead to illicit carnal desire, and second that such appetite is characteristic of all men and women. If Desdemona is not like all other women (as, clearly, she is not), then any defamatory generalization about women cannot be held to apply necessarily to her.

At the base of Iago's derogatory premise about human nature is his assumption that it is only 'natural' for young men and women to seek out their own age and race. 'Unnaturalness' is at the heart of Iago's insulting characterization of the elopement as bestial: it is not 'natural' for blacks and whites to have sex together. Desdemona's father Brabantio lamentably succumbs to this specious line of reasoning: since it is inconceivable 'For nature so preposterously to err', he is convinced that Desdemona must have been drugged or enchanted. Again, we see the warped logic of conclusions derived from racist premises. These kinds of argument are most fatal when they are adopted, at Iago's prompting, by Othello himself.

'And yet, how nature erring from itself –' The word 'yet' gives away Othello's acceptance of a seemingly logical proof. If nature 'in all things tends' to avoid miscegenated marriages, then what Desdemona has done is a wilful act of 'Foul disproportion, thoughts unnatural'. Once Othello has acceded to this false premise and its consequent arguments about her, his faith in her dies. His fear of his unworthiness grows into a hatred of her for causing him to feel unloved.

At the height of his unhappiness, Othello betrays a number of ways in which his fear and hatred of his wife are related to his feelings about his own parents. When the handkerchief that he gave Desdemona appears to be lost (though in fact it is now in Iago's possession and will be used terribly as specious evidence that she gave it to Cassio), Othello tells his frightened wife what the handkerchief means to him:

> That handkercher
> Did an Egyptian to my mother give.
> She was a charmer, and could almost read
> The thoughts of people. She told her, while she kept it
> 'Twould make her amiable and subdue my father
> Entirely to her love, but if she lost it
> Or made a gift of it, my father's eye
> Should hold her loathèd and his spirits should hunt
> After new fancies.
>
> (3.4.57–65)

The handkerchief, Othello insists, possessed a magical power by which the mother could hold Othello's father to his marital obligation; without it, he would turn away from her and seek some other companion. The implications of Othello's loss of love for Desdemona in the present instance are unmistakable. Othello's family history is, to him, a story of male fear of the woman and a need to break away from her unless she can tie him to her by a magical spell. 'There's magic in the web of it,' he says of the handkerchief. Marriage is a kind of enslavement of the male against his better judgement.

Othello's most bitter denunciation of Desdemona is that she has betrayed and unmanned him just as his mother did his father, and that his recourse must be to retaliate. She has inflicted upon him the shame of being labelled a cuckold, and thus to be 'A fixèd figure for the time of scorn / To point his slow and moving finger at'. Yet even this is not the worst; he could bear that if it were all.

> But there where I have garnered up my heart,
> Where either I must live or bear no life,
> The fountain from the which my current runs
> Or else dries up – to be discarded thence!
>   (4.2.59–62)

In his diseased imagination, Othello is sure that Desdemona has 'discarded' him.

Othello is persuaded that he can no longer receive life-giving sustenance at 'The fountain from the which my current runs / Or else dries up'. The implied generalization here about women embraces Desdemona and Othello's mother. Othello seems to anticipate Freud's idea that a man marries in order to recover the lost mother who sent him out into the world some time ago; a forbidden, incestuous desire for the mother's body is transferred allowably onto another, younger woman. By having sex with her, he enters once again, vicariously, the maternal body from which he was ejected. He finds once again the nurturing warmth needed to assure him that he is a lovable person.[1] Othello compares his feelings about his wife and his mother in just these terms. To the vast extent that Othello now bases his whole happiness on the protective nurturing that a woman can offer, moreover, he places himself at the mercy of the woman and her power to discard him. This is what Othello is convinced that Desdemona has done. Once he is persuaded of this, he needs very little 'evidence' to go ahead and act on his certainty.

Iago's insidious success in making Othello irrationally jealous forms a bond of hatred between them. Iago has found another male to share his own spiritual torment, and he has proven to his satisfaction that other men are, like him, prone to this unhappiness. He has won what jealous children want: he has won Othello back from Desdemona. Bound together in hate, Iago and Othello can now join in destroying the hated enemy: woman. Othello thinks he is killing an adulteress. Iago knows that she is innocent and pure; and that is why she must die. As a refutation of his low premise about all women, she must die.

Iago cannot succeed in destroying Othello without Othello's cooperation; as in *Macbeth*, the devil's work cannot proceed without the victim's willing compliance. That is why, in Iago's master plan, Othello must kill Desdemona with his own hands. He does so. Yet a countermovement in the play's final action separates the two men from each other in a crucial redeeming move for Othello. Having killed his wife, Othello must now learn, from Emilia, that his wife was innocent. Emilia loses her life in daring to confront her husband Iago, whom she now finally realizes to be the villain she has suspected. This is another crucially recuperating move at the play's end. Iago's villainy stands fully exposed for all to see, and as a consequence he is to be punished to the full extent of the law by the Venetian state. Othello now understands fully the enormity of Iago's crime and his own terrible act. Even more importantly, he knows the truth about Desdemona.

Too late to recover her and the blissful happiness he has thrown away, Othello nonetheless recovers his faith in her innocence. He understands that his hatred of her and his fear of women were the features of a nightmare from which he now awakens. He takes his own life as expiation. He is a greatly tragic figure because, like Oedipus, he is so wisely able to judge and sentence himself and then carry out that sentence. He accepts the blame for his failure and sets himself up as a public example:

> When you shall these unlucky deeds relate,
> Speak of me as I am; nothing extenuate,
> Nor set down aught in malice. Then must you speak
> Of one that loved not wisely but too well;
> Of one not easily jealous, but, being wrought,
> Perplexed in the extreme.
>
> (5.2.351–6)

In the battle of good and evil contending for his soul, Othello now realizes, Desdemona has represented the good and Iago the evil. 'Oh, the more angel she!' cries Emilia in her grief for her dead mistress. Desdemona, insists Emilia, was 'heavenly true'. Iago, conversely, is called a 'devil', a 'viper', and a 'demi-devil'. Othello hyperbolically looks down at Iago's feet to see if he has cloven hoofs as the devil is fabled to have. Iago is not the devil, of course, any more than Desdemona is literally an angel. Iago is a man; that is what is so terrifying, that a human could be so like the devil.

Othello too is a 'devil' to Emilia, and he himself wonders if his soul will not merit being hurled from heaven for fiends to snatch at it. 'Whip me, ye devils, / From the possession of this heavenly sight! / Blow me about in winds! Roast me in sulfur! / Wash me in steep-down gulfs of liquid fire!' Yet he too is a human being, not a devil, and he is capable of genuine remorse as Iago is not. Othello's soul struggle has such emotional impact on us because the cosmic dimensions of the conflict are so all-embracing, as in *Macbeth*. The story is at once deeply human and universal.

Antony and Cleopatra, Shakespeare's other great love tragedy of his mature career (*Romeo and Juliet* being much earlier), does not engage with the concepts of good and evil. As in the earlier plays based on Roman and Greek history (*Julius Caesar, Troilus and Cressida*), Shakespeare finds classical civilization liberating. The mores of Christian culture apply only indirectly and inferentially if at all. In questions of political struggle, and above all in matters of sexuality and pleasure-seeking, *Antony and Cleopatra* translates us into the alien and fascinating worlds of ancient Rome and Egypt. Here Shakespeare is able to examine issues of adultery and hedonism in ways that would not be feasible in an early modern European setting. This is not to privilege one over the other, or to claim that Shakespeare endorses the liberation of the psyche in a pagan context. It is to suggest instead how much he delights in varying approaches to the large questions of personal choice and moral behaviour. The unfamiliar world of *Antony and Cleopatra* is set in dialogue and debate with the more explicitly Christian worlds of *Hamlet, Othello*, and *Macbeth*.

Antony stands between two worlds. He revels with Cleopatra in Egypt, and yet part of him is intensely Roman. 'A Roman thought hath struck him', Cleopatra observes, when the arrival of a messenger from Rome has, for the moment, banished Antony's mirth. The play's opening scene, set in Egypt, brilliantly juxtaposes Antony's two worlds for us. He enters in procession with Cleopatra and her glittering entourage of fan-bearing eunuchs and exotic ladies. Evidently Antony is drunk. We are invited to observe this spectacle through the disapproving gaze of two Roman soldiers, one newly arrived from Rome, the other explaining to him what has been going on in Alexandria. 'Look, where they come', says the soldier who has been in Egypt for a while with Antony. 'Take but good note, and you shall see in him / The triple pillar of the world transformed / Into a strumpet's fool.' To the speaker, this sad picture shows the decline of a great warrior into sensual enslavement. Antony's goodly eyes, 'That o'er the files and musters of the war / Have glowed like plated Mars, now bend, now turn / The office and devotion of their view / Upon a tawny front'. Antony has become 'the bellows and the fan / To cool a gypsy's lust'. He has evidently forgotten the great Roman truths, that one must 'know oneself' (*nosce teipsum*) and that one must practise moderation. Antony's self-indulgent behaviour 'O'erflows the measure'.

This is the Roman view of greatness: self-discipline, moderation, moral probity, and attention to duty. Shakespeare derives the view in good part from his major source for this play, Plutarch's Life of Antony in his *Parallel Lives*. In Plutarch's estimation, Antony is a clear example of tragic failure. A great general has allowed himself to be conquered by his sexual desire for a woman. Cleopatra is admittedly no ordinary woman; Plutarch's description of her first meeting with Antony, which Shakespeare versifies nearly word for word, freely grants that she is supremely skillful at being seductive. One can understand why a man would hunger after her. Still, that is all the more reason for the man to be on his guard. Temptations are there to be overcome in the name of moral duty and love of the Roman state. Having failed to observe this call of duty, the once-great Antony is now no more than a shadow of his former self.

This Roman perspective is highly moral and principled. The lack of a Christian perspective does not mean that morality is irrelevant. Pagan culture at its highest, in ancient Rome, is fully capable of devising its own strict moral standards without Christian revelation. What is more, Antony accepts and endorses this Roman morality. When he awakens in the morning after a night of revelling with Cleopatra, he is generally ashamed of his over-indulgence and neglect of duty. When messengers arrive from Rome, his own malfeasance is borne in upon him and he finds himself having to apologize for his behaviour to those messengers and to Antony's fellow-triumvir who sent them, Octavius Caesar. In response to such promptings of guiltiness, Antony returns to Rome, patches up his quarrel with Octavius, and confirms an alliance between them by marrying Octavius's sister.

Egypt is indeed, from the Roman perspective, a place of enervation and licence. Cleopatra's ladies-in-waiting, Charmian and the rest, vie with one another in dreaming of how many lovers they might take and how many children they might bear. 'Oh, excellent!' exclaims Charmian. 'I love long life better than figs.' They jest bawdily about men's sexual anatomies; Iras, when asked amusedly where she would choose to have her 'inch of fortune', replies, 'Not in my husband's nose' (1.2). The penis would be a better place to have her husband endowed with an adequate size. This is all very strange, and yet it is captivating. Egypt possesses a kind of vitality that is infectious. And Cleopatra is supremely vital.

Cleopatra knows how to tease Antony, to keep him on tenterhooks. She loves practical jokes, like arranging for a diver to attach a salted, dead fish covertly to Antony's fishing line in the water, so that she can laugh at him when he reels in his catch and wants to brag to her of his prowess. She boasts to Charmian of her wiliness in playing with her man by incessantly crossing his moods; to Charmian's anxious warning that Cleopatra should give in to Antony instead of irritating him, Cleopatra replies, 'Thou teachest like a fool: the way to lose him'.

Cleopatra is, as Enobarbus admiringly describes her to his fellow Romans, a woman of 'infinite variety'. She knows how to stage herself like a goddess, as when she first appears to Antony in a barge on the River Cydnus. She masterfully arranges all the opulent details: the poop of beaten gold, the purple sails, the oars of silver, the flute music, the 'pretty dimpled boys' on each side of her 'like smiling Cupids' with 'divers-coloured fans'. Though she is past her younger days – her 'salad days', as she calls them – she knows how to compensate for any physical effects of ageing by surrounding herself with impressive props. Most of all, she knows how to be resourceful in varying her pleasures.

> Other women cloy
> The appetites they feed, but she makes hungry
> Where most she satisfies; for vilest things
> Become themselves in her, that the holy priests
> Bless her when she is riggish.
>
> (2.2.246–50)

Cleopatra is paradox, and as such she partakes of a kind of divine mystery. She is an incarnation of the Lucretian Venus, an impossible contradiction of holiness and eroticism that prompts even the 'holy priests' of the temple to bless her when she is 'riggish' or lustful. To Enobarbus, at least, sexuality in her is transcendent, metaphysical. She is a strange goddess like the Isis (often mentioned in the play) whom the Egyptians worship, wife of her own brother Osiris and symbolic of the female reproductive power of nature.

Antony is, by this analogy, the Osiris to Cleopatra's Isis; that is, he can aspire to represent the male reproductive principle in nature. He is also, in a recurrent image in the play, the Mars to Cleopatra's Venus. This enduring myth could be interpreted in two divergent ways in the Renaissance, however. In one version, Mars is the manly, heroic figure protecting the woman, while she provides beauty and soft graces with which to adorn his life – much the way Othello imagines himself at first in relation to Desdemona. In a contrasting interpretation, Mars is besottedly enslaved to the woman's beauty, emasculated by her charm and no longer a great warrior. Other legends alluded to in this play incorporate the same idea: as a great follower of his ancestor Hercules, Antony is the heroic achiever of astonishing deeds, but at times his behaviour invites comparison with the Hercules whom the Amazonian Omphale, Queen of Lydia, enslaved and set to work at her loom while she assumed his lion skin and club. (Compare the scene, 2.5, in which Antony is described as drunkenly allowing himself to be dressed up in Cleopatra's intimate garments, her 'tires and mantles', while she 'wore his sword Philippan'.)

The Roman officers to whom Enobarbus describes the wondrous variety of Cleopatra are bedazzled by what they hear, and pruriently curious (as are we); they long to see, even if they know they must not touch. Octavius Caesar, on the other hand, is revulsed by the reports coming out of Egypt. Antony is said to 'tumble in the bed of Ptolemy' and 'reel the streets at noon', losing all dignity, while Rome and the triumvirate are endangered by the threat mounted by Sextus Pompeius, would-be inheritor of the Republican mantle of his great forbear, Pompey the Great. Octavius is repelled by sensual enervation, and prefers to remember Antony's great days as a fearless warrior. Octavius becomes the chief spokesman for the Roman point of view, and it is a perspective that is openly hostile to Egypt and Cleopatra.

Much can be said in favour of the Roman point of view. Antony's story, read from the Plutarchan vantage point, is one of nearly uninterrupted decline. He is losing power quickly in the Middle East, the part of the world assigned to him in the division of the triumvirate. Octavius rules over Europe, and Lepidus over Africa; Antony is supposed to reign supreme in the Middle East. Yet even his own commanders in the area are disillusioned. Ventidius, having won a great victory on Antony's behalf over Pacorus in Parthia, knows that he dare not succeed too well lest he awaken Antony's envy; such men as Antony like to take credit for what their subordinates accomplish for them. To smooth over his differences with Octavius, Antony agrees to marry Octavia, but then deserts her for Cleopatra. (Shakespeare greatly shortens the time required for this desertion to take place, thereby accentuating Antony's disloyalty to his marriage vows.) Once back with Cleopatra and now at war with Octavius, Antony disastrously follows her advice at Actium, agreeing to fight at sea rather than on land where he is stronger, and turning tail in the midst of the sea fight when she retreats in panic. Antony knows that he should not have given her command in the first place, and certainly should not have allowed himself to be towed after her as if tied to her rudder. As one of his commanders, Scarus, puts it, 'I never saw an action of such shame. / Experience, manhood, honour, ne'er before / Did violate so itself.' Back in Egypt, Antony finds that his men are deserting him, even the officer who means most to him personally, Enobarbus.

Today we might say that Antony is experiencing a midlife crisis. His compulsive gambling with his own happiness, his infidelity to his marriage, his taking huge risks to prove to himself his own manliness, his mercurial changes of mood, all suggest a response characteristic of many men in their middle years to their own ageing and loss of physical and sexual prowess. Antony fears and resents Octavius in part because Octavius is a younger man. 'To the boy Caesar send this grizzled head, / And he will fill thy wishes to the brim / With principalities,' he caustically advises Cleopatra in response to an offer from Octavius that she yield Antony up and put herself in Octavius's protection. Antony sends a personal challenge to Octavius, prompting Enobarbus to conclude that Antony is unhinged. The instability, the panic, and the self-hatred all betray a fear of approaching decline and death.

Such a chronicle of incessant failure, for which Antony is directly responsible, would seem to bolster Plutarch's argument that Antony's story is a simple object lesson in which others may see the perils of enslavement to a woman. Yet *Antony and Cleopatra* becomes at last a tribute to the greatness of the lovers and a celebration of their mythic immortality as Isis and Osiris. How does Shakespeare accomplish this transformation, and why? One possible approach to the question is to ask who Octavius really is, and what he represents.

Octavius is the embodiment of the Roman virtue of attentiveness to duty. He is a workaholic, and never misses an opportunity to advance his own interests and those of his followers. By the same token, he is what we would call repressed. He drinks sparingly, if at all. When he tries the wine on board Pompey's ship off Misenum, he is distressed by the way it befuddles his intellect, even if only briefly. 'I could well forbear't,' he protests, as his companions become more and more drunk. 'It's monstrous labour when I wash my brain / And it grows fouler' (2.7). He is personally distressed by accounts of Antony in Egypt 'tippling with a slave' and engaging in fisticuffs 'With knaves that smell of sweat'. His recollections of the Antony he once admired are of a man who could withstand pain and hunger with almost masochistic self-discipline, crossing the Alps in winter and drinking 'the stale of horses' and eating 'strange flesh' for lack of other sustenance (1.4). This bracing, Spartan existence excites Octavius's imagination, whereas the thought of Egyptian sybaritism fills him with loathing. The Roman way of life has become, in Octavius, an obsession no less driving than Antony's lust for life. The true Roman ideal of 'nothing in excess' (compare the Greek *medan agan*) seems to have been lost in the battle of polarities.

Part and parcel of Octavius's obsessive pursuit of self-control and of worldly success is his deeply cynical view of women. He trusts women no more than he trusts alcohol; both represent the threat of loss of male control so aptly represented in the recurrent image of Hercules spinning for Omphale. The only woman that Octavius can care for at all is his sister, Octavia, whose very name, following Roman custom, betokens the extent to which she is a diminutive, feminized corollary to the male Octavius. A Roman woman's first duty is to the senior male head of her household and, when she is a married, to her husband. One sign among many of Antony's failures as a man, in Octavius's view, is that Antony let his first wife, Fulvia, conduct the affairs of that union and even don military gear to fight Antony's wars in his absence. As for Octavia, Octavius does love her as 'a great part of myself' (suggesting that his regard for her is really a form of self-regard), but such fondness is not enough to keep Octavius from using her calculatedly. He knowingly pushes her into a marriage that he wants and expects to fail, since he can then go to war with Antony for having dishonoured his sister. Such is the extent of his devotion to the most important woman in his life, and, so far as we know, the only person toward whom he has any feelings of domestic intimacy. Octavius is not married. Others may find time for that, but not he.

Toward Cleopatra, Octavius feels a contempt that borders on fear. He is profoundly cynical about all women, and most of all her. If, as he advises his follower Thidias, 'want will perjure / The ne'er-touched vestal', what cannot he obtain from Cleopatra once she can no longer rely on Antony for support and is at the mercy of Octavius's armies? 'Women are not / In their best fortunes strong', and Cleopatra is neither strong nor in a fortunate position. Octavius dispatches Thidias to entice Cleopatra with vaguely-worded offers. 'Promise, / And in our name, what she requires; add more, / From thine invention, offers' (3.12). Promise her anything you can think of. Thidias does so, and is ordered to be whipped by a furiously jealous Antony, who begins to suspect that Cleopatra might listen to Octavius's offers.

Might Cleopatra actually 'pack cards' with Octavius, as her lover fears? She has been loyal to Antony during his long absence in Rome and Athens, during which time he has married Octavia and begun to raise a family. Yet she has had famous lovers before, notably Pompey the Great and Julius Caesar. She is renowned as a seductress, and she is not getting any younger. Antony is clearly coming to the end of his career, if not of his life, while Octavius is the man of the hour. An accommodation with Octavius would enable Cleopatra to continue to rule in Egypt under his shroud, 'The universal landlord'. Why not? Cleopatra cagily does not tip her hand. In her conversation with Octavius's ambassador Thidias she leaves every possibility open; that is why Antony has Thidias whipped. Perhaps she is waiting to see just what Octavius has in mind.

Her stratagem of vamping one of Octavius's officers, Dollabella, to find out Octavius's plans for her strongly suggests that she is still considering her options. Like Charmian, or like Falstaff for that matter, Cleopatra loves life 'better than figs'. One's options are so restricted once one is dead. Yet there are limits; she is not interested in a life of servitude and humiliation. Once she learns the truth of what she has feared, that Octavius plans to lead her back to Rome in triumph, she knows at once that she will commit suicide rather than submit to indignity. She knows Octavius now for what he is. He is no man for her.

Octavius's plan to return to Rome with her as his captive is manifestly designed to overmaster the unruly woman who has enslaved Pompey, Julius Caesar, and Antony. Cleopatra is no doubt right in surmising that she and her women are to be shown to the Roman citizens, who, with their 'greasy aprons, rules, and hammers', will lift them up to the view. Ballad-writers and itinerant actors will lampoon her Egyptian revels (5.2).

Octavius wants to put Cleopatra back in her cage and thereby re-assert male mastery over female licentiousness. The processional entry into Rome will be a public relations triumph for him. It will also be a personal triumph, attesting to his having resisted and humiliated the very woman who, in his view, enslaved his one-time hero Antony. Octavius will be man on top.

Antony and Cleopatra suffer defeat and death. They lose to Octavius, and Antony for his part knows that he is to blame for his own terrible failures. Yet the last act of the play is triumphant in a way that a story of such failure might not seem to anticipate. Cleopatra presides over that last act, once Antony has died in her arms. His death is the result of a miscalculation for which she holds herself at least partly to blame; frightened by his loss of control and fury at her, she has feared for her life and has sent Antony word of her own death as a ruse to fend him off. He takes his own life in remorse, as she had partly feared. Their last moments together are moments of reconciliation and of concern for each other. They come together to be everlasting partners in death.

What they have dared to do, at the ruinous cost of failure and death, is just what Octavius has found most threatening to his own protective male ego: they have dared to be as much like each other as they know how to be. They do their best to transcend the barrier of gender that separates men from women. Cleopatra determines to die 'after the high Roman fashion', even if she employs a very Egyptian asp as death's agent. 'My resolution's placed', she tells her women, 'and I have nothing / Of woman in me. Now from head to foot / I am marble-constant.' Antony, for his part, embraces all that Egypt has come to mean for him, weeping for pardon, dreaming of an eternal life with Cleopatra where they will 'couch on flowers', hand in hand, to the envy of all the other ghosts in the Elysian Fields. Despite all that has happened to them, despite all their quarrels, he chooses her and is not afraid of her as woman. He is willing to be subsumed into her magnificent life force.

Cleopatra sees their end as a triumph over Octavius and all that he represents about repression of life's most vital spirit. The asp at her breast, if it could speak, would be able to 'call great Caesar ass / Unpolicied'. She has outwitted Octavius Caesar at his own game. He wanted to take her back to Rome, but all he can do now is bury her dead body. By agreeing to bury her together with Antony, he seems to concede that he has lost that game. The lovers will not be a subject of derision and moral disapproval: 'No grave upon the earth shall clip in it / A pair so famous,' he pronounces. Aided by the dramatist, Shakespeare, who has told their story in an immortal play, Antony will live in our imagination as a giant figure, one whose 'legs bestrid the ocean' and whose 'reared arm / Crested the world'. Cleopatra will be remembered as a royal figure, robed and crowned, embracing death as she triumphantly declares, 'I have / Immortal longings in me'. Antony and Cleopatra stand before us as humanly frail persons who have been redeemed by the power of poetry and by the daring of their unconventional eagerness to dissolve their separate identities in the paradox of oneness.

Antony and Cleopatra's attempt to transform themselves beyond the boundaries of gendered difference is all the more remarkable in the context of Shakespeare's dramatic depictions of sexuality in the other plays we have been exploring. In *Hamlet* and *King Lear*, sexual desire is too often the source of evil, and must yield place to friendship, or filial piety, or a servant's loyalty to a master, as the site of nurturing relationships. In *Macbeth*, marital intimacy is where temptation and male enslavement to evil begin. *Othello* portrays mutuality in marriage in glowing terms only to undermine happy desire with suspicion and hatred between the sexes. Othello's brief experience of loving a woman because she is attractive to other persons as well collapses into protective and fearful jealousy. Achieving a whole relationship, in which the partners can trust each other to surrender their autonomy in a mutual gesture of union, turns out to be extraordinarily difficult in Shakespeare's plays. Even the earlier comedies, despite their generally happy endings, find themselves at times nearly overwhelmed by misunderstanding and mutual mistrust. In this large context, what Antony and Cleopatra attempt is indeed extraordinary. They fail, but they are immortal because of what they tried. What is more, the distinctly alien culture of the ancient world in which they make this attempt may well be an essential part of what makes the whole story possible. Shakespeare finds, in the otherness of a culture so markedly unlike his own, a place of liberated imagination.

Before we speculate that Shakespeare has personally fought his way through to a new and wiser understanding of human sexuality and of the constraints of gender barriers, however, we need to consider the evidence of other late plays. The women in them are apt to be baleful figures, devouring, menacing, implacable. Lady Macbeth's ambition for her husband to become king is especially frightening because it is diabolical. 'Come, you spirits / That tend on mortal thoughts', she apostrophizes, 'unsex me here / And fill me from the crown to the toe top-full / Of direst cruelty!' She appears to be thinking of devils, of familiar spirits, of agents of evil not unlike the Weird Sisters. 'Come to my woman's breasts / And take my milk for gall, you murd'ring ministers' (1.5).

Lady Macbeth imagines herself feeding these demonic agents, just as witches feed familiar spirits or attendant demons, with their breasts; she substitutes this nourishment for the milk she might otherwise provide for her children. She has 'given suck', she claims at one point, though her marriage with Macbeth appears doomed to be childless; the former promise of childbearing has given way to an imagined intimately physical contact with devils. Her fantasized partners in this obscene intimacy are like succubi or incubae, renowned and feared as demonic beings that have sexual intercourse with humans in their sleep. Sexuality and evil are intertwined in the portrayal of Lady Macbeth as the devouring female presence who goads her husband into murdering Duncan by taunting him with unmanliness: 'When you durst do it, then you were a man'.

Macbeth cannot rule in his own household; the success of the murder depends on a domineering female presence. Macbeth's nemesis, Macduff, wins the battle between them at the end in part because he is not 'of woman born', having been delivered by Caesarian section. He owes nothing to the matronly mother who, in this frightening vision, brings males into the world and then disables them. Women are expunged from the final ordering of affairs in *Macbeth*.[2]

The domineering female is not a new presence in this play; she in fact is there from the start of Shakespeare's career. Joan of Arc, in *1 Henry VI*, offers to 'lop a member' of her body off and give it to her attendant fiends 'In earnest of further benefit', one that is plainly sexual. Joan's trafficking with the devil is further manifested by her donning men's apparel in order to defeat the English with her French forces. She temporarily overpowers the hero of the play, Lord Talbot, who recognizes her for the witch she is. 'Heavens, can you suffer hell so to prevail?' he implores, and eventually Joan is brought to account by the English and burned at the stake.

Talbot's relationship is altogether more cordial and chivalric with the Countess of Auvergne, who attempts to dominate him in the spirit of Tomyris, the heroic Amazonian Queen of the Massagetae, who reportedly slew Cyrus the Great and ordered his head to be placed in a wineskin filled with blood. In the present instance, Talbot is too resourceful and self-knowing to fall prey to the schemes of his would-be captor, and overwhelms her instead with courtly generosity. This episode of Talbot's successful encounter with a would-be dominating woman is an invention of Shakespeare's, added to show by contrast with the more prevailing pattern of gender relationships in these history plays that men and women can get along handsomely so long as they mutually agree that the man should be in charge. Especially if the woman is French.

Another threatening Frenchwoman in the early history plays, Margaret of Anjou, is not manifestly a witch, but she is no less scary as a towering feminine presence. Henry VI is captivated by her picture and becomes enslaved to her charms even before he has actually seen her. She, meantime, is involved in an intimate relationship with the Duke of Suffolk, who is so spellbound by her that he negotiates a disastrous marriage between her and the infatuated Henry VI so that Suffolk may have her close to him. The catastrophe of civil war, then, is set in motion in part by Henry VI's enervated and foolish attachment to a determined, managerial woman.

Throughout the *Henry VI* plays and *Richard III*, Margaret continues to be an ominous presence in England's affairs. When the press of battle proves too much for her mild-mannered and ineffectual royal husband, Margaret herself dresses and acts like a man, fighting Henry's battles for him. She calls savagely for revenge for the death of her kindred, especially her son Edward, and indeed is an active agent of that revenge: when, in *3 Henry VI*, she and her allies capture Richard Duke of York, scion of the Yorkist claim to the throne, Margaret mocks him with a paper crown, shows him a handkerchief that she has dipped in the blood of York's slaughtered young son Rutland, and joins with Clifford in stabbing Richard to death. Richard of York's condemnation of her before he dies reinforces the similarity between Margaret and Joan of Arc:

> She-wolf of France, but worse than wolves of France,
> Whose tongue more poisons than the adder's tooth!
> How ill-beseeming is it in thy sex
> To triumph like an Amazonian trull
> Upon their woes whom fortune captivates!
> (1.4.111–15)

In *Richard III*, though politically powerless now as the dowager queen of the defeated Henry VI, Margaret remains as a baleful presence, very much feared as a prophetess; and indeed her cursing helps shape the pathway to King Richard III's defeat.

The Scythian Queen Tamora in *Titus Andronicus* is another early instance of the terrifying Amazonian woman. The new emperor Saturninus is quickly enslaved to her will, even though she is a captive and even though Saturninus must sacrifice a far more politically advantageous match with the daughter of Andronicus in order to have Tamora. She pursues revenge against Titus for having slain her eldest son Alarbus in a ritual sacrifice, and eggs on her sons' lustful determination to rape Titus's daughter Lavinia, turning a deaf ear to Lavinia's pleading that she respect the chastity of a fellow-woman. She and her two remaining sons butcher Lavinia's husband, Bassianus. She manages the affairs of her compliant husband. Most tellingly, perhaps, she carries on a vigorous liaison with Aaron the Moor (who, like Othello, is black, not Arabic), and bears him a mulatto child. Animal sexual vitality is characteristic of Shakespeare's threatening females. That vitality is frequently demonic.

It should not surprise us, then, to encounter men in Shakespeare's plays who fear women as cuckolders and who seek desperately for mates whose appetites can be managed. 'Oh, curse of marriage', Othello laments, 'That we can call these delicate creatures ours / And not their appetites!' Othello's implicit assumption is that men own women and therefore ought to be able to control their appetites. Indeed, it is this claim of an unalienable right to own women's bodies that makes men afraid.

Posthumus Leonatus, the male lead in *Cymbeline*, holds the same opinion, and with similarly disastrous results. He has cherished Imogen as his wife, he tells us, primarily because she has seemed so timorous about sexual intercourse, even with him, her lawful husband:

> Me of my lawful pleasure she restrained
> And prayed me oft forbearance; did it with
> A pudency so rosy the sweet view on't
> Might well have warmed old Saturn, that I thought her
> As chaste as unsunned snow.
>
> (2.5.9–13)

Imogen's seemingly repressed sexuality actually excited desire in Posthumus, because it betokened her virgin pureness and her unlikeliness to wish to couple with another man.

Like many males, Posthumus is obsessed with sexual possessiveness. His punishment is to suffer terrible pangs of jealousy; though his wife is innocent, he is too ready to believe the worst of women, like Claudio in

Much Ado about Nothing or Othello in *Othello*. Iachimo, the villain of the play, is a tempter much like Iago, bent on revenge against women and urgently in need of recruiting other men into a companionship of hatred. Posthumus is easily led this way. He is half persuaded that his own mother must have been faithless to her husband and that he, Posthumus, is a bastard. 'Is there no way for men to be', he asks, 'but women / Must be half-workers?' He craves to expunge any element in him of femininity and to be beholden to no woman. Like Othello, he equates his presumably faithless wife with his mother, despite the fact that his mother 'seemed / The Dian of that time'.

This fear of bastardy runs throughout Shakespeare. It is a predictable fantasy of the male who is frightened by woman's 'appetite'. At times it can be humorously described, as when Falstaff, play-acting at being King Henry IV, admonishes his son (played by Prince Hal in his own person): 'That thou art my son I have partly thy mother's word, partly my own opinion, but chiefly a villainous trick of thine eye and a foolish hanging of thy nether lip that doth warrant me'. Benedick, in *Much Ado about Nothing*, jests with Leonato as to how he knows that the daughter given him by his wife was in fact his. A man cannot be biologically sure, in this early modern culture, who fathers his children; they are delivered from the womb of his wife, so they are plainly hers, but whose seed implanted the baby in that womb? The bastard Philip Faulconbridge in *King John* is sure that his putative father played no part when he, Philip, was engendered, and he is right: Richard Lionheart was the true father. Edmund, in *King Lear*, is proud to have been conceived out of wedlock in a moment of fierce passion rather than owing his existence to routine marital mating in 'a dull, stale, tirèd bed . . . 'tween asleep and wake'. This is a major reason why men in Shakespeare often regard the prospect of marriage as one of putting their heads in a noose.

The macho instinct for possessiveness of women can get men into serious trouble – trouble that they bring on themselves. Posthumus, in *Cymbeline*, makes the mistake of betting on his wife's chastity. Goaded by Iachimo, he enters into a bet that Imogen cannot be seduced. Iachimo takes the bet, visits Imogen during Posthumus's absence, and, though entirely unsuccessful in his attempts to seduce her, manages to enter her bedroom while she sleeps and to note down intimate personal effects that can persuade Posthumus that Iachimo has indeed slept with her. The bet was rash, and was prompted by a competitive rivalry among men to boast of their wives' chastity and obedience. Such a boast plainly bespeaks a need to assert masculine aggression: I am so manly that I can claim as my own the most beautiful woman in the world, who is more chastely loyal to me than any other man's wife or mistress. Such a wager can only lead to disaster. It did so earlier in Shakespeare's poem *The Rape of Lucrece* and, in a more comic version, at the end of *The Taming of the Shrew*.

Women in Shakespeare, especially in the very early and the late plays, are apt to be either seductresses or devouring female presences, or both. Volumnia, in *Coriolanus* (*c.* 1608), is the mother of the protagonist. She is the author of his life and, as it turns out, of his defeat and death as well. She embodies the legend of Althaea and her son Meleager, a story to which Shakespeare repeatedly alludes. When Althaea gave birth to her son, the Fates appeared to her and declared that the son should live only so long as a brand that was on the fire was not consumed. Snatching the brand from the fire, she preserved it carefully. Later, Meleager happened to quarrel with her brothers by taking sides against them over a great boar that Artemis had sent to ravage Calydon. When Althaea learned that her son had killed her brothers, she cast the fatal brand into the fire. As it consumed itself to ashes, Meleager fell dead. The legend is, in essence, a fantasy of maternal control over the life and death of the male child. Like some sort of terrifying goddess, the mother has the power to take back the life she first bestowed. The Fates are female. So are the Weird Sisters.

Volumnia wants her son to be like her. Like Lady Macbeth, she is frustrated by the lack of opportunity for advancement given exclusively to men in her culture, and resolves, by way of revenge, to control and destroy through a man that she can manipulate. In Volumnia's case, this is her son. We get some sense of how she has raised him from the way in which she encourages the manly aggressiveness of Coriolanus's young son Marcius. The child loves to run after butterflies, catch them and let them go repeatedly, and then tear them apart with his teeth. 'Oh, I warrant, how he mammocked it!' declares a friend, and Volumnia nods approvingly: 'One on 's father's moods' (1.3). She wants Marcius to grow up to be like his father.

Volumnia lives vicariously through her son's violent militarism. The bond between them is close – indeed, uncomfortably so. 'If my son were my husband', she ventures, 'I should freelier rejoice in that absence wherein he won honour than in the embracements of his bed where he would show most love.' This speech superimposes the son upon the husband in a way that is positively incestuous. What 'he' does she mean that claims the 'embracements' of the marital bed? Her son takes the place, in her imagination, of her husband. As such, he will show best devotion to her not by sex but by gaining honour in war.

Volumnia has trained her son to be a fighter. It is vitally important to her that she has borne a son, not a daughter. 'I sprang not more in joy at first hearing he was a man-child', she declares, 'than now in first seeing he had proved himself a man.' She is herself dauntingly masculine in her preference for blood rather than feminine graces. In her view, 'The breasts of Hecuba, / When she did suckle Hector, looked not lovelier / Than Hector's forehead when it spit forth blood / At Grecian sword, contemning'.

As her warrior son-husband, bringing home his trophies of victories as votive offerings to her, Coriolanus is a brilliant success. Intrepid, charismatic, contemptuous of fear, he manages war against the Volscians as no other general could do. His men forgive his abruptness because he is such an inspiring leader, willing to put his own life on the line. He in turn loves his best soldiers, saving his scorn for those who hold back in the battle. The trouble begins in the play when Volumnia decides, with other patricians of Rome, that Coriolanus is needed as a political leader to combat the growing authority of the people's tribunes.

Coriolanus knows that he is no politician. Short-tempered and vitriolic in his denunciation of human folly, he concedes that he lacks all semblance of ability to negotiate and compromise. 'Know, good mother', he pleads with Volumnia, 'I had rather be their servant in my way / Than sway with them in theirs' (2.1). He would rather serve the state his way, as soldier, than seek political power. He is right. Yet Volumnia insists on having her way.

When, after repeated protests against his autocratic manner by the tribunes and people, Coriolanus departs from Rome an exiled and embittered man, and takes up with his old enemy Aufidius in revenge against his ungrateful city of Rome, Coriolanus finds himself confronting an impossible paradox: to burn down Rome is to destroy his family, and, most perilously of all to him, his mother. Others plead with him in vain to spare the city; his mother alone prevails. He accedes; what else can he do? His career is in ruins, and his very life endangered by his violating of his vow to Aufidius to attack Rome, but to Coriolanus it appears that he has no choice. His mother has done this to him.

> O mother, mother!
> What have you done? Behold, the heavens do ope,

The gods look down, and this unnatural scene
They laugh at.

(5.3.182–5)

Why is it 'unnatural'? Partly, perhaps, because it shows so many strange inversions: the male controlled by the female, the enemy of Rome forced against his will to become the city's preserver, the ally of Aufidius now become a traitor to his vow. Partly, too, the scene is incestuous because the pull of motherhood suffocates him with Volumnia's insistence that he act as the man to whom she is wedded through their mother–child bond. Like Althaea's son, Coriolanus must serve her turn at the expense of his very life. Coriolanus sees what is grimly comic in this pitiable spectacle. Volumnia has demoted him, a supposedly grown man, to the status of being her child. If she is to live vicariously through him, he will be the sacrificial figure. Volumnia has, as it were, thrown the brand into the fire.

Coriolanus's demoted status as a punished child is underscored by Aufidius's contempt for his defection. 'Thou boy of tears!' he taunts Coriolanus. You cry-baby! The taunt does its work: Coriolanus can stand anything but to be called 'boy'. It denies his manhood, the essence of his being. Aufidius has his excuse at this point and cuts Coriolanus down, aided by others who are waiting for Coriolanus's fall. Yet it is his mother who has done this to him, in his own estimate. The mother has had the power to end his very existence by depriving him of his manhood.

Only one other Shakespearean tragedy ends as bitterly as this one. *Timon of Athens*, written perhaps about the same time as *Coriolanus* and left unfinished (and perhaps collaboratively written, with Thomas Middleton), embodies the sort of furious paranoia that can afflict human beings as they confront old age, declining potency, and a loss of hope for the future. Mainly the play is about ingratitude, about Timon's mounting anger at the forgetfulness of his friends when he finds himself in financial need. He is in straits because he has been overly generous to others – a circumstance they now conveniently forget. What appalls him most is that they see no obligation to repay his kindnesses to them. 'I am Misanthropos and hate mankind,' he concludes. The bitterness leads to exile, to renunciation of the entire human race, and to a lonely death virtually unmarked by an oblivious generation of ingrates.

In the centre of Timon's misanthropic, apocalyptic vision of the end of human society is his loathing of sexuality and the woman's reproductive capacity. Money and whoring are inseparably linked in his imagination. Money is 'damnèd earth' to him, a 'common whore of mankind'. It will prompt marriages with worn-out widows so eaten with disease that 'the spital house and ulcerous sores / Would cast the gorge at'. When he accidentally finds buried gold, he gladly bestows it on two prostitutes, Phrynia and Timandra, who happen upon his isolated cave. Like Lear, Timon curses humankind by wishing on it the diseases of wealth and venereal infection. 'Consumptions sow / In hollow bones of man!' he mockingly instructs the two women.

> Down with the nose,
> Down with it flat; take the bridge quite away
> Of him that, his particular to foresee,
> Smells from the general weal. Make curled-pate ruffians bald,
> And let the unscarred braggarts of the war
> Derive some pain from you.
>
> (4.3.153–64)

The consumptions he thus wishes on humanity are the wasting diseases of sexual commerce. Collapse of the nose and loss of hair are common symptoms of syphilis. Timon does not mean that only the two whores to whom he speaks are to blame, of course; he indicts all women, and he indicts men as their 'customers', even in the speciously legal game of marriage. 'Maid, to thy master's bed!' he cries. 'Thy mistress is o'the brothel.'

Timon's misogyny and misanthropy are thus all-embracing. He refuses to be reconciled even to his loyal and sympathetic servant, Flavius. He will not accept Apemantus's offer that they join together in mocking a bad world. Timon's assault on hypocrisy is devastating because of its breadth and universality. The corruptions of human life undo every semblance of order and decency.

> Piety and fear,
> Religion to the gods, peace, justice, truth,
> Domestic awe, night rest, and neighbourhood,
> Instruction, manners, mysteries, and trades,
> Degrees, observances, customs, and laws
> Decline to your confounding contraries,
> And yet confusion live!
>
> (4.1.15–21)

The last of Shakespeare's tragedies ends in nightmare and despair.

CHAPTER EIGHT

◆

The Lean and
Slippered Pantaloon

Ageing Fathers and their Daughters

*A father's love for a grown-up daughter is the most dangerous of all
infatuations.*

G. B. *Shaw*, Major Barbara, *act 2*

Although Shakespeare's preoccupation with fathers and daughters is lifelong, it gains a special intensity in his late tragedies and in the plays of
the years 1606–11, generally known as the romances. Throughout Shakespeare's career, the mother is usually absent. Baptista Minola has no wife
to help him find husbands for Bianca and Kate in *The Taming of the Shrew*.
The Duke of Milan, in *The Two Gentlemen of Verona*, struggles alone, as
a parent, to hinder the love-match of his daughter Sylvia with Valentine.
So too with Old Egeus and his daughter Hermia in *A Midsummer Night's
Dream*. Although Portia has no living mother or father in *The Merchant
of Venice*, her father is a towering presence in her memory, whereas the
mother is never mentioned. Shylock, in the same play, is deserted by his
daughter Jessica in an elopement; we learn the name of his wife, Leah,
but she has apparently been dead for some time. Leonato faces, without
a married partner, the crisis of a slander against his daughter Hero in *Much
Ado about Nothing*. Cressida in *Troilus and Cressida* is dependent on the
will of her father, and left to her own devices by him; the mother is
nowhere mentioned. In *All's Well That Ends Well*, the heroine often
remembers her physician father and his legacy to her of a medical cure;
we learn nothing of Helena's mother. In Shakespeare's early tragedy, *Titus
Andronicus*, Lavinia's extended family has no mother. (Queen Tamora,
who is a mother of two young men, is the exception that proves the rule:

as a mother, she is perfectly terrifying.) In many cases the family config-
uration lacking a mother is to be found in Shakespeare's sources, but that
is only to say that the motif is common in fictional narrative and that
Shakespeare found it compellingly attractive.

More instances suggest themselves. Glendower's Welsh daughter in *1
Henry IV* marries Lord Mortimer; how she was mothered we do not learn.
So too of Margaret in *1 Henry VI*, daughter of Reignier, Duke of Anjou.
Ophelia in *Hamlet* is emotionally dependent on her father and her
brother, as well she might be, having no living mother to whom she might
turn. And so on to Desdemona in *Othello*, the three daughters of King
Lear, Imogen in *Cymbeline*, and Miranda in *The Tempest*.

Pericles and *The Winter's Tale* are special cases. *Pericles* features two
daughters with highly visible fathers and absent mothers (Antiochus'
daughter and Thaisa) together with the play's heroine, Marina, whose
mother is presumed dead during the years of her growing up. (Still
another daughter, Philoten, daughter of the Governor of Tarsus and of
Dionyza his wife, does not actually appear in the play; Dionyza, like
Tamora in *Titus Andronicus*, is terrifying as a mother.) Perdita in *The
Winter's Tale* is, like Marina, dependent on her father because her mother
has apparently (though not actually) died. In both *Pericles* and *The
Winter's Tale* the family of father, mother, and daughter is reunited at last.

Otherwise, few exceptions are to be found to the almost universal
paucity of daughters with mothers. The exceptions are Juliet in *Romeo
and Juliet*, the Princess Elizabeth in *Richard III*, Katharine of France in
Henry V, Diana Capilet in *All's Well That Ends Well*, and Ann Page in *The
Merry Wives of Windsor*. Cassandra in *Troilus and Cressida* is the daughter of Priam and Hecuba, though Hecuba does not appear in the play.
Some of these are minor characters for whom the relation to the father is
not particularly at issue.

Possible explanations of this lifelong preoccupation with fathers and
daughters are varied. Theatre historians, noting the fact that female roles
were generally played by boy actors who were sometimes in short supply,
have wondered if Shakespeare simply lacked the theatrical resources to
bring on many mothers. This theory would not explain, however, why
mothers are so often not even mentioned, or are mentioned only glanc-
ingly. Absent mothers are not uncommon in Shakespeare's sources and
elsewhere in prose fiction (as in Dickens's *Little Dorrit*, *A Tale of Two
Cities*, and *Our Mutual Friend*, for example), suggesting that the pattern
is a convention of story-telling and folktale not limited to Shakespeare.[1]

MR. WILLIAM SHAKESPEARES

COMEDIES,
HISTORIES, &
TRAGEDIES.

Publifhed according to the True Originall Copies.

LONDON
Printed by Ifaac Iaggard, and Ed. Blount. 1623.

Plate 7 Engraved portrait of Shakespeare by Droeshout from *Mr. William Shakespeare's Comedies, Histories, and Tragedies*, 1623, the so-called First Folio. The Bodleian Library, Oxford, Arch. G.c.8.

Young men as well as young women often have dominant fathers but lack mothers in his plays: Prince Hal in the *Henry IV* saga is one of many.

Still, when we consider what Shakespeare does with fathers and daughters, we can begin to wonder if the relationship did not have for him a special and personal meaning. He was, after all, the father of two daughters and no living son after the death of Hamnet in 1596. His strong sense of the importance of progeny as a means of achieving a kind of immortality, depending primarily on the son (as in Shakespeare's Sonnets), could rely, after Hamnet's death, only on the daughters. Shakespeare may have had a special fondness for his elder daughter, Susanna; as we have seen, he bought for her and her physician husband, John Hall, a splendid house in Stratford. Most importantly, the late plays associate the father–daughter relationship with ageing and retirement. The marrying of the daughter to the younger man is not always an easy thing emotionally for the father. Prospero in *The Tempest* achieves this difficult transition gracefully, but in a way that suggests the conscious resolution of a problem that the dramatist has been mulling over for some time.

The relationship is often fraught with difficulties, as one would expect in plays; drama requires conflict. In the early comedies, like *A Midsummer Night's Dream*, the conflict is the conventional one of comedy going back to Plautus and Terence: the father objects to the daughter's romantic attachment. He need not give his reasons, as indeed Egeus does not; his will is law. Such fathers are blocking figures, placed in comedy to be outwitted and outmanoeuvred by clever young men and women. Jessica elopes in *The Merchant of Venice*. Juliet secretly marries Romeo. Bianca, in *The Taming of the Shrew*, displeases her father by her clandestine attachment to a young man (Lucentio) who appears to be a mere servant. The lovers Pyramus and Thisbe arrange a secret meeting in the Ovidian story that Shakespeare parodied so deliciously in *A Midsummer Night's Dream*. Sylvia's father in *The Two Gentlemen of Verona*, the Duke of Milan, does everything in his power to prevent her marriage to Valentine. These fathers represent the norms of parental authority, against which young love must strive because it is misunderstood. It is a necessary plot device more than an attempt to see deeply into the father–daughter relationship.

In *Othello*, on the other hand, the conflict is deep and hurtful. Desdemona knows that she has wounded her father's heart by her elopement with Othello. She is everything to Brabantio, all that he has left in life. In the presence of the Venetian senate, Brabantio asks his daughter a question that implies her absolute obligation to him: 'Do you perceive in all this noble company / Where most you owe obedience?' The postulated obligation is one that she accepts, though she goes on to explain how it is that she now must transfer her allegiance to a younger man:

> My noble father,
> I do perceive here a divided duty.
> To you I am bound for life and education;
> My life and education both do learn me
> How to respect you. You are the lord of duty;
> I am hitherto your daughter. But here's my husband,
> And so much duty as my mother showed
> To you, preferring you before her father,
> So much I challenge that I may profess
> Due to the Moor my lord.
>
> (1.3.182–91)

Marriage is, in this perspective, a rite of passage (so called by Arnold van Gennep) through which the woman moves from one patriarchal household to another, transferring her loyalties in the process to a younger man. It is an unsettling process, like all rites of passage. Desdemona's point is that it is also natural. She is accused of being romantically involved with a practitioner of witchcraft. Her answer is that her marriage to Othello, however unusual its particular circumstances of inter-racial coupling and the secrecy of elopement, is essentially what happens in any marriage. Her mother left *her* father to marry Brabantio; why should not she, Desdemona, leave her father to marry Othello? This is how the cycle of generations proceeds.

The trouble is that Brabantio cannot see it that way. Acknowledging that his daughter is already married and that he as father can do nothing to undo the tie, the old man resigns her to her husband with the worst grace possible. 'I here do give thee that with all my heart / Which, but thou hast already, with all my heart / I would keep from thee', he tells Othello. He warns the new husband that he had better keep a sharp eye on his wife, since, as the elopement proves, women are too often duplicitous: 'Look to her, Moor, if thou hast eyes to see. / She has deceived her father, and may thee.' This warning note comes back into Othello's mind, prompted by Iago, when he begins to be jealous of Desdemona. 'She did deceive her father, marrying you', Iago points out, and Othello can only agree: 'And so she did'.

Both fathers and younger men view themselves in *Othello* as the victims of women's wiles. The men are frightened, baffled, angry. The unexpected way in which Brabantio and Othello turn out to be so alike suggests that Brabantio is jealous. He has fended off other wooers of his daughter, even if, under the prospect of a miscegenated alliance, he allows belatedly that he would prefer even Roderigo to be his son-in-law rather than Othello. Desdemona has kept house for him. She has taken the place of his wife. They have lived together, received visitors together. Her departure is an unbearable shock. She learns later that her father has died of a broken heart: Gratiano's news from Venice is that 'Thy match was mortal to him'.

Cordelia is similarly on the verge of marriage at the start of *King Lear*. The giving of her hand in marriage by the father is complicated by the fact that she is being sought by two wooers, the Duke of Burgundy and the King of France. Lear appears ready to auction her off to the highest bidder, like Baptista Minola in *The Taming of the Shrew*. Yet Burgundy is not prepared to take her without a handsome part of the kingdom as a dowry, and Cordelia forfeits that dowry by her refusal to flatter Lear with hyperbolical promises of unending devotion. Why is she silent when Lear turns expectantly to her, his favourite daughter, after he has heard Goneril and Regan swear that their father to them is 'Dearer than eyesight, space, and liberty'? The question haunts us; our interpretation of the play depends on how we answer it.

Cordelia is about to marry. She is very like Desdemona, both in her unassailable virtue and in her strongminded view of what marriage means. It means leaving the father for another lord and master. Like Desdemona, Cordelia readily acknowledges what her father has provided for her. 'You have begot me, bred me, loved me.' She has no hesitation in granting that she owes him a special reverence for this. 'I / Return those duties back as are right fit, / Obey you, love you, and most honour you.' Yet marriage brings with it new obligations and loyalties:

> Why have my sisters husbands if they say
> They love you all? Haply, when I shall wed,
> That lord whose hand must take my plight shall carry
> Half my love with him, half my care and duty.
> Sure I shall never marry like my sisters
> To love my father all.
>
> (1.1.96–104)

The sadness is that Lear, like Brabantio, cannot see the wisdom and necessity of this. Cordelia has promised him half her love, and she means to abide by the agreement. That is enough; that is what a reasonable observer (Kent, for example) might call 'natural'. But it is not enough to satisfy Lear's self-blinded feelings of entitlement to all.

With wonderful insight, *King Lear* sees the problem of fathers and daughters from both sides. Lear is overwhelmed with feelings of ingratitude, at first toward Cordelia and then, in deadly earnest, toward Goneril and Regan. 'Ingratitude, thou marble-hearted fiend!', he lashes out at Goneril when she demands that he 'disquantity' his retinue of a hundred followers. 'How sharper than a serpent's tooth it is / To have a thankless child!' he cries (1.4). 'To take't again perforce! Monster ingratitude!' (1.5). When Regan insists that she will receive him with no more than twenty-five followers, he tries to argue her down by reminding her that 'I gave you all,' only to be cut off by her curt reply: 'And in good time you gave it' (2.4). Lear has an undoubted point: Goneril and Regan are indeed ungrateful.

Yet they have a point as well. Lear is autocratic and ceaselessly selfish. When he returns from hunting to Albany's castle in Scotland, he expects to find food on the table for himself and his entourage. Peter Brook's 1970 film based on the play uses the camera to visualize what it might actually be like to have a hundred knights and all their servants crowded into a medieval castle on top of the usual occupants. Clouds of dust, noise, quarreling, and crowding at tables are the inevitable consequence. One can well believe that Goneril is impatient with Lear for striking a gentleman of her household 'for chiding of his fool'. Ageing parents can be an intolerable burden. There appears to be some sense in the proposals of both Goneril and Regan that Lear might comfortably be attended to by servants in their households.

Yet we are aware that both daughters are finding excuses. Knowing from considerable experience that their father has 'ever but slenderly known himself' and that his habitual self-centredness is now exacerbated by 'the infirmity of his age', they have plotted together from the very start to deny him the privilege of a hundred knights to which they implicitly agreed by their statements of love and fealty; that benefit was a condition of the contract. They intend to stick together in hounding the old man until he leaves them alone.

The play resonates with us today because it deals so honestly with the seemingly impossible problem of what to do with ageing parents, especially when they grow personally difficult. Goneril and Regan know what they want to do: abandon Lear to whatever he can find elsewhere, be it in a place unprotected from the weather or in his grave. Their lives have no room for a tedious, disagreeable, dependent, and demanding old father.

Cordelia, who tried most honestly to make clear to her father her need for a new life of her own in marriage, has no hesitation in knowing what she must do when Lear is abandoned by her sisters. She must return to England and devote her life, if necessary, to caring for him. This is not what she wanted to do. It means leaving her husband; we never see them together after the first scene. It means invading England with a French army supplied by her husband, the French king, and thus engaging in a treasonous act against her native country. Most of all, it means sealing herself off from the rest of the world in the suffocating bond of a family relationship from which she hoped to escape through marriage. Yet she sees herself as having no choice. She tends to her father uncomplainingly, tenderly, lovingly. She offers the one thing that can restore his sanity, because his insanity is so much a product of his feeling that he has wronged Cordelia unforgivably. She can cure that affliction by her silent forgiveness, or, rather, by her letting him know that forgiveness is not even necessary. 'No cause, no cause,' she says with her simple eloquence, when her father, having just come back to sanity, admits that she might well have 'some cause' for hating him. Simply by being there when he awakens, Cordelia knows that she can provide Lear with the assurance of love that he is certain he has forfeited.

Cordelia does not manifest the same happiness as does her father when they are captured and sent to prison together. To Lear, being with her is all that matters now. He is ecstatic. She says only that she is concerned about his welfare. 'For thee, oppressèd king, I am cast down; / Myself could else outfrown false Fortune's frown' (5.3). Like Edgar, like Horatio in *Hamlet*, Cordelia finds what comfort she can in stoical indifference to hostile fortune. A life together with her father is not what she would have bargained for, if it ever occurred to her to bargain with life. The too-close dependence on Cordelia sustains him, but, as we have seen, cannot be his for long because he wants it too badly, craves it as his right to happiness. Cordelia is too wise to rest her hopes on such a fragile proposition that one deserves to be fortunate. She is thus the necessary sacrifice.

The muted note of incestuous attachment in Lear's or Brabantio's clinging to their daughters is only a kind of whisper; it is incestuous solely in the sense that Freud uses the term to characterize such an overly dependent relationship between father and daughter (or mother and son). The attachment is 'erotic' only to the extent that one's whole emotional being is engaged and that physical separation is an agony. In *Pericles*, on the other hand, incest is real. Antiochus, King of Antioch, lives in secret incestuous pleasure with his daughter. One of Pericles' first tests, as the wandering hero of this romance, is to solve the riddle of Antiochus's incest. Pericles has arrived at the palace of Antioch in search of a bride. Like Bassanio in *The Merchant of Venice*, he must compete for the prize of the princess's hand in marriage by answering a riddle. The penalty for failure is death. The princess is thus like the golden apples in the Garden of the Hesperides, handsome but 'dangerous to be touched' and guarded by 'deathlike dragons'. The riddle is as follows:

> I am no viper, yet I feed
> On mother's flesh which did me breed.
> I sought a husband, in which labour
> I found that kindness in a father.
> He's father, son, and husband mild;
> I mother, wife, and yet his child.
>   (1.1.65–70)

As a riddle, this one is not tough to solve. It speaks from the point of view of the daughter, for whom Antiochus is at once father and husband; she, as his child, is also his wife and prospective mother of his children. Incest famously complicates family relationships in this way: her own son will be her brother, and so on. She consumes and destroys her own mother by sleeping with her father. As Pericles puts it, in soliloquy, she is 'an eater of her mother's flesh / By the defiling of her parents' bed'. This confounding of family ties is traditionally one of the great proofs that incest is unnatural.

For Pericles, then, the problem is not how to solve the riddle but how to extricate himself from an impossible situation. His danger is increased by Antiochus's suspicions that Pericles has indeed solved the riddle, which means of course that Pericles understands the terrible truth of the incest. Antiochus hires an assassin; Pericles flees.

When he ends up next in the court of Simonides, King of Pentapolis, another monarch with another daughter of marriageable age, the contrast could not be more instructive. Simonides is as generous and gracious as

Antiochus was calculating and suspicious. Simonides' relationship with his daughter Thaisa is admirable. Part of his dear love for her is that he hopes to see her well married to a young man of her own preference. She again has many wooers, competing for her not by means of addressing a menacing riddle but by showing knightly prowess in a tournament. When Pericles turns out to be Thaisa's choice, he is Simonides' choice as well. Like Prospero in a later romance (*The Tempest*), Simonides play-acts the jealous father only to make the resolution of courtship all the more joyous. Pericles and Thaisa wed and proceed to have a daughter, Marina, named so because she is born at sea.

The contrast between two fathers, one of them unwilling to part with his daughter to a younger man and the other lovingly aware that his daughter will want to have a family of her own, makes abundantly clear the hazards of incest. Why is this instructive antithesis so important to the play of *Pericles* as a whole? What do Pericles' early encounters with fathers have to say about his own relationship, years later, with his daughter Marina?

That situation is given a special urgency by the fact that Marina's mother appears to die at sea, leaving Pericles alone to raise Marina. From the point of view of the story-teller, we can say that the narrator chooses to remove Thaisa from the narrative so that the story may focus on Pericles and Marina; the decision to remove Thaisa is a fictional choice. Shakespeare, as usual, is relying for plot on a source, in this case the often-told story of Apollonius of Tyre, renamed Pericles in Shakespeare's version, but we can also ask what drew Shakespeare to a story told in this manner. The relationship of Pericles and Marina is certainly at the centre of the play.

By any objective account, Pericles would appear to be an oddly distant parent for Marina. He commits her to the care of Cleon, Governor of Tarsus, and his wife Dionyza. Dionyza turns out to be a wicked stepmother out of a fairy tale, so jealous of her own daughter Philoten's fondness for Marina that the mother conspires to have Marina murdered. The young lady escapes, but is then captured by pirates and sold into slavery in Mytilene, where she is pressured relentlessly to become a prostitute. The governor of Mytilene, Lysimachus, hoping to be her first customer, is instead converted by her radiant goodness into a virtuous wooer. Pericles has obviously lost track of Marina. Only when his ship comes to anchor at Mytilene, with Pericles himself in wordless despair over some unspoken sorrow, does he find her again. She is brought to his ship because Lysimachus sends for her as a miracle worker. The miracle does work; Pericles is strangely moved by her voice, and at last recognizes his own daughter.

What has caused Pericles to sink into a catatonic state of unresponsive despair before her arrival? The play provides no clear answer, but allows plentiful room for speculation. Some burden of guilt hangs over him. Perhaps it is the result of an incomplete working out of his relationship with his daughter. He has observed the object lesson of incest in his early adventures, but has not applied that lesson to his own family. Perhaps, too, he feels guilty about his seemingly dead wife, Thaisa.

Thaisa's death puts a heavy burden of responsibility on Pericles. She is very pregnant when they take a journey by sea, and gives birth to their daughter Marina at the height of a terrible storm. When the sailors demand that her body be thrown overboard because of their superstitious belief that the wind 'will not lie till the ship be cleared of the dead', Pericles reluctantly complies. He sees that this is merely their superstition, but the master of the vessel is insistent. Pericles would seem to have had no other choice. Yet the gesture is emblematic: he abandons her to the deep. In view of the fact that a similar abandonment recurs in *The Winter's Tale*, the event is a momentous one. The fiction of *Pericles* concerns a man who throws his wife overboard and leaves his daughter precariously to the care of others for a long time. What is more, the wife is not actually dead.

Thaisa washes ashore and is brought back to life, miraculously it would seem, by a gentleman of Ephesus who dabbles in the 'secret art' of medical properties dwelling in herbs, metals, and precious stones. She becomes a high priestess at the Temple of Diana in Ephesus, to which Pericles is ultimately directed by none other than the goddess Diana herself, appearing to him in a vision. The story is manifestly one of dream-work. The sequence of the play's recuperative action is meaningful in these terms. Pericles is reunited first with his daughter, who, like Cordelia in *King Lear*, knows how to provide needed emotional sustenance for the long-suffering hero simply by being at his side when he wakes out of a trance-like state. She accepts him as her father, redeeming him from his sorrows through her forgiving love. Like Cordelia, she never mentions anything for which she needs to forgive him. The huge difference, of course, is that Pericles gets to keep his daughter, as Lear did not. Romance redeems tragedy by working through the potentially unhappy situations that tragedy has postulated and then finding a resolution.

Pericles gets to reclaim Thaisa as well. Like her daughter, she has no words of reproof for her husband, who undoubtedly can be described as a 'wandering' husband by the very nature of the story's peripatetic cast. Has he been a guilty husband as well? To all appearances, not. He is the wandering hero of romance. Yet the depth of feeling at the end of *Pericles* attests to its symbolic character. This play, on one level at least, is a fantasy about a husband who jettisons his wife and lives apart from his family, burdened increasingly with unease until an unexpected and miraculous union reveals to him that his family life, seemingly lost forever, is still intact.

This is an appealing dream of wish fulfillment, and one that may have meant a lot to Shakespeare. Some time after his hasty wedding to a woman considerably older than he in late 1582, and after they had produced three children in their first two and a quarter years of marriage, Shakespeare left Stratford for London. As we have seen in Chapter 1, he and Anne had no more children. He must have returned home from time to time, and certainly provided for his family, buying handsome properties and acquiring other real estate in his home town. He did not retire until some time after 1611, and even then he seems to have come out of retirement occasionally to write in collaboration, especially with John Fletcher, his successor as chief writer for the King's Men. Shakespeare wrote *Pericles* and the other late romances some time before he retired, when the prospect of being reunited with Anne Hathaway and his two daughters, both of whom were living in Stratford, loomed on the immediate horizon.

This is not to argue that *Pericles* and the other romances are autobiographical in any direct way. We do not know what Shakespeare's relationships with his immediate family were really like. We should assume that his primary reason for going to London was to find opportunity for the kind of work at which he quickly came to excel. We can speculate, however, that the story of Pericles' separation from and eventual reunion with wife and daughter was just the kind of tragicomic dream to give Shakespeare the chance to express, in a play, the sorts of feelings that a man might have in rejoining his wife and daughter after so long a separation.

Cymbeline is like *King Lear* in that both plays are named after legendary kings of England in the shadowy prehistory that England's early chroniclers, beginning with Geoffrey of Monmouth (*c.* 1136), had filled largely with fictitious names and exploits in order to account for the long years of which little or nothing was known: Lear or Leir, Gorboduc,

Ferrex, Porrex, Cymbeline, and others. Most of these are entirely fictitious. A Celtic chieftain named Cunobelinus or Cymbeline did rule over
a large territory in southern England during the first three decades of the
new millennium, becoming the most powerful monarch in Britain and
enjoying friendly relations with Rome; he died only a year or two before
the Claudian invasion of 43 CE. Other than when it is describing the incur-
sions of the Roman army, however, *Cymbeline* tells a romantic yarn that
is without historical basis and is taken chiefly instead from Boccaccio's
Decameron. Cymbeline was included in the great Folio edition of 1623
among the tragedies, along with *King Lear*, despite its happy ending. The
play represents itself for the most part as a sombre historical drama in
which tragedy is narrowly averted.

The title figure, King Cymbeline, is significantly like Lear. He is old
and autocratic, and he drives away his beloved daughter Imogen when
she imprudently but virtuously marries the gentleman of her choice,
Posthumus Leonatus, who is below her in social station. Again like Lear,
Cymbeline turns to other members of his family, who prove vicious: his
second wife and her son by her former marriage, Cloten. Cloten is thus
Imogen's half-brother through family connection only; they share no
heritage of blood.

Blood will tell in a narrative of this sort. Cymbeline's long-lost sons,
Arviragus and Guiderius, who have been taken into the wilderness by a
virtuously outspoken and therefore banished courtier named Belarius
(compare Kent in *King Lear*), are unaware of their royal identity and yet
instinctively behave like princes. They are immediately drawn to Imogen,
the sister they have never known, when she takes refuge in their cave and
is found by them when they return from hunting. Though she has disguised herself as a young man, instinct and royal blood draw the family
together in love and mutual respect until the workings-out of the romantic plot can reunite them all with Cymbeline and thus restore to him his
eldest son and heir, along with his other rightful children.

This romantic plot is the stuff of folktale. We recognize in the story of
the discovery of Imogen by her brothers a version of the nursery tale of
'Scrapefoot' or The Fox and Three Bears, better known today in its sentimentalized form as Goldilocks and the Three Bears, in which the bears
return to their lair to discover that someone has been eating their por-
ridge and sleeping in one of their beds. Similarly, the saga of young men
who are raised far away from the court in an entirely natural environment
and yet manifest princely behaviour is a variant of the legend of Parzival.

Moreover, the motif of the heroine in disguise as a young man named Fidele takes us back to Shakespeare's Julia (in *The Two Gentlemen of Verona*), Portia, Rosalind, and Viola. In his late tragicomic romances, Shakespeare is revisiting the imaginary landscape of his earlier romantic comedies, while still preoccupied with the emotional and spiritual crises of his tragedies. He is concerned in *Cymbeline* both with the father–daughter relationship and with sexual jealousy, as in *Othello*.

Both Cymbeline and Posthumus Leonatus do their best to be undeserving of Imogen. The father, in a towering rage, drives her into flight from the court for refusing to marry Cloten and taking instead 'a beggar'. Posthumus, as we have seen, wagers on her virtue and then believes a villainous slander against her. Both men are eventually brought to their senses. Posthumus, after having hired his loyal servant Pisanio to kill Imogen (a task that Pisanio virtuously refuses to carry out), belatedly comes to believe that, like Othello, he has slain an innocent and has thus destroyed all his hopes of happiness. He joins Cymbeline's army against the Roman invaders as a British peasant, hoping to die in battle, but lives to become the hero of the day in the company of two fierce and unknown fighters who turn out to be Arviragus and Guiderius. The King, disabused finally of his faith in his wife when he learns that, in dying, she has confessed to a plan to poison her husband, embraces his long-lost daughter and two sons, forgives Belarius for having abducted the two princes, makes peace with Rome, and even pardons the villainous Iachimo.

The god Jupiter, descending in thunder and lightning, presides over all with his providential blessing. 'Whom best I love I cross, to make my gift, / The more delayed, delighted,' he assures those who have suffered so many disappointments. 'Be content' (5.4). As the Roman general, Caius Lucius, puts it, 'Some falls are means the happier to arise'. The shape of tragicomic romance is manifest in these utterances. As a genre it prolongs separation, misunderstanding, and estrangement in order to increase the satisfaction of the play's characters, and of the audience as well, when all is finally resolved. Human misery is providentially explained: it is a form of testing by the gods with the benign intent of ultimately increasing human happiness by showing how dearly bought that happiness can be.

Despite the upbeat ending, however, the pathway to it is littered with demonstrations of human failure. Cymbeline does not deserve to have his daughter and his sons restored to him; he has done everything in his power to destroy them. Posthumus is fully as guilty. Cymbeline is thus a

Lear given an undeserved second chance, while Posthumus is an Othello who tries to kill his wife and then is allowed to have her back only because he did not succeed in killing her. The gods protect us against our own worst selves. At the same time, the stagey epiphany of Jupiter in act five is plainly a *coup de théâtre*, calling attention to itself as theatrical artifice. Tragicomedy offers us assurance that the worthy characters of the play, however flawed, will ultimately find forgiveness and reconciliation. Even the villainous Iachimo is reclaimed (though Cloten and his wicked mother are not).

The Winter's Tale again revisits the interconnected motifs of sexual jealousy and the strong emotional bond between father and daughter. Leontes, King of Sicilia, persuaded that his wife has been untrue to him, tries to kill his infant daughter by ordering a courtier, Antigonus, to abandon the baby on a deserted foreign shore. As in *Cymbeline*, the daughter lives because of kindly human intervention, and perhaps through the intervention of nature as well: the famous bear that pursues Antigonus offstage ('*Exit pursued by a bear*') and then proceeds (as we are told) to gnaw on his shoulder bone chooses not to molest the child. The father is spared the consequences of his own infanticidal wish; the child lives to be her father's daughter once more. The fantasy of guilt, long separation, and reunion is, as in *Pericles* and *Cymbeline*, a legend of family conflict, sorrow, and recovery.

Once again it bears an intriguing if uncertain relationship to the circumstances of Shakespeare's own impending reunion with his family in Stratford in the years around 1609–11, when the play appears to have been written. At all events, the story is essentially about an ageing man for whom a recovered daughter's love (as in *King Lear*) means more than all the world. That precious love also leads him back to a wife who, as in the case of *Othello* and *Cymbeline*, the husband believes himself to have killed through his senseless, insane jealousy. Leontes is a man who thinks he has killed both his wife and his only daughter.

Leontes has lost his only son as well; young Mamillius dies of grief at his mother's disgrace. We explored in Chapter 4 the possibility that this sad event might represent a kind of dream-work on Shakespeare's part in coming to terms at last, after some fourteen years, with the fact of his own son Hamnet having died in 1596 – a coming to terms after a number of intervening dramatizations of bringing a seemingly lost son back to life, as in *Twelfth Night* and *Cymbeline*. The family constellation of *The Winter's Tale* certainly does seem recognizable as fantasy on Shakespeare's part: a father who has so alienated himself from wife and daughter that they are in effect dead to him, and a son who is truly dead. We can perhaps see why Shakespeare was attracted to this story. As usual, he did not invent the plot; it came to him pretty much intact from Robert Greene's *Pandosto: The Triumph of Time* (1588). Shakespeare did not invent it, but he did find it and he chose to dramatize it.

In *Pericles*, the hero does not kill his wife; she dies at sea and is thrown overboard with Pericles' reluctant consent, for which reason, perhaps, he seems to carry the event with him as a burden of guilt. In *The Winter's Tale*, Leontes really thinks he has succeeded in killing Queen Hermione. He is too ready to believe that she has been sexually unfaithful to him, even though no tempter like Iago eggs him on. Leontes suffers, like Othello, the common male affliction of fearing the woman's bodily appetites and the warmth of her innocent love for another man, in this case Leontes' best friend and fellow-monarch, Polixenes. Leontes' broodings on jealousy are as frighteningly unhappy as any in Shakespeare's great tragedies. In his bleak ruminations on human sexuality, Leontes warns all married men to be wary of their wives:

> There have been,
> Or I am much deceived, cuckolds ere now;
> And many a man there is, even at this present,
> Now while I speak this, holds his wife by th' arm,
> That little thinks she has been sluiced in 's absence
> And his pond fished by his next neighbour, by
> Sir Smile, his neighbour. Nay, there's comfort in't
> Whiles other men have gates and those gates opened,
> As mine, against their will. Should all despair
> That have revolted wives, the tenth of mankind
> Would hang themselves.
> (1.2.190–200)

The images in this passage, of open gates, of water in a pond being sluiced off, are disturbingly anatomical in their representation of the ungovernable female body. Leontes goes on to lament that he has 'No barricado for a belly', which will 'let in and out the enemy / With bag and baggage'. Leontes cannot free his tortured mind from the obsessive picture of another man's genitalia moving in and out of his wife's body.

Even his most loyal courtier, Camillo, cannot convince Leontes that he suffers a self-inflicted folly. Leontes' lack of any evidence other than

Hermione's loving cordiality toward their guest and the fact that Polixenes came to pay his long state visit some nine months ago, when Hermione became pregnant, does not deter him from believing something that his own frail inner nature demands that he believe about himself, that he is a cuckold. As Emilia observes in *Othello*, some men are jealous 'for they're jealous'.

Leontes suffers a prolonged agony of guilt for having, as he thinks, killed his wife with grief over her own public shame and the death of their son Mamillius. For sixteen years, if we are to believe the story, the King begs Antigonus's wife Paulina to act as his conscience and remind him incessantly of his crime so that his sorrow will not diminish. Even after sixteen years have passed, he refuses to heed his courtiers' admonitions that he has performed 'A saintlike sorrow' and has, by now, 'paid down / More penitence than done trespass'. Surely the heavens have forgiven him by this time; cannot he not forgive himself? He does not think so, and Paulina is at his side to remind him not only that Hermione is gone but that he killed her. Paulina knows that the time for renewal and forgiveness has not yet come, though it is close at hand. The timing must depend on the recovery of Leontes' daughter. As in *Pericles*, the reunion with wife and daughter must be meaningfully interconnected. It betokens the renewal of the generations, that great cycle through which nature perpetuates itself.

The Winter's Tale's most significant variation in Shakespeare's twice-told tale of the recovered daughter and wife is that we as audience are assured that Hermione is really dead. Unlike Pericles' wife Thaisa, who is dead to him but is known by us to be safely alive once she has washed ashore, Hermione is reported to us as dead. Antigonus relates how she has appeared to him in a dream, as one of 'the spirits o'the dead', warning him that he will never see his wife Paulina again because of his unhappy role in abandoning Hermione's infant daughter to the elements. Having said this, 'with shrieks, / She melted into air', Antigonus wonderingly recalls. Though generally sceptical about dreams, he is convinced of this one: 'I do believe / Hermione hath suffered death'. Hermione disappears from the play other than as the long-dead wife for whom her husband continues to perform such penitence.

The theatrical advantage of misleading the audience in this fashion – something that Shakespeare does nowhere else – is that the dramatist is thus able to bring Hermione back to life in a way that seems magical. The statue of Hermione, kept in seclusion by Paulina, comes to life in her husband's presence. 'It is required / You do awake your faith', Paulina admonishes the royal visitor to her gallery. Such an awakening from a seeming death is sure to seem miraculous. In human terms, we understand that Paulina has simply kept Hermione with her, hidden from Leontes over many years until penitence has done its slow work. Yet the reunion is something that passes human understanding.

As in *Pericles*, this reunion of husband and wife must be preceded by the recovery of the lost daughter. The reunion of father and daughter is no less an event of almost incomprehensible joy. Shakespeare prudently keeps it offstage so that it can be described for us in terms of paradox: it is 'a sight which was to be seen, cannot be spoken of'. The whole story of Perdita's having been found by shepherds on the seashore in Bohemia and raised as a shepherdess only to turn out to be a princess is 'Like an old tale still, which will have matter to rehearse though credit be asleep and not an ear open'. Shakespeare courts the improbable in order that it may be wondrous.

As a fable about father, daughter, wife, and son, *The Winter's Tale* provides a meaningful fantasy. The father in this play is more guilty of desertion of his wife than in *Pericles*. He is directly responsible for the loss, and he is inconsolable. He lives apart from his family while his one surviving child, a daughter, grows up to young adulthood. Only then does he find a happiness that, like Cymbeline's, is all the more precious for being undeserved; he has been truly penitent, but feels that nothing he does can atone for his crime. The happiness takes the form of recovering a daughter who is now the age of the wife he once married. His wife has aged too: the sculptor's skill 'lets go by some sixteen years and makes her / As she lived now'. Yet despite that ageing Leontes realizes that he loves her as much now as he ever did. The most precious recovery for Leontes is to discover that he loves and trusts the wife he once spurned and hated. He sees that former hatred and fear of Hermione as entirely the result of his own failing as a suspicious man, not as a result of anything she did. He is not afraid of her ageing body. 'Oh, she's warm!' he cries, as he touches her. 'If this be magic, let it be an art / Lawful as eating.' This is a fantasy that Shakespeare, about to retire and go back to Anne Hathaway in Stratford, could not have resisted.

Prospero in *The Tempest* is given a chance to succeed in doing what his predecessors – Polonius, Brabantio, Lear, Pericles, Cymbeline – have done so imperfectly or not at all: be a loving father to the daughter he cherishes more than all the world and yet allow and encourage her to marry the young man of her choice. Prospero has made many mistakes in his life, especially in his negligent ruling of Milan, but he is determined to give Miranda both the love and the freedom she needs to be her best self.

The lack of any single narrative source for *The Tempest* invites us to consider this play as one in which Shakespeare's narrative choices are especially significant. Shakespeare gives his protagonist no wife. Prospero had a wife, to be sure, when Miranda was born; he refers to her (only once) as a 'piece of virtue' who assured Prospero that Miranda was his daughter, but even this glancing reference depends for its humour on the painful old joke that fathers cannot be sure who has sired the children born of their wives' loins. The dream of living out the end of life in the company of wife and daughter seems to have faded. Instead, *The Tempest* is a fantasy about living out the end of one's life with a daughter and a son-in-law who might feel, as Ferdinand does, that to live forever with 'So rare a wondered father and a wife' would be 'paradise'.[2]

Prospero feels tremendously in himself the tug of possessive longing for his daughter. After all, he has lived with Miranda as his sole companion and mate, other than Caliban, for nearly all her fifteen or so years. (Miranda was nearly three when they came to the island some twelve years ago.) *The Tempest* is, in one sense, the fictional enactment, on a deserted island, of the life that Lear dreamed of with Cordelia. Like Lear, Prospero has been banished and deprived of power, so that he has nothing left but his daughter. Like Lear, Prospero has learned to be more than content with that, having discovered through suffering that the love of a daughter can compensate for every imaginable worldly loss. The pull of attachment is extraordinary. Yet Prospero appears to know, too, that the very nature of such an attachment means that he must yield to the cycle of nature through which she will become the wife of a young man and the mother of a new family. Prospero sees that he is growing old, and he accepts the consequences of that unavoidable decline.

Prospero does not want his daughter's love for Ferdinand to be too easy. Because they are on a desert island, and because Prospero has managed through his magical powers to cause Ferdinand to be separated by the storm from the rest of the Italian party with whom he was journeying, Miranda and Ferdinand are quite alone except for her father. (Caliban is confined to his rock.) Why should not Ferdinand and Miranda couple, once they have discovered that they truly love each other and have said vows of perpetual obligation? Those vows, especially when said in the presence of another person, would bind them as fast as the saying of the marriage service in an English church. A witness is in fact present, in the person of the invisible Prospero. No church is to be found on the island, no priest to pronounce them man and wife. What is there to hinder them from becoming man and wife in a state of nature, as it were?

Yet Prospero does not want this to happen. Nor do Miranda and her young man, as it turns out. A major reason for their desire to wait until they are properly married seemingly has to do with Caliban. He represents an entirely opposite point of view on the morality or amorality of sex. Having been born on the island to the witch Sycorax, who then died, Caliban has been brought up in the household of Prospero as a kind of companion and brother for Miranda. The family intimacy evidently was such that when Caliban started to feel the promptings of the reproductive urge, Miranda must have struck him as the inevitable target. After all, they were much alike in their shared destinies, in that each was the sole child of a single parent banished to this island. Why not capitalize on this shared destiny? Caliban made his move which, when urgently resisted, turned into an attempted rape. The angry father enslaved Caliban at this point, forcing him to carry firewood. Yet Caliban was then, and remains now, unrepentant of the attempted violation. 'Oho, oho! Would 't had been done!' he exclaims. 'Thou didst prevent me; I had peopled else / This isle with Calibans.' Caliban believes in the mating instinct in its purest form: a pleasurable act that procreates the species.

Caliban's view is at odds with that of Miranda, Ferdinand, and her father, all of whom, as good Western Europeans, subscribe to the teachings of the church forbidding sex before marriage. Who is right? The debate is a lively one, prompted in good part by Shakespeare's reading in Montaigne, where he encountered a challengingly sceptical view of traditional Western values. Europeans might stand to learn something about themselves by looking at their frequently corrupted civilization from the perspective of those so-called savages who, as Montaigne imagines them, live communally without laws, contracts, money, or organized religions.

The debate is not resolved in favour of free love, in Montaigne or in Shakespeare, but it does raise questions. In *The Tempest*, the contrasting perspectives on sexual desire serve to highlight the differences between Ferdinand and Caliban as potential mates for Miranda. The two males are alike in that, at different times in her life, they enjoy a proximity with her and a desire for her. The resemblance is reinforced by the emblematic action of carrying logs; when Ferdinand is forced to carry firewood for Prospero, he re-enacts the stage gesture that we especially associate with Caliban. Yet these similarities only underscore the differences. To Ferdinand and Miranda, physical sex without a lasting bond of spiritualized friendship is lust, animal lust. Caliban is an animal to them in this regard.

Ferdinand is as eager physically to have sex with Miranda as is Caliban. On the day of their wedding, he confesses, he will think that either 'Phoebus' steeds are foundered / Or Night kept chained below'. The day will seem endless until he can be in bed with his beloved. He says this, however, in the context of what he has already promised his bride-to-be and his prospective father-in-law, that nothing could prompt him to break his resolution of chaste postponement:

> As I hope
> For quiet days, fair issue, and long life,
> With such love as 'tis now, the murkiest den,
> The most opportune place, the strong'st suggestion
> Our worser genius can, shall never melt
> Mine honour into lust, to take away
> The edge of that day's celebration.
>
> (4.1.23–9)

Not even being on a desert island alone with this beautiful young woman could tempt him to succumb to the promptings of his 'worser genius', his carnal desire. He subscribes to the orthodox Christian view that the heavens themselves will punish transgressions of this sort, and that a long life of marital happiness depends on restraint before marriage. He has internalized a set of values that have become second nature to Miranda, under her father's tutelage and presumably in response to her own inner sense of decency.

Because Prospero does not want sexual desire to be too easily achieved and marriage too lightly undertaken, he devises for himself the role of the angry father. He becomes the blocking figure of earlier comedy, like Egeus in *A Midsummer Night's Dream* or the Duke of Milan in *The Two Gentlemen of Verona*. That he does so in play, with the virtuous intent of giving the young people something to worry about and manoeuvre their way around, is evident in his asides to us and his soliloquizing when he is alone: 'So glad of this as they I cannot be, / Who are surprised with all; but my rejoicing / At nothing can be more' (3.1). At the same time, we sense that Prospero is working his way through the very real emotional difficulty that has earlier afflicted Brabantio, Lear, Cymbeline, and

Leontes. The play-acting, in other words, is for himself as much as for the young people. Prospero needs to act out the part of the jealous, possessive father in order to expunge that feeling as much as he is able. The effort needed is not small. Prospero's imperiousness, his irritability, his struggle to forgive his enemies are all part of his awareness that he is on the verge of momentous events in his life: the marriage of his daughter to a younger man, his retirement from his art, his return to Naples and then Milan where 'Every third thought shall be my grave', and eventually his death. The concatenation of these rites of passage may help explain why the relationship of father and daughter is so precious and yet deeply troublesome: it coincides with the end of everything. That ending will be the burden of our next and final chapter.[3]

CHAPTER NINE

◆

Last Scene of All

Retirement from the Theatre

But on he moves to meet his latter end,

. . . .

Bends to the grave with unperceived decay,
While resignation gently slopes the way.

Oliver Goldsmith, The Deserted Village, *107–10*

Prospero gives up much more than his daughter at the end of *The Tempest*. By freeing Ariel, he relinquishes the power to do things that are, to a remarkable degree, what a poet-dramatist does in the theatre. Prospero is the author and stage-manager of all that occurs on his island of the Tempest. Aided by his magical knowledge derived from his beloved books and assisted by Ariel, he creates a huge storm, lands the shipwrecked Italian party on one part of the island, stage-manages the meeting of Ferdinand and Miranda on another, puts Alonso and the other Italians through a nightmare of vexation, aborts a conspiracy on the part of Stephano, Trinculo, and Caliban to seize power, and orchestrates a finale of resolution in which even the shipwrecked vessel turns out to be per-fectly unharmed. He does all this and then deliberately breaks his magic staff, vowing to drown his book. The very last thing he does in the play, before speaking the epilogue in quite a different dramatic persona, is to free Ariel. 'Then to the elements / Be free, and fare thou well!' To come to the end of *The Tempest* is to realize that we have come to the end of something very big.

Ariel must represent something like the creative spirit. Ariel is not human; Ariel is immortal. One does not know whether to refer to

Ariel as 'he' or 'she', because Ariel has no gender. The conventional 'he' employed in the play is a compromise. Ariel has no amorous attachments. He plainly enjoys Prospero's company and works collaboratively in carrying out Prospero's managerial schemes. At the same time, Ariel leaves Prospero at the play's end without hesitation or so much as a farewell. Ever since the play began, Ariel has wanted to be free. He has bargained with Prospero for what he can get, and then accedes to the contract drawn up between them. 'After two days / I will discharge thee', Prospero promises, and Ariel cheerfully agrees. 'That's my noble master! / What shall I do? Say what? What shall I do?' As long as the obligation is for only two days, Ariel is ready for anything.

In order to understand the way in which Ariel embodies the creative and artistic spirit that enables Prospero to do his work, we need to consider the terms of his servitude to Prospero and how it began. As Prospero forcefully reminds him, Ariel was once a servant of the witch Sycorax, Caliban's mother, and was imprisoned by her in a cloven pine tree for having been too delicate a spirit 'To act her earthy and abhorred commands'. We are not told what these commands were, but the clear implication is that they were evil. Ariel chose to suffer the torments of imprisonment in the cloven pine for twelve years rather than carry out Sycorax's wishes. When Prospero offers to free Ariel on condition that Ariel become Prospero's servant for some limited period of time, Ariel accepts with alacrity if also with occasional reminders that he wishes ultimately to be freed. Ariel, then, perceives a world of difference between serving Sycorax and serving Prospero. One practises black magic, the other practises white magic. Ariel will lend countenance to the one and not the other.

Certain humans, then, who are gifted with a special aptitude for magical things, may enlist the aid of a supernal, immortal force to help them in their work. The assistance will be only for a time, and will help only those who are pursuing benign ends. This paradigm suggests that the distinction Ariel makes between benign and evil ends is absolute, timeless, and universal. The distinction belongs to the invisible world of which he is a part and to which he will return when he has left Prospero's service. The mortal artist will eventually die, having accomplished what time and his energy have permitted. The creative spirit lent to him for a while, somewhat like the inspiration of a Muse, will endure forever. So will the works of art thus created.

As magician and artist, Prospero behaves very much like a theatre manager and dramatist. The plot of *The Tempest* is his plot. Stage movement, entrances, and exits are under his control. He does not create the characters or make choices for them, but he controls their environment to such an extent by means of his theatrical illusions that their choices are far less free than they individually suppose. Antonio and Sebastian, for example, think that they are free agents who can remain awake while their companions sleep and thus be able to exploit the opportunity for assassination; Antonio and Sebastian will kill King Alonso and his entourage and thus seize control of the island. Yet we know that they are being watched by Ariel, who, perfectly visible to us as audience, is understood to be invisible to the Italian shipwrecked party. Ariel is there because Prospero has foreseen the danger and has dispatched Ariel to forestall murder.

The metaphoric implications of this stage action seem clear: we humans are being watched by some unseen presence without our conscious awareness. At least on the island of the Tempest, villainy will not go unchecked. Some invisible being knows our very thoughts. Yet this overseeing force is not a divinity. On his island, Prospero assumes the role of God: he is both stage-manager of the drama he creates and supreme arbiter of his cosmos.

On the more broadly comic level, Stephano and Trinculo are also being watched. Ariel takes a Puck-like pleasure in mimicking their voices to foment a quarrel. He stands invisibly behind Trinculo and exclaims 'Thou liest!' in Trinculo's voice, thereby goading Stephano into striking his partner for the seeming insult. Again, the episode has a more serious intent. Stephano and Trinculo are devising a plot to take over the island, with Caliban's help. These two Neapolitans are debased comic versions of the better-educated villains, Antonio and Sebastian. They must be overseen by an invisible presence so that their planned rebellion can be aborted. Ariel does his job with dramatic flair, leading the hapless comics through stagnant pools so that they smell of horse-piss, distracting them from their attempted assault on Prospero's cell, and chasing them with '*divers spirits, in shape of dogs and hounds*'. Together with Ariel, Prospero assumes the role of stage-manager and God.

A managerial figure of this sort runs the risk of losing the audience's sympathy. His arrogation of authority seems hubristic; his manner is often harsh. To many readers today, in fact, Prospero comes close to being sadistic. His enslavement of Caliban smacks of colonialism, even if Prospero did not come to the island with an exploitive purpose and leaves at the end without attempting to set up any commercial ties with mainland Italy. (The real colonialists are Sebastian, Antonio, Stephano, and Trinculo, all of whom would take Caliban back to Italy as a freak in a lucrative sideshow if given the chance.) Prospero's treatment of Alonso and the rest can seem unfeeling, even brutal. They go through a kind of torture: tables appear laden with food and then disappear mysteriously, Ariel hovers over them '*like a harpy*' in order to cow them with a sermon on their sinfulness, and the like. Most of all, Prospero allows Alonso to believe that his son is dead by drowning. Prospero is playing with their lives and threatening their happiness.

We must allow all this to be true, and yet we can also observe that Prospero, in so doing, is behaving exactly like the providential tragicomic force that oversees the action of a play like *Pericles*, *Cymbeline*, and *The Winter's Tale*. That is, he creates the illusion of loss in order that the regaining of a happiness once thought to have been destroyed will be all the more sweet. At Jupiter put it, in *Cymbeline*, 'Whom best I love I cross, to make my gift, / The more delayed, delighted'.

At the same time, this tragicomic principle, presided over by Prospero in *The Tempest*, is not simply a theatrical trick of delayed pleasure. It also incorporates a deeper idea of penitence, remorse, and restoration of the spirit through sombre reflection on one's shortcomings. Ariel, as the harpy, bids Alonso consider that the drowning of his son was a consequence of Alonso's own sinfulness in helping to oust Prospero from his dukedom of Milan. Alonso is responsive to such instruction; he knows that he bears a very heavy burden of guilt. Yet remorseful despair is not sufficient; in fact it is a destructive spiritual response. Alonso must be led beyond despondency and despair to an awakening belief that he can be forgiven if he is truly sorry. His agony of self-accusation is thus potentially curative, as it was for Leontes in *The Winter's Tale*. The evidence is that this process works for Alonso; his son is restored to him. That gift, so much like the restoration of Perdita to Leontes or Imogen to Cymbeline, is a token of new hope for a fallen, imperfect human being who, despite his weakness, can hope for help of a redemptive sort from some power larger than himself.

For Prospero to play the role of forgiver of Alonso is truly hubristic. Yet he knows that he must do so. The one piece of advice he gets from Ariel is precisely that: to forgive. Ariel reports to his master that Alonso and the rest are so humbled, so distracted and sorrowful, that if Prospero were to see them in this condition his affections would become tender and compassionate. 'Dost thou think so, spirit?' asks Prospero, to which the spirit replies, 'Mine would, sir, were I human'. Prospero readily agrees that he now needs to side with his 'nobler reason' against his 'fury'. 'The rarer action is / In virtue than in vengeance.' When his onetime enemies are fully penitent, he sees that he must forgive them.

This lovely passage suggests both how hard and how necessary it is for him to forgive. The desire for revenge touches him deeply. He has his former enemies in his power. They have done him terrible wrong in deposing him and sending him out to sea in an unseaworthy vessel with his infant daughter, presumably to their deaths. He has mulled over the injury for twelve years, with no one to share his anger, not even the dear daughter to whom he finally reveals the truth as she reaches puberty. Prospero plays God with them, but he acknowledges his own human frailty as well; that is partly why he must forgive them. No less importantly, he can hope that some of his motive in subjecting them to the illusion of danger and loss is to make them better people. In the case of Alonso especially, he may have some real hope. Sebastian and Antonio are no doubt villainous beyond reclamation, but one does the best one can.

Prospero is fully aware that his power as artist–magician extends only to his island and its immediate environs. He had no such power in Italy, and will not have that power when he returns to Milan. He is unable to alter the course of the sea vessel carrying the Neapolitan party, as they sail from a wedding in north Africa back to Naples, until they are within his magical orbit. 'By accident most strange', he explains to Miranda, 'bountiful Fortune, / Now my dear lady, hath mine enemies / Brought to this shore.' The opportunity thus afforded Prospero will last only for a brief time; if he neglects the chance now, his fortunes 'Will ever after droop'.

The island, in this sense, is very much like the theatre in its relation to ordinary life. Persons from that outside world enter the theatre for a time, where they are subjected to strange, magical shows that move the audience in strongly emotional ways. The audience then disperses as its individual citizens return to their normal lives. The theatre experience is 'unreal' in that it is a fiction. What effect will it have on their lives? No more and no less, perhaps, than the experience of being on the island of the Tempest will have on the lives of Alonso, Sebastian, and the rest once they are back in 'reality'. The island experience will then be remembered as a dream.

One visitor to the island is perhaps more likely than the rest to be inspired by its magical vision: Gonzalo. This devoted old courtier, who saved the lives of Prospero and Miranda twelve years ago by provisioning their boat, is a dreamer. He notices miraculous things. He alone, on the beach, sees that the garments worn by the survivors of the shipwreck are unstained by the salt water, retaining their freshness as if they were new-dyed. Such a thing is indeed remarkable. Perhaps Gonzalo is dreaming to think that such a thing could have happened; more likely, the others, in their preoccupations with despondency and self-advancement, are not attuned to magical things.

Gonzalo's dream is of an island utopia. It is taken out of the pages of Montaigne's essay on cannibals. While the others worry about sheer survival or plot to murder their companions, Gonzalo imagines what it would be like to start life afresh on some island, far, far from European civilization. He imagines an island off the coast of the Americas, it seems, like the Bermudas (mentioned in the text) or the island of Thomas More's Utopia near the South American coast, though practically speaking the island they are on must be in the Mediterranean. In Gonzalo's utopia there will be no money, no commerce, no social distinctions, no need for legal contracts or jails. His vision is mad, in the sense that all utopias are mad, including King Lear's and Gloucester's ideas for a radical redistribution of all wealth so that rich and poor alike will be the happier. Utopia is a vision of the artist. It exists, like the island of the Tempest, someplace and noplace. It exists in time and it is timeless. Gonzalo is attuned to the vision of the artist because he is a dreamer. Antonio and Sebastian scoff at him, laughing as they point out the self-contradictions and impossibilities in his utopian scheme. Gonzalo doesn't mind. Art is supposed to be impractical. If it compromised with the real world it would fail to do its visionary job of teasing our minds with wonderful impossibilities.

Another creature of the artistic world called the island of the Tempest is Caliban. He is, after all, the one character in the play who was born here and the only one that will remain when the others sail back for Italy. If the island represents the world of Shakespeare's theatre, what is Caliban doing there? In some ways, he is the one figure most perfectly attuned to its haunting natural beauty. Years ago he was able to show Prospero and Miranda where to find the island's fresh springs and brine pits. He offers to show Stephano and Trinculo the best places to pick berries and fish or find firewood. He will harvest pignuts for them with his long nails, and instruct them how to snare 'the nimble marmoset'. To him, 'the isle is full of noises' that hum about his ears, waking him and sending him off to sleep again. In his dreams, the clouds 'open and show riches / Ready to drop upon me'. Caliban responds to his natural environment in a way that is at least partly denied to his more 'civilized' visitors. At such moments, his voice speaks poetry as fetchingly graceful as any in the play. That voice is integral to the artist's world. In colonialist terms, we share his resentment that his island, in which he lives so perfectly in harmony with nature, has been invaded by Europeans. 'This island's mine', he complains to Prospero, 'Which thou tak'st from me.'

At the same time, Caliban represents the limits of unreconstructed, 'uncivilized' nature. He evidently had no language before Prospero and Miranda arrived to teach him how to name the sun and the moon. Language has taught him only how to curse, in his angry view, but perhaps language at its best is capable of better things than that. If nothing else, language has given Caliban a vehicle of expression through which to describe, for us, what is so magical about the island's beauty. As the place of art, then, as theatre, the island is a forum about language, about culture. In its precincts, the characters debate and act out what is best and worst about human nature and about civilization.

Presiding over this debate about culture and the moral vision of art is Prospero, the artist and magician. He takes the place of God, or the gods, in many ways. With Ariel's assistance he devises a masque for the wedding of his daughter and Ferdinand in which the gods come down to earth to bless the event. Juno descends in a chariot from the roof over the theatre to converse with Iris and Ceres; they bring with them the bounty and foison of a generous earth to help celebrate. An antimasque of reapers and nymphs dances a graceful dance. All is theatrical illusion, of course. The three goddesses are really Ariel and his assistants in costume. So was the harpy that lectured Alonso and the rest on their sinfulness. No gods appear in *The Tempest* that are not the creation of Prospero and Ariel. Destiny and Providence take the shape of an ageing father who has learned to play god in his magical space, in his theatre, through the power of his intellect and his gift for being in tune with an eternal creative spirit embodied in Ariel.

Prospero does allow for the role of a larger Providence beyond the sphere of his island-theatre. When Miranda asks him how the two of them managed to find the island and come ashore when they were cast adrift in a boat, Prospero's answer is 'By Providence divine'. To be sure, Providence in this case has taken the form of a kindly old Neapolitan, Gonzalo, who gave them fresh water and enough food to stay alive, but still Prospero is entirely willing to grant that Providence has had its eye on him and his daughter. A larger force than he can comprehend oversees the hoped-for happy ending, as in *Cymbeline, Pericles,* and *The Winter's Tale.* Ferdinand is convinced that Providence had a hand in his finding Miranda and winning her love: 'by immortal Providence she's mine'. Yet within the confines of the island of the Tempest, Prospero is ruler. There, he is the creator of illusion and the designer of delayed happiness.

Prospero knows that such power, even if limited to the world of the artist and his theatre, is hubristic. Shakespeare borrows language from Ovid's depiction of that ominous practitioner of the occult, Medea, to tell us what it is that Prospero can do. With the aid of his spirits, Prospero has 'bedimmed / The noontide sun, called forth the mutinous winds, / And twixt the green sea and the azured vault / Set roaring war'. He has split apart the mighty oak tree with Jove's own lightning bolt. Graves at his command have opened to let forth their occupants. This last achievement particularly sounds both blasphemous and artistically creative: Prospero has raised the dead just as a great dramatist can bring back Julius Caesar or Marc Antony or Cleopatra to speak as though they were alive. The artist is, by his very nature, close to being a blasphemer.

Prospero recognizes and acknowledges this inherent danger in artistic creation. That, presumably, is why he must 'abjure' this 'rough magic' by breaking his magical staff and drowning his book. He is mortal, as Ariel is not; the creative spirit will pass to other human beings while Prospero, in King Lear's phrase, 'Unburdened crawl[s] toward death'. The artist lays aside his task that is at once an enormous burden and the most important, sustaining thing in his life. His mood is one both of acceptance and of emotional struggle. He is at the point of his life's most difficult rite of passage, along with the partial loss of his daughter: resignation and death.

Ever since people began writing about *The Tempest,* they have been struck with the perception that the play is Shakespeare's farewell to the theatre.[1] The case for this reading of the play is hypothetical and can easily be sentimentalized, but there is much to be said for it nonetheless. *The Tempest* was given first place in the collected volume of Shakespeare's plays known as the First Folio of 1623. Its editors, Shakespeare's longtime friends and colleagues in the acting company, seem to have felt that *The Tempest* shows Shakespeare at his very best. They commissioned a scribe, Ralph Crane, to prepare a careful transcript for the printer in order to ensure high quality of editing and printing.

Arguably, Shakespeare himself wrote *The Tempest* as his 'last' play as a way of demonstrating the things he could do best. It is short, and it is neatly 'regular' in terms of dramatic structure: that is, it obeys the unities of time and place called for in classical dramatic theory. All the action occurs on the island, and within 'two days' or less – the period of time during which Ariel agrees to serve Prospero before Ariel is freed. The play has dramatic unity of action: it features a comic subplot, but one that is well integrated into the main action. In other plays, Shakespeare could show a blithe disregard for the so-called unities: *The Winter's Tale*, for example, falls into two halves with a separation of sixteen years in the interim, and moves back and forth between the widely separated kingdoms of Sicilia and Bohemia. (It also gives Bohemia a seacoast, an inaccuracy to which Ben Jonson objected.) *The Tempest* encompasses a story of twelve years and more, but it achieves unity of time by beginning just before the conclusion and by telling the rest of the story through recollection. Similarly, *The Tempest* imagines two contrastingly separate locations, the island itself and mainland Italy, but limits its depiction of actual events to the island. Shakespeare, with a mere flick of his powerful wrist, shows that he can practise the unities, all right, in case anyone was in doubt.

At the same time, *The Tempest* revels in magically 'impossible' events of the sort that neoclassical critics like Ben Jonson found grotesque and indecorous. Throughout his career, Shakespeare has brought onstage fairies, ghosts, demons, and monsters to mingle with his more recognizably human characters. He loves the device of bringing 'invisible' spirits onstage right amongst the humans, as when Puck plays games with the four young lovers in *A Midsummer Night's Dream*, or when the ghost of Hamlet senior appears to his son but not to Gertrude, or when Macbeth can see Banquo's ghost while the other dinner guests cannot. *The Tempest* is, as it were, Shakespeare's affirmation, in answer to his critics, that his plays choose to be what John Lyly called a 'mingle-mangle', mixing clowns and kings, fairies and mortals, the divine and the human.

By the same token, Shakespeare's plays are often strikingly aware of themselves as theatre. He loves the device of the play-within-the-play because it allows him to show us audiences onstage watching plays and commenting on them. In *A Midsummer Night's Dream*, for example, Theseus, Hippolyta, and the young lovers gather in celebration of the royal wedding to watch some performance arranged for their delectation by the master of ceremonies, Philostrate. The purpose of watching a play, interestingly enough, is to while away the time until the married lovers may go to bed and consummate their various marriages. The pattern of frustrated expectation, delay, and eventual resolution that governs the structure of a well-made play also provides the form of this evening's entertainment. The entire play of *A Midsummer Night's Dream* is consciously conceived as shaped by this pattern: Theseus begins it by observing that 'Four happy days' will bring in both a new moon and the celebration of his marriage to Hippolyta. As duke, Theseus might easily hasten on the day of marriage if he wished, and indeed he chafes at the waning 'old moon' that 'lingers my desires / Like to a stepdame or a dowager / Long withering out a young man's revenue', and yet he chooses to abide by the self-imposed delay. It represents the kind of virtuous restraint of sexual desire urged by Prospero on young Ferdinand in *The Tempest*, while at the same time the announced four-day time span neatly structures for us, at the start of *A Midsummer Night's Dream*, the shape and duration of the dramatic action we are about to witness. The play will end when Theseus and Hippolyta marry. But then another pause gives the shape of frustrated delay to the fifth act, like a false cadence at the end of a Beethoven symphonic movement: the lovers may not retire to bed until they see 'Pyramus and Thisbe'. They are both amused and amiably frustrated by the delay.

'Pyramus and Thisbe' is, of course, a delicious sendup of all sorts of bad playwriting in the Elizabethan theatre, with its wooden verse, its predictable rhymes (love and dove), its inept rhymes (dumb and tomb, good and blood), its inappropriate metaphors (Thisbe's 'yellow cowslip cheeks' and eyes as 'green as leeks'), its melodramatic gestures (especially Pyramus's prolonged death agonies), its bathetic appeals to the 'Sisters Three' and 'ye Furies fell' and 'Oh, wherefore, Nature, didst thou lions frame?', its calamitous descent into banality ('Oh, dainty duck! Oh, dear!'), and so on. More significantly, perhaps, this play-within-the-play affords Shakespeare an opportunity to write about theatrical illusion: how it works and how it connects artistic vision to the mundane world in which ordinary mortals live.

The rude mechanicals who stage 'Pyramus and Thisbe' for the court of Theseus are vibrantly attuned to drama's potential for mimesis. They are so worried about frighting the ladies with a lion in their play that they arrange for the actor to show half his face through the lion's neck and preface his performance with a little cautionary statement of assurance that he is not really a lion but Snug the joiner. Bottom the weaver is denied his wish to play the lion along with all the other parts because he would 'fright the Duchess and the ladies, that they would shriek; and that were enough to hang us all'. Snout the tinker is drafted to play a wall because the lovers, Pyramus and Thisbe, separated by the partition of their parents' houses, must whisper to each other through the chink in a wall. In order to provide for moonshine as called for in the story, and out of fear that the moon may not be visible on the night of performance, Starveling the tailor agrees to 'present the person of moonshine' complete with the lantern, dog, and thornbush thought to be the attributes of the man in the moon. To these amateur actors, dramatic representation is all too real.

Their attempts at mimesis are of course laughable, but they do have the crucial effect of calling everyone's attention to the importance of imagination in making possible the full experience of dramatic performance. Shakespeare is talking about the particular kind of theatrical world he creates. It calls for the audience to use its imagination. Elsewhere, notably in *Henry V*, the chorus begs the audience, 'On your imaginary forces work'. When the actors talk of horses in *Henry V*, 'Think . . . that you see them / Printing their proud hoofs i'th' receiving earth'. Without the audience's active participation in the experience of theatre, the playwright and the actors can get nowhere. Mimesis is an illusion through which the part stands for the whole; a handful of actors cannot represent the great battle of Agincourt unless the audience suspends its disbelief during the play and imagines that it sees a whole army of warriors.

This idea of metonymy, or the part for the whole, resonates throughout the Shakespearean canon. Its tone is at once self-deprecatory and proud. On the one hand the artist and his acting company throw up their hands in mock despair. 'Can this cockpit hold / The vasty fields of France? Or may we cram / Within this wooden O the very casques / That did affright the air at Agincourt?' The 'wooden O' calls attention to the theatre building itself, the Globe, newly erected in 1599 partly for this play. Can a manmade wooden structure on the Bankside of the Thames in London represent the greatest battle in English history? Perish the thought. On the other hand, the artist knows what he is doing, and he is proud of his sleight of hand. He invites the audience into a friendly conspiracy: they will pretend they are looking at horses and armed soldiers, while he as artist will give them the magnificent language to make that pretence both possible and convincing.

Theseus, in *A Midsummer Night's Dream*, nicely captures both the self-deprecatory and the proud tone of the dramatist's manifesto. To his bride's complaint, about 'Pyramus and Thisbe', that 'This is the silliest stuff that ever I heard', he offers a thoughtful reply. 'The best in this kind are but shadows', he allows, and then follows up that concession with an appeal to imagination: 'the worst are no worse, if imagination amend them.' Daringly, Shakespeare calls attention to the similarities between 'Pyramus and Thisbe' and the larger play in which this interlude resides. Both are imitations, and both are therefore inherently limited as to the degree they can hope to achieve verisimilitude. But why strive for verisimilitude anyway? Is not the imaginative experience the more rewarding? It involves the audience in the very creative process. The more a play is verisimilar, the more it runs the risk of showing the audience a mere picture of their daily lives. Mimesis of this sort can be rewarding in its own way, but with imaginative theatre the possibilities are more open-ended. Shakespeare seems to be formulating a paradox, in fact: theatre of imagination thrives on its very limitations. The more the audience must meet the actors halfway, the more involved that audience is likely to become in a sense that something 'real' is happening to them.

Theseus is a useful analyst and theoretician of the theatrical experience because he is sophisticated, gracious, and well-educated; at the same time, there are limits to his wisdom. His finest statement about theatre of imagination is prefaced with his sceptical declaration that, to him, 'antique fables' and 'fairy toys' are 'More strange than true'; he finds them more quaintly interesting than convincing. He is an observer, distancing himself from the creative process even while he analyzes it. In his view, poetry is a kind of madness, akin to falling in love:

> Lovers and madmen have such seething brains,
> Such shaping fantasies, that apprehend
> More than cool reason ever comprehends.
> The lunatic, the lover, and the poet
> Are of imagination all compact.
> One sees more devils than vast hell can hold;
> That is the madman. The lover, all as frantic,
> Sees Helen's beauty in a brow of Egypt.
> The poet's eye, in a fine frenzy rolling,
> Doth glance from heaven to earth, from earth to heaven;
> And as imagination bodies forth
> The forms of things unknown, the poet's pen
> Turns them to shapes and gives to airy nothing
> A local habitation and a name.
>
> (5.1.4–17)

How fine of Shakespeare, to give this splendid celebration of the evocative power of poetry to a sceptic who is inclined to put down poetry as mad nonsense! Theseus describes precisely the kind of poetic drama that Shakespeare has been writing in *A Midsummer Night's Dream*: a drama that gives to 'airy nothing' a place in the theatre, providing fairies and monsters with 'a local habitation and a name'. His theatre is essentially different from drawing-room comedy in its insistence on juxtaposing heaven and earth, the immortal and the mortal, the fantastic and the ordinary. Theseus thinks, like Plato, that such imaginings are lies, not to be believed. Yet the description of such a vital 'frenzy' makes us wonder if visionary madness is not to be preferred to the limited truths of our daily lives. Shakespeare seems to be apologizing for Furor Poeticus – apologizing in both senses, of making apologies for it and yet defending it against its enemies.

A Midsummer Night's Dream is thus self-descriptively a kind of mad, visionary poetry. It is also, as its title suggests, a dream. The traditional metaphor of life as a dream coalesces with the idea here that theatre is also a dream, with the result that both life and theatre take on aspects of the experience of dreaming. Puck pursues these ideas in his concluding epilogue to the audience:

> If we shadows have offended,
> Think but this, and all is mended,
> That you have but slumbered here
> While these visions did appear.
>
> (5.1.418–21)

Going to the theatre is like going to sleep. You sleep; you dream; you don't know at first if the dream was real or not, even though it certainly did seem real. Then you waken and wonder what it all meant. Your life is somehow touched by the experience, and yet your life goes on as it did before. As Keats puts it so beautifully: 'Fled is that music; do I wake or sleep?'

Puck is, like other defenders of the imaginative poetic experience in Shakespeare, both defensive and proud. The show he has helped to stage-manage for the audience is a 'weak and idle theme, / No more yielding but a dream'. In part, this is a canny self-deprecatory move on the part of the Epilogue, on behalf of the entire acting company and the dramatist: if this spectacle seems frothy and insubstantial to you, we didn't promise you anything else. Yet the metaphor of dream is endlessly inviting, to 'tease us out of thought, / As doth eternity', to quote Keats again. What is 'real' in a play like this? Are we supposed to 'believe' in the fairies? On one level, of course not: they were actors, not fairies or anything else. On the level of popular lore about fairies, *A Midsummer Night's Dream* is deliberately playful: some people believe in fairies, and, more broadly, one can at least think hard about invisible presences all around us providing a kind of supernatural dimension to our otherwise earthbound and dreary existence. Perhaps, as Hamlet says to Horatio, there are more things in heaven and earth than are dreamt of in our philosophies.

On the level of philosophical debate about reality, an even more profound reversal seems to occur. Are the fairies real? In one sense, they are far more real than we who watch or read the play. We will be gathered to our ancestors in the fullness of time, and eventually forgotten – most of us, anyway. Puck, Oberon, Titania, and Bottom the Weaver are immortal. They have survived already for four centuries and more, and show no signs of old age yet. The paradox is one with which Plato loved to puzzle his student readers in fourth-century Athens. What is more real, a particular table or the idea of a table? A particular table has texture, solidity, and mass; it can be used as a practical table. Eventually, however, it will decay or be turned back into its constituent elements in some way. The idea of a table will endure. So too with a tree, which guarantees its immortality by flourishing, generating seed, and dying, so that the idea of a tree will be perpetuated by what Edmund Spenser calls 'mutability'. 'O chestnut tree, great-rooted blossomer', Yeats implores that tree, 'Are you the leaf, the blossom or the bole?' 'How can we know the dancer from the dance?' It is only through incessant change that constancy can be perceived as a pattern, an idea. Puck and Oberon share that characteristic of an idea. That is why Puck can afford to apologize in the midst of his boast of being a mere 'shadow'. He is laughing at us mere mortals.

Twelfth Night gives us another perspective on theatre as mimetic illusion. This play, like so many of Shakespeare's, takes pains to remind us that we are in the theatre, especially as we watch the subplot of Malvolio, Sir Toby, Sir Andrew, Maria, Fabian, and Feste. Sir Toby and his friends serve as a mirthful audience for the spectacle of Malvolio 'practising behaviour to his own shadow' with his affected mannerisms and then finding the ambiguous letter seemingly written for his benefit by the Countess Olivia but really authored by Maria. The clowns punctuate his reading of the letter, and his teasing out of it a meaning suited to his own self-love, with their satirical barbs, much like the onstage audience of

'Pyramus and Thisbe'. Afterwards, they savour the experience like an appreciative theatre audience. 'I will not give my part of this sport for a pension of thousands to be paid from the Sophy,' Fabian declares. And when they have confronted Malvolio and have heard him persist in his imagined new role as Olivia's favoured wooer, the comedians are sure they have never seen a more delicious dramatic performance. 'If this were played upon a stage, now', comments Fabian, 'I could condemn it as an improbable fiction.' The very absurdity of Malvolio's self-infatuation is part of what makes it so richly enjoyable.

Malvolio is a well-suited target for satire – indeed, just about the most pointed satire that Shakespeare ever wrote, other than in *Troilus and Cressida* – because he is an enemy of merriment and hence a foe of the kind of theatre that *Twelfth Night* represents. Malvolio believes in sobriety. That is presumably why the Countess Olivia retains him as her chief steward; he helps maintain the decorum that belongs to a house in mourning for the death of the Countess's brother. He tries to suppress the noisy merrymaking of Toby, Andrew, and Feste by inquiring in acid tones if they intend to make 'an alehouse of my lady's house' with their catches and their quaffing of much liquor. He has a point, surely, for the party has lasted into the wee hours of the morning; at the end of the scene (2.3), Toby concludes that ' 'Tis too late to go to bed now', and so he and Andrew resolve to warm up some more imported Spanish wine. Even Maria, no friend of Malvolio's and quite devoted to Toby, tries to warn them that their caterwauling is sure to awaken Olivia and prompt her to commission Malvolio to turn them all out of doors. Toby is an impecunious relative of Olivia's and a kind of Falstaffian moocher whose continued presence in the house is a drain on Olivia's patience and her pocketbook.

Malvolio's sobersided performance of duty would be acceptable as a counterweight to Toby and Andrew's excessive merriment were it not for the fact that Malvolio is a hypocrite. Secretly he longs for the pleasures of this world and for the authority to control others, both of which can be best attained by his becoming 'Count Malvolio'. He fantasizes about sharing Olivia's daybed and, even more than that, about putting Toby and Andrew in their place. He is vulnerable to Maria's scheme of the planted letter, supposedly written by Olivia, because Malvolio has long dreamed of being her favourite. What might otherwise be entrapment is justified, according to the satirical code governing this part of the play, by the fact that Malvolio is drawn into a 'crime' of social aspiration in which he is an active participant. Malvolio brings his downfall on himself, albeit with the eager assistance of those who hate him for being a killjoy.

Maria describes Malvolio as sometimes 'a kind of puritan'. Nowhere else does Shakespeare use this term (though Angelo's being 'precise' in *Measure for Measure* hints at a similar inclination), and seldom if ever does Shakespeare take such potent aim at a topical target. When challenged for her reasons in saying 'puritan', Maria backs off and settles for declaring that Malvolio is a 'time-pleaser' and 'affectioned ass' who is far too well 'persuaded of himself'. Still, the word 'puritan' has been thrown up for consideration. Is Malvolio a puritan? Only, in Maria's view, to the extent that puritans too are likely to be hypocrites of this sort. Maria draws back from labelling puritans generally in this way, but issues an implicit warning: if any puritans are like Malvolio, they deserve to be outwitted and humiliated. Puritanism was a hot-button issue when Shakespeare wrote *Twelfth Night* around 1600–2. Some reformers were vociferous in their opposition to the theatre, so much so that the authorities in London (where the longing for religious reform was particularly strong) took every excuse they could find to close down the playhouses. Playwrights like Ben Jonson and Thomas Dekker were soon to spice up their plays with openly satirical sketches of puritan hypocrites, anticipating some of the points that Molière would caricature later in seventeenth-century France in his *Tartuffe*. Shakespeare, with characteristic tact, avoids any wholesale indictment of puritanism. At the same time, he sounds a warning that has a direct bearing on the world of the theatre. If Malvolio is hostile to the liberation of the human spirit that theatre can help celebrate and enhance, then there is no room for him in the concluding harmonies of this play.

Feste, as Malvolio's nemesis and opposite number, is the apostle of merriment. Olivia's presumed reason for keeping Feste around as her fool is that she wishes to be cheered up from time to time, just as she also prefers at other times to be watched over by the melancholy Malvolio. Feste's gnomic advice to Olivia, when it is his turn, is that she give up her self-willed mourning for a dead brother in favour of a full participation in life's joys; her brother is in heaven, and she is still on earth, where she has an obligation to be happy. Feste's songs celebrate the age-old notion of seizing the moment of pleasure while one is still young:

> What is love? 'Tis not hereafter;
> Present love hath present laughter;
> What's to come is still unsure.

In delay there lies no plenty.
Then come kiss me, sweet and twenty;
Youth's a stuff will not endure.
(2.3.47–52)

This is the gospel of innocent hedonism that often takes the name of Epicureanism, though Epicurus' thought is much more complex than a simple urging to seize the moment of pleasure.

At any rate, the battle is joined between Lent and Carnival in this play, and Carnival consistently wins the contest for our hearts. Toby's riposte to Malvolio, when he is attempting to break up their late-night party, has become famous, if only through the title of Somerset Maugham's novel, *Cakes and Ale*: 'Dost thou think, because thou art virtuous, there shall be no more cakes and ale?' The point is well taken. Malvolio has a right to be 'virtuous' (translate here as self-righteous) himself, but he has no right to impose his sense of moral propriety on others. If he is a moral censor, then he is too like those who keep trying to close down the London theatres, and are also hostile to maypoles, village fairs, and the church-ales or festive gatherings at churches that Toby may be referring to. The only way to respond to such would-be arbiters of personal behaviour is to lay a trap for them made out of their own vulnerability to self-regard and a secret, hypocritical longing for the very pleasures they would deny to others.

Malvolio is harshly handled in this unusually satirical play, so much so that he is able to cry, with understandable feeling, 'Madam, you have done me wrong, / Notorious wrong'. Olivia is not primarily to blame, actually, but she has countenanced the imprisonment of her steward out of fear for his sanity. Her response to his outburst is properly gracious and generous; using his very words, she allows that Malvolio 'hath been most notoriously abused', and no doubt agrees with Orsino that Malvolio should be pursued and entreated 'to a peace'. Whether Malvolio can be placated, however, remains doubtful. His warning shot as he stalks away is that 'I'll be revenged on the whole pack of you'. He cannot have known, of course, that puritan reformers would close all English theatres in 1642, at the outbreak of war between militant reformers and supporters of the monarch and the Established Church. Still, Malvolio certainly did know that the opponents of revelry had means at their disposal to close the theatres in the 1600s whenever outbreaks of plague or any other excuses presented themselves. *Twelfth Night* comes close to being militant in its defence of merrymaking. Shakespeare's theatre could not afford to let the killjoy challenge go unanswered.

Shylock, in *The Merchant of Venice*, is another enemy of merriment who is banished from the inclusive gathering at the play's end. He is thus, like Malvolio, a killjoy enemy of the spirit of hedonistic pleasure and carnival that also includes theatre. Shylock dislikes music, banishing it from his house. 'Lock up my doors', he orders his daughter Jessica, 'and when you hear the drum / And the vile squealing of the wry-necked fife, / Clamber not you up to the casements then, / Nor thrust your head into the public street / To gaze on Christian fools with varnished faces.' Because he will not have such sounds of merriment enter his house, he orders Jessica to 'stop my house's ears – I mean my casements' (2.5.30–5). Shylock prefers the literal word of 'casements' – windows – to the metaphoric 'ears'.

Shylock is precise and legalistic with words, since they are used to draw up legal contracts. When young Bassanio comes to him asking for a loan and bidding him be 'assured' that Shylock can feel safe in taking Antonio's bond, Shylock's answer is sharp and quick: 'I will be assured I may'. Bassanio meant that Antonio is to be trusted; Shylock means that he will protect himself with legal guarantees. He concedes that Antonio is a 'good' man – that is, a good credit risk. To Bassanio, 'good' means 'morally upright'.

The painful issue in *The Merchant of Venice* of hostility between Christian and Jew is thus exacerbated by the contrast between merriment and denial. The Christians have much to answer for in this play in their antipathy toward Jews: Antonio's spitting on Shylock's Jewish gaberdine, Gratiano's jeering cries during the courtroom scene. At the same time, the play does equate hedonism and camaraderie with the Christian way of life in Venice. Friendships are common, and are loving: Antonio risks his life for his friend Bassanio, and the young man would do the same for the older man. The play begins with Salerio and Solanio inquiring into Antonio's sadness; they wish to cheer him up. The joyous celebration in Belmont at the play's end, with its crowd of companions and lovers, is only the final confirmation of a play-long celebration of friendship and mutuality.

At times, to be sure, hedonism betrays its thoughtless excesses, as in the drunken revelling of *Twelfth Night*. When young Lorenzo and his friends steal Jessica out of her father's house to be Lorenzo's bride, they dress themselves appropriately as '*masquers*' in a spirit of carnival. They take with them more than Jessica. She throws down a casket filled with treasure, and then, not content with that, goes back for 'more ducats'. No doubt she regards this wealth as her dowry, but it is stealing. Lorenzo later confesses as much, albeit ambiguously, when he describes how Jessica did 'steal from the wealthy Jew'. This phrase suggests both that she stole away and that she took Shylock's money with her. To compound this injury with further insult, the young people go on a spending spree, giving a ring in return for a monkey. The ring (ironically anticipating the so-called 'ring episode' at the end of the play) turns out to be one that Shylock was given by his wife-to-be, Leah, when he was a bachelor. These young Christians are free with wealth rather than hoarding it, and elsewhere we are invited to approve of such openness, but in this instance the eloping couple offend human decency by their thoughtless freedom with Shylock's personal heirloom.

At its best, the ethic of hedonism defines itself as risk, most of all risk for others. Bassanio loves risk; he stakes everything on a journey to win the lady of Belmont. Antonio expresses his love for Bassanio by taking the risk on him, a risk that begins as financial and then becomes physical and life-threatening. Bassanio describes the risk he wants to take as like shooting an arrow after one that has gone astray, double or nothing. It is reckless (practically speaking, this is a dumb way to try to find a lost arrow), but by the same token it is generous. Bassanio needs to borrow money because he has spent it too freely. We are drawn to this openness and sharing, even while we see its hazards.

Shylock takes no risks, and he hates stealing. 'Thrift is blessing, if men steal it not,' he avers. He speaks admiringly of Jacob, who, as we read in Genesis 27, made a deal with Laban that Jacob would get all the particoloured sheep in their herd, whereupon Jacob set up variegated wands or sticks before the sheep during their act of copulation. The device worked: the ewes delivered parti-coloured lambs, 'and those were Jacob's'. 'This was a way to thrive, and he was blest.'

Shylock aspires to thrive in just such a way, by driving hard and even devious bargains. He lends out money at interest, something that Christians like Antonio deplore because it makes barren money reproduce itself unnaturally, as it were. Historically, of course, this Christian disapproval of usury oozes with hypocrisy: Jews were allowed to practise usury because money was needed to capitalize the monarchies of Western Europe, and then the Jewish moneylenders were deplored as unsanctified because they performed a morally contaminated act. Shakespeare's play does not seem, however, to accuse Venice directly of this kind of hypocrisy.

So far as we can tell, Shylock practises usury because it suits him. Antonio, conversely, practises not usury but commerce; he takes risks, trusting to ships that are vulnerable to storms and piracy. Such risks are not only allowable but are sanctioned by the Christian ethic of taking chances and lending to a friend without interest.

The uncomfortable polarity in *The Merchant of Venice* between the old dispensation and the new meets its severest test in the trial scene in act four. Shylock demands vengeance, and appears to have the law on his side. He has a signed contract, and the contract has expired. The forfeiture is stipulated as a pound of Antonio's flesh. Such a ritual cutting and murder awakens painful memories of the crucifixion of Christ; history is about to repeat itself. Antonio is the intended sacrificial victim, willing to die out of love for his friend Bassanio. Bassanio can seemingly do nothing, even by offering, with money received from Portia, vastly more than the original borrowed sum. As a commercial city, Venice needs to abide by the terms of legal contracts; otherwise, merchants will no longer trade there. The opposition seems painfully clear, with the vindictiveness of the older dispensation holding sway, temporarily at least, over the Christian charity of the new.

The conflict is of course severely complicated by the hypocrisies of Lorenzo and his friends, by Shylock's eloquent plea that he is being persecuted as a Jew ('Hath not a Jew eyes?'), and, in the trial scene, by the hair-splitting interpretation of Shylock's contract by means of which Portia, disguised as young Bellario, gets the case thrown out of court: Shylock is to have the flesh but not a drop of blood, and is to have precisely a pound of flesh, no more and no less. In the last analysis, nonetheless, Shylock must lose because, like Malvolio, he is a spoiler in a play about the difficult quest for human happiness. Jessica is accepted into the communal, celebratory life of Belmont because she embraces its premise of a shared, hedonistic commitment to friendship and risk. Shylock is forced to convert to Christianity, but he cannot and will not become a willing Christian. Today we honour him for that and deplore the forced conversion especially (modern stage productions generally cannot stomach it), but he chooses the wrong side from a theatrical point of view. To the extent that Shakespearean theatre celebrates the spirit of carnival, Shylock is doomed to play the role of the blocking figure.

Throughout his career, Shakespeare never tires of calling attention to the contrivances through which theatre achieves its magical effects. One such moment, as we have seen, is the coming to life of Hermione's statue in *A Winter's Tale*; our uncertainty as to whether the seeming miracle is 'real' or a theatrical contrivance says much about the nature of theatrical illusion. Another particularly stunning moment occurs near the end of *Antony and Cleopatra*, when Cleopatra realizes that Octavius Caesar intends to take her back to Rome as his trophy. She imagines what the scene will be like:

> The quick comedians
> Extemporally will stage us and present
> Our Alexandrian revels; Antony
> Shall be brought drunken forth, and I shall see
> Some squeaking Cleopatra boy my greatness
> I'the posture of a whore.
>
> (5.2.216–21)

How intrepid of Cleopatra, and of Shakespeare, to call attention to the fact that Cleopatra is being played onstage by a boy actor! Shakespeare loves risks too, it seems. Yet he knows what he is doing. By reminding the audience that it is involved in the creation of an illusion, the dramatist enlists the support of that audience in a congenial conspiracy to build a theatre of the imagination. Such a theatre is invulnerable because we know it is a fabrication. We helped make it so.

The Tempest engages our complicity in a speech that is often imagined to be Shakespeare's farewell to the theatre. Having staged for the wedding couple a masque in their honour, Prospero as playwright–magician stops to consider what he has accomplished.

> Be cheerful, sir.
> Our revels now are ended. These our actors,
> As I foretold you, were all spirits and
> Are melted into air, into thin air;
> And, like the baseless fabric of this vision,
> The cloud-capped towers, the gorgeous palaces,
> The solemn temples, the great globe itself,
> Yea, all which it inherit, shall dissolve,
> And, like this insubstantial pageant faded,
> Leave not a rack behind. We are such stuff
> As dreams are made on, and our little life
> Is rounded with a sleep.
>
> (4.1.147–58)

Plate 8 A playhouse based on the Swan Theatre, *c.* 1595, drawing by C. Walter Hodges. Reprinted by permission of Oxford University Press.

Prospero's reference to 'the great globe itself' would surely have been recognized by his audience as alluding to the Globe Theatre, the building in which they are seeing *The Tempest*. The theatre is a little model of the world in which we live. Its 'heavens' look down from above upon the main stage, representing the world of human activity. The underworld lies below. All is insubstantial, since the actors are only playing their parts and the building itself will one day disappear, but so will the gorgeous palaces of our mortal existence. Life itself is illusion in that sense. It is accordingly like a dream. We are such stuff as dreams are made on, and so is theatre. Life, dream, and theatre all coalesce in a vision of a pageant that will dissolve and fade, and yet is eternal in the living memory of our imaginations. In an epilogue, Prospero emphasizes that this living memory all depends on us as audience. Unless we applaud, Prospero can never be set free.

I hope that this book has made its point in reinforcing this great Shakespearean theme of theatre as dream, as imagination, and thus as a representation of what is at once evanescent and immortal in us. Shakespeare's writing career takes on the character of Jaques' speech on the Seven Ages of Man in *As You Like It*. He writes comedies of courtship when he is a young man. More or less simultaneously he is interested in how young people – men especially – try to find out who they are as sons of their fathers and as persons with a destiny to achieve something. Once he has reflected on these processes of maturation, Shakespeare then seems drawn to more painful issues of sexual jealousy and compulsive sexual longing, disillusionment about political life, scepticism about providentiality and the existence of the gods, the difficulties of trying to achieve compatibility, temptation to commit crimes for the sake of self-advancement, and male fears of domination by controlling women. The inevitable process of ageing brings with it fears of lost male potency and of diminishing options for self-fulfillment, and anxiety about the approach of death. Family conflicts in these later years centre on resentment of ungrateful children, especially daughters. At the same time, in a crucial recuperative move, daughters turn out to be the means to recovery of the endangered self. So do long-lost wives, although here the vision is more fleeting and is abandoned, significantly, in the play that Shakespeare may have billed as his farewell to the theatre.

This is not to argue a close autobiographical reading of Shakespeare's plays. He did not have to kill his wife to write *Othello* or assassinate a king to write *Macbeth*. We do not know that he experienced midlife crisis, though medical specialists tell us that most men do, in one form or another. We can hope that the unstable vision of a reunion in retirement with a long-lost wife does not hint at disappointment. We do know, on the other hand, that Shakespeare wrote poetry and plays about love when he was young and plays about ageing when he was old. He chose stories to dramatize that engaged his imagination with topics relevant to his current and constantly shifting position in the cycle of the Seven Ages. This, I would argue, is one key to the mystery of why he engages our imaginations so deeply. He writes of desire, jealousy, ambition, ingratitude, misanthropy, and charitable forgiveness because he has known what it is like to be there. He sees into the conditions of human happiness and unhappiness with unequalled sympathy and insight because he is a genius but also because he knows how to respond to and portray what other people are going through. This uncanny ability to put himself in other people's minds and situations is what is often called, in Keats's memorable phrase, Shakespeare's 'negative capability'.[2] It is one of his extraordinary gifts to the human race.

CHAPTER TEN

♦

Shakespeare Today

I puked and cried – that's what Mom said.
School sucks. Why can't I stay in bed?
I want that girl. What is her name?
I'll kick some ass and stake my claim.
I'm fat? So what? I've won the game.
I limp these days, and feel the gout.
Say, now, what was that all about?
John D. Smith, 'Seven Ages of Man'¹

What can it mean for us personally, today, to think of Shakespeare's Seven Ages? In what way is the idea relevant? After all, despite its apparent time-lessness as a generic group portrait of the human experience, the idea is couched in terms that are about four hundred years old. The word 'man' to which Jaques applies his description of the 'seven ages' of life is not just a semantic nicety, using the word 'man' to represent the whole human race, as in the German *man*; as we have seen in Chapter 1, Shakespeare's conception of human experience is that of the male, progressing from the kind of education that the young 'schoolboy' enjoyed in his day (the King Edward VI school in Stratford-upon-Avon had no female pupils), to a male-oriented encounter with the opposite sex in the shape of 'his mistress' eyebrow', to soldiership that is 'Jealous in honour, sudden, and quick in quarrel', to official status as a 'justice' who is 'Full of wise saws and modern instances', and then to 'the lean and slippered pantaloon' of old age in which the garments are those of an elderly gentleman. Even the approach of death in Jaques' wry harangue (*As You Like It*,

2.7.138–65) is explicitly male, as the 'big manly voice' of the imagined voyager through life turns again 'toward childish treble', so that the very phenomenon of 'second childishness' is pictured as a reversal of the physiological process in which the adolescent male discovers, through the deepening of his voice, that he is now an adult.

Other difficulties intervene in a search for relevance today. Shakespeare's language is Elizabethan English, filled with expressions that need glossing: the male infant 'Mewling' (crying with a catlike noise) in the nurse's arms, the soldier 'bearded like the pard' (wearing a bristling leopard-like moustache), the soldier 'jealous in honour' (quickly aroused to anger in a quarrel about honour), the justice's belly lined with good 'capon' (rooster castrated to make the flesh more tender), his speech full of wise 'saws' (sayings) and 'modern instances' (commonplace illustrations). The old man is characterized as 'the lean and slippered pantaloon' (a feeble old man, dressed as a ridiculous stage type out of Italian *commedia dell'arte*) wearing his 'youthful hose' (trousers saved from his younger days) that are now too wide for his 'shrunk shank' (withered calves and thighs), while his childish treble voice 'pipes / And whistles in his [its] sound'. Words that seem misleadingly familiar to us are sometimes quite different in their connotation, such as 'his' meaning 'its' in the sample just cited, or the phrase 'mere oblivion', which doesn't mean 'merely', but rather the total forgetfulness that often comes with senility. 'Jealous in honour' uses 'jealous' in a way that is no longer familiar; it hearkens back to the earliest meanings of the word in English, taken in the fourteenth century from medieval French and late Latin, signifying 'vehement in feeling, wrathful, furious'. The borrowed French of 'Sans teeth, sans eyes, sans taste, sans everything' requires translation for those not familiar with French.

Shifts in social custom are apparent everywhere in this familiar speech, distancing the reader or viewer from the immediacy of a readily understood personal experience. The nurse holding the infant is presumably a wet nurse, hired by the baby's family in a day when such nursing on a twenty-four-hour basis was cheap and widely available (like Juliet's Nurse in *Romeo and Juliet*). We see the schoolboy with his 'satchel' or schoolbag on his way to school, with never a school bus or family van in sight. The soldier encounters a type of warfare like that we have seen in Shakespeare's history plays, wholly unfamiliar today. The justice has a 'pouch' by his side, in which to keep safe his money and personal items. The idea of an old man still wearing the trousers of his youth is unfamiliar to our world of planned obsolescence and changing styles. To understand why he is a 'pantaloon' requires, or is at least assisted by, a knowledge of the Italian *commedia dell'arte* as a type of comedy written in stock scenes and peopled by stereotyped characters like the doddering old man. Shakespeare is in many ways a male writer inhabiting his own sixteenth- and seventeenth-century world. He is very English.

Despite all these hurdles, and in some ways because of them, the pursuit of Shakespeare is truly a lovely quest. I consider myself extraordinarily lucky to have devoted much of my teaching career to him. I have taught many other writers as well, from Homer and Herodotus and Thucydides to Geoffrey Chaucer, Edmund Spenser, Philip Sidney, John Donne, George Herbert, John Milton, John Dryden, Alexander Pope, Jonathan Swift, Henry Fielding, Jane Austen, Charlotte and Emily Brontë, William Wordsworth, John Keats, Walter Scott, Gustave Flaubert, Charles Dickens, George Eliot, William Thackeray, Stendhal, Leo Tolstoi, Thomas Hardy, Mark Twain, Henry James, Edith Wharton, Marcel Proust, T. S. Eliot, William Butler Yeats, Wallace Stevens, Albert Camus, E. M. Forster, and William Faulkner; and much of my teaching has been in the whole history of Western drama, from Aeschylus, Sophocles, Euripides, and Aristophanes to Christopher Marlowe, Ben Jonson, Thomas Middleton, Thomas Dekker, Molière, William Wycherley, William Congreve, Richard Sheridan, Henrik Ibsen, Anton Chekhov, August Strindberg, George Bernard Shaw, Oscar Wilde, John Millington Synge, Sean O' Casey, Samuel Beckett, Bertolt Brecht, Harold Pinter, Tom Stoppard, Caryl Churchill, and many more. By teaching in interdisciplinary humanities programs, I have been able to keep in touch with a wide range of great books. Still, I keep coming back to Shakespeare every year – literally, in the classroom, every year, for about forty-five years and counting.

People do ask me, as I'm sure they ask others, don't you get bored with teaching Shakespeare so often? Aren't you in danger of burning out? The answer is no, absolutely not. The students keep coming, and their enthusiasms and new questions are a wonderful stimulant. So too with reading what is written about Shakespeare, attending conferences, engaging in scholarly debate on still-burning issues: what was his relationship to Catholicism? Can we learn about his own beliefs and experiences from what he wrote? Why did he retire at what is for us a relatively early age, before he was fifty? What do his plays reflect in the way of racial and ethnic prejudice? What do they suggest about power struggles between men and women, between King and Parliament, England and the rest of the world? If Shakespeare can in some ways be Our Contemporary (to use the famous phrase of Jan Kott), is he so because he seems attuned existentially to a world on the brink of apocalypse or because he offers a vision of hope? The very fact that such issues are hotly debated today reflects a desire on the part of all of us to ask that this great writer give voice to the condition of life as we know it.

Speaking for myself, I can say that Shakespeare remains eternally fresh and excitingly new because he changes so as his texts respond to our questionings. The idea that 'Shakespeare' is a constantly evolving, multivocal, resonant, and richly ambivalent text is one main reason that I feel lucky to have lived through, and to have taught my way through, the last half century. Readers today are often baffled and put off by the technical language of much postmodern criticism and its roster of new ideologies: the so-called 'New' Criticism, New Historicism, Cultural Materialism, deconstruction, poststructuralism, feminist interpretation, psychoanalytic interpretation, semiotic theory, audience response criticism, reader response criticism, and still more. Jargon is undoubtedly a problem in some recent critical writing; trendiness and obfuscation are perhaps inevitable in a time of intellectual revolution. Younger scholars entering the competitive world of the academic marketplace are under practical pressures to publish and under personal necessities of resolving their own identity crises by finding a label for what it is they do. Ideological rivalries encourage young teachers to find out who the Enemy is, and to move ahead in the academic world by overthrowing older and presumably outmoded ways of thinking about Shakespeare (or any other subject). These are the hazards. As the Duke asks, rhetorically, in *Measure for Measure*, 'what's yet in this / That bears the name of life?' (3.1.38–9). Yet, as Friar Laurence says in *Romeo and Juliet*, 'I do spy a kind of hope' (4.1.68). 'Hope', incidentally, is a word that Shakespeare uses with astonishing frequency. The hope lies in Shakespeare's malleability. He is eternally relevant because he responds acutely to virtually any question that is put to him, and does so often by disconcerting us with questions of his own.

Thus it is that we are so often left with uncomfortable challenges by modern criticism and performances of the plays instead of reassuring verities. No longer would it be possible, I suspect, for anyone to write a book called *The Meaning of Shakespeare*, as Harold Goddard did in 1951. That book is still in print, from the University of Chicago Press, and does rather well, in fact, owing presumably to a widespread longing to identify '*the* meaning' of Shakespeare. Today, something like it would have to be called '*The Meanings of Shakespeare*', or else more simply abandon the word 'meaning' entirely. The word 'meaning' raises a red flag to many a modern critic, and rightly so; as a teacher, I usually cringe when I read a student's paper attempting to explain what Shakespeare's 'meaning' is, not because I don't long to know the answer, but because posing the question that way leads so often to reductive answers. To see *Macbeth* as an object lesson in the great commandment, 'Thou shalt not kill', is to invite judgemental interpretation of killing as sinful. It reduces the play to the level of any 'crime does not pay' narrative, and it seeks a utilitarian answer to the great purposefulness of literature by turning that literature into homily. Shakespeare does not write sermons, thank goodness. One of the many great paradoxes about Shakespeare is that he can dramatize moral values so lucidly and humanely without doing so as a moral essayist. Even when we sense that Shakespeare encourages us to sympathize with a whole set of what might be called moral values, he never preaches. Clearly we are invited to admire Desdemona and Cordelia and Viola as loyal, decent, caring characters; conversely we are shown what is so deplorable in Edmund, Iago, Richard III, Claudius, Goneril, and Regan. Even here the characterizations are immensely subtle, so that we strive to understand what has led these characters to behave as they do, and cannot help applauding the brilliance of their performance as intriguers. In ways such as these, Shakespeare engages with topics that are intensely meaningful while at the same time demonstrating how a quest for 'the meaning' or 'the intent' can lead one astray into certitudes that are commonplace.

The longing for reassurance is understandably acute in view of our century-long experience with global war and other severe dislocations. Goddard's *The Meaning of Shakespeare* (1951) marks, in a way, the end of an era, along with E. M. W. Tillyard's *The Elizabethan World Picture* (1943), with its portrayal of the great intellectual and spiritual coherences that presumably held together the world of Shakespeare and his contemporaries. More in keeping with the ferment of post-World-War-II disillusionment was Jan Kott's *Shakespeare Our Contemporary* in 1964, looking at Shakespeare as an existential author attuned to the horrors of the Jewish holocaust and the enslavement of Eastern Europe (where Kott had grown up) behind Stalin's Iron Curtain. Kott saw Shakespeare as a dramatist of the Absurd, as defined by Antonin Artaud (*The Theatre and Its Double*, 1958) and later by Jerzy Grotowski (*Toward a Poor Theatre*, 1968). Kott's challenging interpretation had an immense effect on theatrical performances of Shakespeare, as seen for example in Peter Brook's *A Midsum-*

mer Night's Dream (1970), with its intensely metatheatrical demystifying of fairy magic; gone were realistic scenery and fairies with gossamer-winged costumes in favour of a white box filled with circus-act performers on trapezes. Brook's *King Lear* (1962, filmed in 1970–1) was no less revisionary and Kott-inspired: in a bleak, wintry landscape, Lear stood revealed as a selfish old man capable of ruining the lives of his daughters, while those who persecuted him were ready to use any cruelty at their disposal. Gloucester's eyes were scooped out with a spoon; Cordelia's neck snapped as she was hanged in prison; Goneril dashed out the brains of her sister Regan before hurling her own head against a huge rock. All the characters were stripped of heroic stature. These were, after all, the years of the Cuban missile crisis and its threat of nuclear war with the Soviet Union, growing unrest over the Vietnam War, the assassinations of Jack and Robert Kennedy and Martin Luther King, Jr, incessant conflict in the Middle East and much of the Third World, and ominous signs of impending ecological disasters.

Under the pressures and challenges of such a changing world, Shakespeare has changed too. Even his texts have been subjected to revisionary analysis. A collection of essays called *The Division of the Kingdoms: Shakespeare's Two Versions of 'King Lear'*, edited by Gary Taylor and Michael Warren in 1983, has been strongly influential in its argument that the two texts (the Quarto of 1608 and the First Folio of 1623) represent two different states of *King Lear*, almost two different plays; and the approach has had no less of an impact on the study of *Hamlet*, with its three early texts (a seemingly unauthorized Quarto of 1603, an authorized second Quarto in 1604 'Newly imprinted and enlarged to almost as much again as it was', and the Folio of 1623). Other multiple-text plays, including *The Merry Wives of Windsor*, *Henry V*, and *Troilus and Cressida*, present similar ambiguities. The great deconstructive insight of Michel Foucault, that we have not a single text but texts, turns out to be importantly true of Shakespeare. To determine what actual words Shakespeare wrote is problematic, and continues to be so.

If this indeterminism is true of the printed texts themselves, multiplicity is inevitably present, and to a larger extent, in modern interpretation of what those words can mean. Performance history offers many instances. Laurence Olivier's film version of *Hamlet* (1948), for instance, announces itself at the start as 'the tragedy of a man who could not make up his mind'. Olivier's model for this thematic emphasis was a psychoanalytic study of the play by a student of Sigmund Freud, Ernest Jones, entitled

Hamlet and Oedipus. Accordingly, the film devotes close attention to the warm encounters between Hamlet and his mother in her private chambers, since Hamlet's unresolved emotional difficulties stem, according to this interpretation, from an incestuous Oedipal attachment to his mother and hence a paralyzing sense of envy at the hated sexual possessor of that mother. Because Grigori Kozintsev's 1964 film, in Russian, sees Hamlet's story from the point of view of a director who had been incarcerated in a prison camp by the Stalinist regime during World War II for his allegedly subversive ideas, this film implicitly defends the integrity of the artist in a totalitarian world. Franco Zeffirelli's *Hamlet* of 1990 is an action film in which the protagonist (Mel Gibson) overpowers and kills his enemies with a dispatch that contrasts markedly with the brooding, melancholy Hamlets of nineteenth-century stage tradition (such as John Philip Kemble and Henry Irving). Gertrude, as played by Glenn Close, is anything but the passively indecisive queen often seen onstage; this Gertrude knows what she wants, namely Claudius (Alan Bates) as her lover and husband. Joseph Papp's *Hamlet* at the Public Theatre in New York, 1968, shocked audiences with its opening tableau of a manacled Hamlet in a coffin-like cradle at the feet of the bed occupied by his mother and hated uncle. At Wisdom Bridge Theatre in Chicago in the 1980s, under the direction of Robert Falls, Claudius was transformed into a television president in the style of Ronald Reagan, appearing on TV monitors for his first public appearance while his advance men busily set up for the cocktail reception at which press reporters would be given the 'spin' of the new administration. Kenneth Branagh's 1989 film broke with tradition by adopting a four-hour uncut text and by depicting Polonius (Richard Briers) as canny and serious rather than, as often seen, a doddering old busybody. In Michael Almereyda's modern-dress film of 2000, the protagonist (Ethan Hawke) is a rebellious youngster with a passion for digital equipment and experimental filmmaking who is understandably alienated by the sybaritic lifestyle of his powerfully rich uncle (Kyle MacLachlan), chief executive officer of Denmark Corporation, and that uncle's creature-comfort-loving new wife (Diane Venora). The universality of *Hamlet* in modern times takes the form of an almost limitless variety.

Examples of such multiplicity of approaches are to be found throughout the Shakespeare canon. *Much Ado About Nothing* has adopted the various guises of the American southwest frontier, with Dogberry as a bumbling sheriff (John Houseman and Jack Landau, Stratford, Connecticut, 1957), early Victorian England of the 1840s (Douglas Seale,

Stratford-upon-Avon, 1958), Regency England of 1811–20 (Michael Langham, Stratford-upon-Avon, 1961), Edwardian England of 1901–10 (William Hutt, Stratford, Canada, 1971), and British Raj India (John Barton, Stratford-upon-Avon, 1976), to name only a few possibilities. A. J. Antoon's production at the Delacorte Theatre in New York in 1972 and subsequently on public television set the play in small-town America during the Teddy Roosevelt era of the 1900s, with khaki-clad soldiers returning from a military campaign (presumably the Spanish-American War), brightly decorated reviewing stands, brass bands, player pianos, barber shops, vintage automobiles, and all the trappings of that long-ago Age of Innocence. Kenneth Branagh shot his 1993 *Much Ado* on location in Tuscan Italy, with loving attention to the boxwood hedges, fountains, and fourteenth-century architecture of the splendid Villa Vignamaggio. Directors have even located *Much Ado* in Messina, Sicily, where Shakespeare imagines the story to take place; Franco Zeffirelli did so in 1965 at London's National Theatre, albeit moving the time frame forward to the early twentieth century. Charles Kean, at London's Princess's Theatre in 1838, was more literal: with lavishly expensive sets, he treated his audiences to an opening view of Messina harbour, showing a lighthouse, various mansions with lighted windows, and the moon rising slowly over the deep blue waters of the Mediterranean. Herbert Beerbohm Tree also, at His Majesty's Theatre in 1905, provided Sicilian landscapes and Italian gardens.

To take another example, *Romeo and Juliet* has led a life in the theatre and on screen as varied as the ever-changing cultures from which those productions have arisen. Henry Irving, at London's Lyceum Theatre in 1882, went in for lavish surroundings – vaulted arches, stone staircases, ironwork grill gates – in his depiction of Juliet's tomb in act five. Mary Anderson, also at the Lyceum, in 1884, outdid Irving with a recreation of the Piazza Dante in Verona, complete with a handsome Renaissance garden. More recent directors have preferred simple sets to allow swift action, as in Glen Byam Shaw's partly abstract and geometrical set, with concentric circles and curved walkways, at Stratford-upon-Avon in 1954. Joseph Papp, at New York's Delacorte Theatre in 1968, constructed a scaffold set with runways extending into the audience. Franco Zeffirelli's 1968 film, exploiting fully the camera's protean eye, takes the opposite tack of providing as gorgeous a scene as possible, with the lovers (Leonard Whiting and Olivia Hussey) confessing their passion for one another in a garden and terrace where they are almost able to touch; later, after their marriage, they are shown briefly in bed. Zeffirelli's Verona is a place of sunbaked streets, piazzas, stone stairs, winding alleys, and inhabitants in colourful outfits copied out of Renaissance paintings. (The actual outdoor filming was done in several north Italian towns more suitably picturesque than modern-day Verona itself.) Baz Luhrmann's *Romeo + Juliet* (1996) sees the play in an updated, postmodern idiom suited to the cultural values of an American city like Miami or Los Angeles, though the outdoor filming actually was done in Mexico City. The mansion of the Capulets is a masterpiece of vulgar conspicuous consumption of wealth; its owner is a Mafia Boss (Paul Sorvino). Capulet's wife (Diane Venora), seen slipping her slender frame into a Cleopatra costume as she prepares for their lavish ball, is a pill-popping, chain-smoking society woman who cannot understand why her laid-back daughter, Juliet (Clare Daines), would be reluctant to marry the prize celebrity bachelor of the social season, Dave Paris (Paul Rudd). MTV film techniques add to the frenzied contemporaneity. Friar Laurence (Pete Postlethwaite) is a New Age priest at home in a modern world of experimental drugs. Juliet's Nurse (Miriam Margolyes) is Hispanic. Romeo (Leonardo Di Caprio) hangs out with his buddies at the seedy Sycamore Grove Amusement Park or the Globe pool room. Mercutio (Harold Perrineau) is a drug-addicted black drag queen. The first street confrontation between Montagues and Capulets culminates in the blowing up of a gas station. Other versions too, including the splendid adaptation *West Side Story* (1961), have pursued analogies to gang warfare in modern cities between ethnically antagonistic populations. Directors have found rich dividends in stressing the contemporary relevance of Shakespeare's love story; even if older and more traditional audiences sometimes balk at the updating and complain of the loss or impairment of much of Shakespeare's language, younger audiences have flocked to these productions. Shakespeare is a constantly evolving cultural phenomenon.

Recent criticism of Shakespeare's plays and poems has had the same effect of opening up a striking and continually new range of possibilities. John Drakakis's collection of revisionist essays, published in 1985 under the title *Alternative Shakespeares*, nicely captures the new spirit of the enterprise: there are many Shakespeares, and they offer bracing alternatives to the more traditional, canonized figure of England's national poet and dramatist. Some studies in this vein are deliberately outrageous, but many are not, and in either case the challenge is liberating. Take *The Tempest*, for example. The traditional reading of Prospero is that he is a

benign if somewhat austere father and duke who has been unjustly banished from his dukedom of Milan to a desert island with no other
company than his only daughter and a strange islander named Caliban.
When his one-time enemies happen to come within reach of his magical
power, he causes a storm to cast them ashore and then subjects them to
a series of humiliating trials, ending in his forgiving them and blessing the
marriage of his daughter Miranda to young Ferdinand. As we have seen
in Chapter 9, this can be read as a kind of self-portrait of the ageing
dramatist himself, preparing for retirement as he stage-manages the lives
of everyone on the island and then bids farewell at last to the potent
visionary art (embodied in Ariel) that has enabled him to do what he has
done. There is much to be said for this reading, surely, and yet it is refresh-
ing to consider a more radical view in which Prospero is overbearingly
cruel and even sadistic in his manipulation of people's lives, and in which
his enslavement of Caliban is the act of a colonial master. Recent stage
interpretations have often depicted Caliban not as a freakish half-human,
as in many a nineteenth-century production, but rather as a thoughtful
and understandably angry Caribbean black male suffering the oppression
of unasked-for European white rule.

Criticism of *The Tempest* has pursued the same point, by emphasizing
Caliban's innocent perception of natural beauty, his mistrust of the colo-
nializing impetus of European language and culture, and his longing to
be free. Even if, as we have seen in Chapter 9, Prospero is not a colonialist in the normal sense of commercial exploitation, he (and Miranda)
do not understand Caliban well, and they do not treat him well. Caliban's
protesting that the island was his before they arrived resonates today in a
modern world that generally views European colonization as a wrong turn
in history. To impose this view of colonization on Shakespeare's island is
of course anachronistic, but it has had the beneficial effect of opening up
a series of debates in which the culture of Western Europe is seen through
the eyes of the New World as in serious moral decline. Prospero's patriarchal ways are perhaps overstated by those critics who see his interfer-
ence in the lives of others as sadistic, but the clash of opinions in recent
criticism does raise crucial issues about a male-dominated patriarchy in
which daughters and subjects alike are under the control of an absolute
authority. Western civilization has a lot to answer for, and a lot to learn
from a dramatic vision in which incommensurate worlds collide and size
each other up. Such debate is the stuff of good drama, and helps explain

why *The Tempest* is so vital to our understanding of ourselves and our culture after a nearly four-hundred-year interval.

Recent critical responses to *Measure for Measure* tell a similar story, and with a similar benefit of opening up a divergence of opinion on the nature of authority. Traditional criticism generally holds to the view that Duke Vincentio disguises his identity for a benign purpose: having failed himself to enforce the harsh Viennese laws regarding sexual promiscuity, he adopts a friar's disguise in order to see what will happen when his subjects think they are not being watched by an overseeing authority. When the test confirms his suspicion that Lord Angelo, now deputy ruler in his stead, is himself all too prone to succumb to sexual temptation, the Duke allows Angelo's attempted seduction of Isabella to proceed, ensuring all the while that the seduction itself will not take place and that her brother, condemned by the law for fornication, will not be executed. The Duke's testing shows to each of these persons an inner weakness that leads to moral collapse and failure, but such failure is ultimately forgivable and is an experience through which they can begin to cope with their own individual inadequacies. Much modern criticism, on the other hand, sees the Duke as sadistic in his manipulations. The critical appraisal is much like that applied to Prospero in its mistrust of a governing figure and its inclination to find in authority the most mean-spirited of motives. No doubt such a critical estimate can be pushed too far as an implied statement about political rule today, as is often the case in modern stage productions (the Duke as a sado-masochistic puritan in 1962 at Stratford-upon-Avon; the Duke as a hypocrite deeply implicated in the moral decline of Vienna at the same theatre in 1974), but it has the liberating effect of asking us to question the Duke's motives and to see him as a remarkably ambiguous human being.

In the same way, contemporary feminist issues have been raised and challenged by interpetations of *Measure for Measure*. Traditionally, as we observed briefly in Chapter 5, Isabella accepts the Duke's offer of marriage at the end of the play; she says nothing, but he is after all the Duke, and he has supported her (after testing her) in her hour of need. A comedy wants a marriage or two at the end to express a hope for the future. Yet *Measure for Measure* is anything but a traditional romantic comedy, and its three marriages at the end are all bizarre. Isabella has devoted herself to becoming a nun; is marriage what she wants, even with a duke? Beginning with Estelle Kohler as Isabella in John Barton's production at

Stratford-upon-Avon in 1970, the unthinkable option suddenly became thinkable: a shocked and bewildered Isabella did not give the Duke the answer he had hoped and expected. Martha Henry, in Robin Phillips's production at Stratford, Canada, in 1975, made a similar choice. The point was made: women and men alike get to choose in such a serious matter as marriage. In a similar way, the concluding marriage of Mariana and Angelo has been seen as problematic: though traditional criticism has assumed that Angelo is grateful and relieved to be forgiven by the Duke at the entreaty of Mariana and is therefore willing to take her now as his bride, in a production by the Shakespeare Repertory Company in Chicago in 1995, directed by Barbara Gaines, Angelo (Greg Vinkler) angrily repelled the arm of Mariana as he stalked offstage in the final scene quite unreconciled to his marital fate. Lucio, too, has become an ingratiating rake in many recent productions, wiser than the Duke and unfairly forced into a marriage with Kate Keepdown.

Contemporary critics and directors have increasingly made of Shakespeare an arena of contestation in which to explore and deconstruct every imaginable political, economic, ethnic, or religious difference of opinion. The issues are those we have examined in the preceding chapters of this book. Is *The Merchant of Venice* a play that endorses anti-Semitism, perhaps unwittingly, or does it offer a critique of that prejudice? Should it be read by high school and college students or pulled from the curriculum? Should *The Taming of the Shrew* be taken out of public and school libraries, as has sometimes happened, because it can be seen as defamatory toward women? Or does it offer a subtle defence of equality between the sexes? Should we see Henry V as a patriotic hero or as the warmongering, self-aggrandizing exponent of a repressive feudal warrior class? (William Hazlitt and George Bernard Shaw are among those inclining to the latter view.) Is *Othello* racist in its depiction of Othello's descent into savagery, however much he is ennobled in his early scenes? Does *Julius Caesar* offer a model of dangerous absolutist dictatorship challenged by noble but defeated champions of liberty, or does it caution against demagogic appeals to mob violence? Is Falstaff a true companion for Prince Hal in the *Henry IV* plays or does he represent the dangers of lawlessness? (In some of these instances, to be sure, both alternatives may be possible and even reconcilable.) Does Antony in *Antony and Cleopatra* lose the world for a worthwhile vision of greatness as Cleopatra's lover, or is he (as Plutarch views him) an enslaved worshipper of erotic beauty who must pay a ruinous price for his transient pleasure? Can the hero of *Macbeth* escape the fate that is predicted for him by the Weird Sisters, or is the nature of fate such that Macbeth can only become what he is destined to be, a murderer and tyrant? Is Malvolio justly punished for his hypocrisy and killjoy spirit in *Twelfth Night*, or has revelry gone too far? Is satire, as it is debated in *As You Like It*, a cleansing moral agent that society needs in order to correct itself, or is it a product of malicious minds intent on getting back at enemies? Does Hamlet really delay excessively in pursuing a necessary revenge, or is he finally in a right state of mind when he puts himself at the disposal of an overseeing Providence? Do the gods exist at all in *King Lear*, and, even if they do, what are we to make of their intent toward humankind?

Instead of answering our questions, Shakespeare seems to question our answers. Never has this seemed more true than in the late twentieth and early twenty-first centuries, as we have been bombarded by terrorism, onrushing social change, looming environmental disaster, and a decline of political discourse into name-calling and confrontation. To me, this is the real way in which Shakespeare can be our contemporary. It is why reading and seeing and teaching Shakespeare remain eternally fresh. It is in this complex sense that Shakespeare's plays and poems best represent what Jaques calls the 'seven ages' of man.

Notes

Chapter 1

1 Nina Tovish has assembled, at the Folger Shakespeare Library in Washington, DC, a computer-based interactive kiosk based on treasures from the Folger collection. It is now on permanent display in the Library. It uses the Seven Ages of Man metaphor to organize and illustrate three different types of information: aspects of Elizabethan/Jacobean life, thematic quotations from Shakespeare's works, and Shakespeare's biography and legacy. The Library's stained glass window and its visual elements are used as an interface to access the information. There is also a section about the Folger Library itself, and of course the window (which supplies the illustration for the cover of this present book). More can be learned about the Seven Ages of Man project by visiting the Lucid Design website: www.luciddesign.com. For titles dealing with the Seven Ages of Woman, see p. 4, and also books with this title by Elizabeth G. Parker, ed. Evelyn Breck, 1960; Sir Compton MacKenzie, 1923; and Mary Ann Dacomb Bird Scharlieb, 1915.

2 Act, scene, and line references in Shakespeare are to my edition, *The Complete Works of Shakespeare*, fifth edition (New York: Longman, 2004). I have modified the text slightly for this book with British English spellings (honour, centre) and an occasional repunctuation.

3 Neither I nor the Twain scholars whom I have consulted been able to find this quip in print among Twain's published works. But I have heard it told several times, and have found scholars quoted on the internet as affirming the veracity of the story (e.g., A. G. Kozak, at the University of California, Berkeley, writing on e-mail to a colleague in the Classics Department at the University of Washington, March 16, 1998). The joke certainly sounds like Twain. Perhaps it is one of the wonderfully funny things he said in his lectures, along with his wry observations on giving up smoking ('Doctors say

that giving up smoking will lengthen your days. They're certainly right about that. I refrained from smoking yesterday, and it was the longest day of my life'; or 'Giving up smoking is the easiest thing in the world. I've done it innumerable times'). The Shakespeare joke is a variant of the facetious observation that the works of Homer were not by Homer but by another person of the same name.

4   I once wrote a limerick on this subject. It imagines a conversation between William Shakespeare and the Earl of Oxford:

> Will Shakespeare to Oxford once said,
> 'My lord, you've an excellent head
>   For a tragical line.
>   *King Lear* is quite fine
> For a chap who for years has been dead.'

Chapter 2

1   'My look-alike, my brother' (Baudelaire, 'To the reader').
2   Laurence Olivier's film version of 1955 portrays Richard of Gloucester (Olivier) as deeply angered by the jibe of his young cousin and namesake, Prince Richard: at the lines 'Because that I am little, like an ape, / He [Edward] thinks that you should bear me on your shoulders' (3.1.130–1), the hump-backed Richard glowers in scorn, the music (by William Walton) rises to an alarming pitch, and the audience is put on notice that the young prince's days are fatally numbered. Precocity in Shakespeare's juveniles need not always be endearing. For an account of young Marcius's aggressive play habits in *Coriolanus*, see Chapter 7, p. 186.
3   Arthur's jump from the castle walls must take place in full view of the audience, and is an electrifying event. At the Swan Theatre in Stratford-upon-Avon, 2001, the body of Arthur seemed to fall from a height of at least twenty-five feet, from an upper gallery, and it landed with a resounding thud. It was, of course, only a dummy, allowed to fall through a trap while the young lad playing Arthur teetered on a narrow railing and then jumped backwards in the gallery out of sight. An amazing theatrical moment.
4   Clearly Shakespeare does not adopt Aristotle's argument that women are incapable of true friendship.
5   Peter Brook's enormously influential production of the play for the Royal Shakespeare Company in 1970, set in a brilliant white theatrical space equipped with trapezes and other circus gear, underscored the competitiveness of the young lovers by encouraging them to be as athletic as possible, chasing and tackling one another, acting out their aggressions in frenetic

physical movement. A similar rivalry is at the heart of *The Two Noble Kinsmen*, a play on which Shakespeare collaborated with John Fletcher in 1613, as Shakespeare was at the point of retirement. The plot, taken from Chaucer's 'The Knight's Tale', pits Palamon and Arcite against each other as friends and deadly rivals for the hand of Emilia.

Chapter 3

1 '*Haec tibi non tenues veniet delapsa per auras: / Quaerenda est oculis apta puella tuis*' (Ovid, *The Art of Love*, 1. 43–4).
2 As for example in the production directed by Michael Kahn at Stratford, Connecticut, in 1967, and in the production directed by Jonathan Miller at the National Theatre in London in 1969 and subsequently shown on ABC Television in the United States on March 16, 1974.

Chapter 4

1 Richard Wheeler, 'Deaths in the Family: The Loss of a Son and the Rise of Shakespearean Comedy', *Shakespeare Quarterly*, 51 (2000), 127–53.

Chapter 5

1 The plays are thus classified in Francis Meres, *Palladis Tamia: Wit's Treasury* (London, 1598).
2 Cressida is a leper in *The Testament of Cresseid* by the late medieval Scottish Chaucerian, Robert Henryson.
3 Compare Ophelia's plight in *Hamlet* when her father has died; Laertes accepts the role as her protector.
4 Angelo need not be played as contrite. In a fine production by the Shakespeare Repertory Company of Chicago in 1993–4, Angelo (Greg Vinkler) angrily spurned the arm of Mariana as they walked away from the Duke's seat of justice, no more ready to accommodate himself to marriage than at the start of the play.
5 As, for example, at Stratford, Canada, in 1975, in a production directed by Robin Phillips with Martha Henry as Isabella.
6 One should bear in mind that *Hamlet* exists in three different early texts, each one with something to contribute to our understanding of the play's textual history. In this present instance, the first folio edition (1623) reads

'Wormwood, Wormwood'. The second, authorized quarto of the play (1604/5) reads 'That's wormwood'. The first, unauthorized quarto of 1603 has nothing corresponding to this utterance. The differences between the second quarto and the folio are not material to the present discussion, but can matter significantly in some situations. *King Lear* presents even more variants between its quarto (1608) and the first folio text; see chapter 6, note 5. Some other plays, including *Othello*, *2 Henry IV*, and *Troilus and Cressida*, are similarly problematic.

7   See also John Updike's version of this prior history to the play in *Gertrude and Claudius* (New York: Knopf, 2000).

Chapter 6

1   *Titus Andronicus* does foreshadow important motifs that we find later in *King Lear*, of questioning divine justice and asking why the gods seem unready to intervene on behalf of the innocent. Of the gloomy spot where Titus's daughter Lavinia has been ravished, her uncle cries out, 'Oh, why should nature build so foul a den, / Unless the gods delight in tragedies?' Prompted by Titus's suffering, Marcus laments, 'O heavens, can you hear a good man groan / And not relent, or not compassion him?' From early in his career, then, Shakespeare saw such troubling philosophical questionings as material for tragedy. He was to return to these matters when, around 1600, he began devoting his energies especially to the writing of tragedy.

2   To be sure, there are useful analogies between ancient Rome and early modern England, especially in Shakespeare's portrayal of mob action. Mark Antony knows that he need only unleash mob violence to defeat the conspirators against Caesar; his manipulation of the crowd in *Julius Caesar* is both awesomely skillful and deeply discouraging to any observers who plead for moderation and common sense. Similarly, in *2 Henry VI*, Shakespeare portrays the irresponsibilities of Jack Cade's rebellion with an exaggerated satirical animus that appeals to a deep mistrust of mob action. In *Richard III*, wise observers deplore the ease with which Richard and the Duke of Buckingham are able to bend the London citizens to Richard's will; though reluctant at first to crown Richard as king, they are too easily bamboozled by Richard's artful display of seeming piety. The wavering multitude is a constant source of uneasiness in *Antony and Cleopatra*, as Antony and Octavius jockey for position; as Octavius observes, 'This common body, / Like to a vagabond flag upon the stream, / Goes to and back, lackeying the varying tide / To rot itself with motion'. In *Coriolanus*, the citizens of Rome are too easily worked up to animosity by their tribunes, who have their own self-serving agenda in fomenting unrest. Throughout Shakespeare, whether in ancient Rome or in

early modern England, commoners are generally decent and perceptive as individuals or in small groups but are worrisome when incited to group action.

3 This truism is not said directly by Hamlet; it is said by Friar Laurence in *Romeo and Juliet*, 4.1.21.

4 See E. M. W. Tillyard, *The Elizabethan World Picture* (London: Chatto and Windus, 1943; New York: Vintage Books, *c*. 1967).

5 This passage appears in the 1608 quarto text of *King Lear*, and not in the first folio text of 1623. The cut materially affects the character of Albany as presented in these two texts. See chapter 5, note 6, on other textual problems in Shakespeare. The following paragraph in this present chapter is similarly based on a quarto-only passage.

Chapter 7

1 See Arthur Kirsch, *Shakespeare and the Experience of Love* (Cambridge: Cambridge University Press, 1981).

2 See Janet Adelman, *Suffocating Mothers: Fantasies of Maternal Origin in Shakespeare's Plays, 'Hamlet' to 'The Tempest'* (Chicago: University of Chicago Press, 1992).

Chapter 8

1 The mother is also generally absent in Verdi's operas (*Il Trovatore* being the exception), as Eric A. Plaut notes in his *Grand Opera: Mirror of the Western Mind* (Chicago: Ivan R. Dee, 1993), in a chapter entitled 'Verdi's *Aida*: Fathers and Daughters'. The huge difference here is that Verdi's fathers are repeatedly the cause of their daughters' unhappiness and death, as in *La Traviata* (1853), where the father, Germont, is unalterably opposed to his son Alfredo's extra-marital relationship with Violetta. *La Traviata* is the most autobiographical of Verdi's operas; his living with Giuseppina Strepponi, the mother of a number of illegitimate children, was vehemently opposed by Verdi's father and even by Verdi's close friend and valued father-figure, Antonio Barezzi, a leading merchant in Busseto. Similar disapproving fathers are to be found in *I Vespri Siciliani* (1855), *Simon Boccanegra* (1857), *La Forza del Destino* (1862), and *Aida* (1871). Only when Verdi himself became a more successful and happy father-figure to Arrigo Boito and to his adopted daughter (Maria-Filomena, a distant cousin) was he free to write *Otello* (1881), with its tragic celebration of a passionate romantic love.

2   Some scholars argue that Ferdinand's line should read 'So rare a wondered father and a wise', since the 'f' of 'wife' and the tall 's' of 'wise' in early modern writing and typography are hard to distinguish, even in the well-printed Folio text. If the word is 'wise', the fantasy is even more complimentary to the father; his prospective son-in-law thinks the father is pretty special.

3   *The Life of King Henry VIII*, written in 1613 after *The Tempest*, is as much a tragicomic romance as it is an English history play, perhaps more so. The romance motif of tragic difficulty resolving itself into a visionary hope for the future is nowhere more evident than in the birth of the princess Elizabeth, who is to become Elizabeth I. She is, of course Henry's daughter, and is characterized in act five as very much his favourite daughter. The birth of Elizabeth not only gives Henry hope; it atones for all that he has been through, and completes his sense of self-identity:

> O Lord Archbishop,
> Thou hast made me now a man! Never, before
> This happy child, did I get anything.
> This oracle of comfort has so pleased me
> That when I am in heaven I shall desire
> To see what this child does, and praise my Maker.
> (5.5.64–9)

As in the more purely fictional romances, the coming together of father and daughter at the play's end signals an end to strife.

Chapter 9

1   Georg Brandes, *William Shakespeare* (1898), was an early proponent of the thesis that *The Tempest* is Shakespeare's farewell to the theatre.

2   In Keats's own words, negative capability is a quality 'which Shakespeare possessed so enormously – I mean when a man is capable of being in uncertainties, mysteries, doubts, without any irritable searching after fact and reason' (letter to George and Thomas Keats, December 21, 1817). It is widely applied today in literary criticism to mean an ability to see things from other people's points of view.

Chapter 10

1   From *In a Fine Frenzy: Poets Respond to Shakespeare*, ed. David Starkey and Paul J. Willis, forthcoming from the University of Iowa Press. The poem appeared originally in *Light*.

Further Reading

I hope that this postscript will do two things: offer some suggestions for further reading, and at the same time acknowledge my indebtednesses in a book that does not provide detailed citation. My indebtednesses are extensive, and will, I am sure, be recognized by scholars in the field of Shakespeare studies and most of all by the persons who have taught me through their personal example and their writings.

Among the critical studies to which I am most generally indebted, let me first name Janet Adelman, *Suffocating Mothers: Fantasies of Maternal Origin in Shakespeare's Plays, 'Hamlet' to 'The Tempest'* (Chicago: University of Chicago Press, 1992), and Richard P. Wheeler, *Shakespeare's Development and the Problem Comedies: Turn and Counter-Turn* (Berkeley: University of California Press, 1981). The central idea of this book, of looking at Shakespeare's writing career as a mirror of the human life cycle as experienced by Shakespeare, is explored with wonderful richness and sagacity in these books and in other critical writings by these two friends.

Here are some critical studies that are essential to more than one chapter:

C. L. Barber, *Shakespeare's Festive Comedy.* Princeton NJ: Princeton University Press, 1959.

C. L. Barber and Richard P. Wheeler, *The Whole Journey: Shakespeare's Power of Development.* Berkeley: University of California Press, 1986.

A. C. Bradley, *Shakespeare Tragedy: Lectures on 'Hamlet', 'Othello', 'King Lear', 'Macbeth'.* London: Macmillan, 1906.

Sigurd Burckhardt, *Shakespearean Meanings.* Princeton NJ: Princeton University Press, 1968.

Stanley Cavell, *Disowning Knowledge in Six Plays of Shakespeare*. Cambridge: Cambridge University Press, 1987.

Jonathan Dollimore, *Radical Tragedy: Religion, Ideology and Power in the Drama of Shakespeare and His Contemporaries*. Chicago: University of Chicago Press, 1984.

Juliet Dusinberre, *Shakespeare and the Nature of Women*. Originally published in 1975; second edition, London: Macmillan, 1996.

Lars Engle, *Shakespearean Pragmatism: Market of His Time*. Chicago: University of Chicago Press, 1993.

Northrop Frye, *Anatomy of Criticism*. Princeton NJ: Princeton University Press, 1957.

Marjorie Garber, *Coming of Age in Shakespeare*. London: Methuen, 1981.

Stephen Greenblatt, *Shakespearean Negotiations; The Circulation of Social Energy in Renaissance England*. Berkeley: University of California Press, 1988.

Stephen Greenblatt, *Will in the World*. New York: Norton, 2004.

Alfred Harbage, *Shakespeare and the Rival Traditions*. New York: Macmillan, 1952.

E. A. J. Honigmann, 'Shakespeare's Second Best Bed', *New York Review of Books*, Nov. 7 (1991), 30.

Robert Grams Hunter, *Shakespeare and the Comedy of Forgiveness*. New York: Columbia University Press, 1965.

Lisa Jardine, *Still Harping on Daughters: Women and Drama in the Age of Shakespeare*. Berkeley: University of California Press, 1989.

Coppélia Kahn, *Man's Estate: Masculine Identity in Shakespeare*. Berkeley: University of California Press, 1981.

David Scott Kastan, *Shakespeare and the Book*. Cambridge: Cambridge University Press, 2001.

David Scott Kastan, ed., *A Companion to Shakespeare*. Oxford: Blackwell, 1999.

Arthur Kirsch, *The Passions of Shakespeare's Tragic Heroes*. Charlottesville: University Press of Virginia, 1990.

Arthur Kirsch, *Shakespeare and the Experience of Love*. Cambridge: Cambridge University Press, 1981.

Claude Lévi-Strauss, *The Elementary Structures of Kinship*. London: Eyre and Spottiswood, Boston: Beacon Press, *c.* 1969–70.

Russ McDonald, ed., *The Bedford Companion to Shakespeare: An Introduction with Documents*. Second edition, Boston and New York: Bedford/St. Martin's, 2001.

Patricia Parker, *Shakespeare from the Margins: Language, Culture, Context*. Chicago: University of Chicago Press, 1996.

Victor W. Turner, *The Ritual Process: Structure and Anti-Structure*. Chicago: Aldine, 1969.

Arnold van Gennep, *The Rites of Passage*, trans. Monika B. Vizedom and Gabrielle L. Caffee. London: Routledge & Kegan Paul, 1960.

Other studies can best be cited by chapters.

Chapter 1 All the World's a Stage: Poetry and Theatre

Stephen Booth, *An Essay on Shakespeare's Sonnets*. New Haven: Yale University Press, 1969.

Park Honan, *Shakespeare: A Life*. Oxford: Oxford University Press, 1998.

S. Schoenbaum, *William Shakespeare: A Documentary Life; William Shakespeare: Records and Images*. In two volumes. Oxford: Oxford University Press, 1981.

Brian Vickers, 'Shakespeare's Use of Rhetoric', in *A New Companion to Shakespeare Studies*, ed. Kenneth Muir and S. Schoenbaum. Cambridge: Cambridge University Press, 1971.

Chapter 2 Creeping Like Snail: Childhood, Education, Early Friendship, Sibling Rivalries

Louis Adrian Montrose, ' "The Place of a Brother" in *As You Like It*: Social Process and Comic Form', *Shakespeare Quarterly*, 21 (1981), 28–54.

David Young, *Something of Great Constancy: The Art of 'A Midsummer Night's Dream'*. New Haven: Yale University Press, 1966.

Chapter 3 Sighing Like Furnace: Courtship and Sexual Desire

Lynda E. Boose, 'The Father and the Bride in Shakespeare', *PMLA*, 97 (1982), 325–47.

William C. Carroll, *The Great Feast of Language in 'Love's Labour's Lost'*. Princeton NJ: Princeton University Press, 1976.

Alexander Leggatt, *Shakespeare's Comedy of Love*. London and New York: Methuen, 1974.

Mary Beth Rose, *The Expense of Spirit: Love and Sexuality in English Renaissance Drama*. Ithaca: Cornell University Press, 1988.

Lawrence Stone, *The Family, Sex and Marriage in England, 1500–1800*. London: Weidenfeld & Nicolson 1977.

Chapter 4   Full of Strange Oaths and Bearded Like the Pard: The Coming-of-Age of the Male

James L. Calderwood, *Metadrama in Shakespeare's Henriad: Richard II to Henry V*. Berkeley: University of California Press, 1979.

David Scott Kastan, *Shakespeare and the Shapes of Time*. Hanover NH: University Press of New England, 1982.

Phyllis Rackin, *Stages of History: Shakespeare's English Chronicles*. Ithaca NY: Cornell University Press, 1990.

Robert Watson, *Shakespeare and the Hazards of Ambition*. Cambridge MA: Harvard University Press, 1984.

Chapter 5   Jealous in Honour: Love and Friendship in Crisis

David Bevington, ed., *Troilus and Cressida*. The Arden Shakespeare, third series. Walton-on-Thames: Nelson, 1998.

Maynard Mack, 'The World of *Hamlet*', *Yale Review*, 51 (1952), 502–23.

Chapter 6   Wise Saws: Political and Social Disillusionment, Humankind's Relationship to the Divine, and Philosophical Scepticism

Fredson Bowers, *'Hamlet as Minister and Scourge' and Other Studies in Shakespeare and Milton*. Charlottesville: University Press of Virginia, 1989.

Paul Jorgensen, *Our Naked Frailties: Sensational Art and Meaning in 'Macbeth'*. Berkeley: University of California Press, 1971.

Maynard Mack, *'King Lear' in Our Time*. Berkeley: University of California Press, 1965.

John W. Velz, 'Undular Structure in *Julius Caesar*', *Modern Language Review*, 66 (1971), 21–30.

Chapter 7   Modern Instances: Misogyny, Jealousy, Pessimism, and Midlife Crisis

Janet Adelman, *The Common Liar: An Essay on 'Antony and Cleopatra'*. New Haven: Yale University Press, 1973.

Ania Loomba, *Gender, Race, Renaissance Drama*. Manchester: Manchester University Press, 1989.

Chapter 8   The Lean and Slippered Pantaloon: Ageing Fathers and their Daughters

Inga-Stina Ewbank, '"My name is Marina": The Language of Recognition', in *Shakespeare's Styles: Essays in Honour of Kenneth Muir*, ed. Philip Edwards, Inga-Stina Ewbank, and G. K. Hunter. Cambridge: Cambridge University Press, 1980.

Barbara A. Mowat, *The Dramaturgy of Shakespeare's Romances*. Athens: University of Georgia Press, 1976.

Chapter 9   Last Scene of All: Retirement from the Theatre

Frank Kermode, *William Shakespeare: The Final Plays*. Harlow: Longman, 1963.

Frank Kermode, ed., *The Tempest*. The Arden Shakespeare. London: Methuen, 1954.

Alvin B. Kernan, *The Playwright as Magician: Shakespeare's Image of the Poet in the English Public Theater*. New Haven: Yale University Press, 1979.

Meredith Ann Skura, *Shakespeare the Actor and the Purposes of Playing*. Chicago: University of Chicago Press, 1993.

Chapter 10   Shakespeare Today

Antonin Artaud, *The Theatre and Its Double*. Translated from the French by Victor Corti. London: Calder and Boyars, 1970.

John Drakakis, ed., *Alternative Shakespeares*. London, New York: Methuen, 1985.

Harold Goddard, *The Meaning of Shakespeare*. Chicago: University of Chicago Press, 1951.

Jerzy Grotowski, *Towards a Poor Theatre*. Ed. Euenio Barba. New York: Routledge, 2002.

Ernest Jones, *Hamlet and Oedipus*. Revised edition. New York: Norton, 1976 (*c*. 1949).

Jan Kott, *Shakespeare Our Contemporary*. Translated from the Polish by Boreslaw Taborski. New York: Norton, 1974 (*c*. 1964).

Meredith Skura, 'Discourse and the Individual: The Case of Colonialism in *The Tempest*', *Shakespeare Quarterly*, 40 (1989), 42–69.

Gary Taylor and Michael Warren, ed., *The Division of the Kingdoms: Shakespeare's Two Versions of 'King Lear'*. Oxford: Oxford University Press, 1983.

E. M. W. Tillyard, *The Elizabethan World Picture*. London: Chatto and Windus, 1943, New York: Vintage Books, *c*. 1967.

Index